THE
OPTIONS
STRATEGIST

How to Invest and Trade Equity-Related Options

EFFECTIVE STRATEGIES FROM BASIC TO ADVANCED

OPTIONS ON ETFs AND INDEX FUNDS

TECHNIQUES TO PROTECT YOUR INVESTMENTS

MARC ALLAIRE

McGraw·Hill

New York   Chicago   San Francisco   Lisbon   London   Madrid   Mexico City
Milan   New Delhi   San Juan   Seoul   Singapore   Sydney   Toronto

Library of Congress Cataloging-in-Publication Data

Allaire, Marc.
    The options strategist / Marc Allaire.
        p.   cm.
    Includes index.
    ISBN 0-07-140895-9
    1. Stock options.   I. Title.

    HG6042 .A45   2003
    332.63'228—dc21   2002191236

1 2 3 4 5 6 7 8 9 0   DOC/DOC   2 1 0 9 8 7 6 5 4 3

ISBN 0-07-140895-9

McGraw-Hill books are available at special quantity discounts to use as premiums and sales promotions, or for use in corporate training programs. For more information, please write to the Director of Special Sales, Professional Publishing, McGraw-Hill, Two Penn Plaza, New York, NY 10121-2298. Or contact your local bookstore.

This book is printed on acid-free paper.

To my wife, Lynda

CONTENTS

INTRODUCTION

THE MAIN PURPOSE OF A BOOK TITLED *The Options Strategist* is self-explanatory: to present and explain different options strategies. Still, the contents and the structure of this book are based on a number of assumptions that we would like to set out.

A major assumption is that people who use options fall into two broad categories: investors and traders. We made this distinction several years ago in a chapter titled "Investing and Trading Strategies for the Individual Investor," which appears in *Options: Essential Concepts and Trading Strategies*. In reality, most options users are neither pure investors nor pure traders. They invest part of their capital and trade with their "mad money." This distinction led us to group the investment strategies in Chapters 2 and 5 and the trading strategies in Chapters 3 and 6. Chapter 7, which deals with the special features of index options, presents both investing and trading strategies.

To understand any option strategy, some theoretical knowledge is necessary, but many options books present all of the theory before explaining any strategies. By the time readers have plowed through the theory, their heads are spinning and they can't see the connection between the theory and the strategies.

We took a different tack. We believe that basic theory is necessary to understand basic options strategies, and more advanced theory is required for more advanced strategies. Thus, the basic theory presented in Chapter 1 should help the reader understand the strategies presented in Chapters 2 and 3. The more advanced concepts in Chapter 4 lay the groundwork for the strategies in Chapters 5, 6, and 7.

Chapter 8 looks at ways to hedge positions in corporate stock and options. Some of the strategies in that chapter could have been included with the other advanced strategies, so readers who don't hold any of their employer's stock should resist the urge to skip Chapter 8. Chapter 9 goes back to theoretical notions, with more in-depth discussions of volatility, time decay, options valuation, and other concepts that were introduced in earlier chapters. Although this information is helpful, it is not critical in implementing trading or investing strategies; hence, there are no strategy chapters that follow Chapter 9. Finally, Chapter 10 discusses tactical considerations, since there is more to using options successfully than simply mastering all of the strategies.

One goal we did *not* have was to maximize the number of strategies covered. Instead, we decided to concentrate on strategies the average investor can implement. In keeping with this restriction, we adhered to two principles: First, not all strategies are created equal and therefore do not get equal time. Compare the number of pages dedicated to the various aspects of buying calls to the number allocated to butterfly spreads. We know from experience that just about everybody who trades options ends up buying calls sooner or later, but very few people ever initiate a butterfly. Second, we found it necessary to present certain strategies just to caution our readers away from them. This may sound negative, but not losing money is just as important as establishing profitable positions when investing or trading with options or any financial instrument.

A participant in one of our seminars said he tried spreads and concluded that they don't work. After a little prodding, we found that if he had been aware of Regulation FD (full disclosure), a more accurate comment would have been, "They didn't work the way I expected them to work," or "They didn't work the way I expected them to work because I didn't know what to expect from these strategies." This trader's knowledge of spreads was probably limited to their risk and reward at just two points in time—the day the trade was initiated and at option expiration. An analysis of an option strategy is often limited to these two dates, but we have gone to great lengths to analyze how options positions can be expected to behave between the trade date and option expiration. Most readers will be surprised at how options can behave, especially in a complex position that involves more than one option.

Certain advanced trading strategies are presented as equity strategies in Chapter 6, and others as index option strategies in Chapter 7. Readers should keep in mind that call back spreads, for example, can also be used with equity options, even though the only example in this book involves index options.

A few housekeeping items regarding the examples in this book: We used both actual stocks and options prices and fictional ones in our illustrations. Readers find it easier to relate to names they know, but to illustrate a point that requires a stock trading at exactly $50, we found it easier to refer to "Nifty Fifty Inc." trading at the required level. As of this writing, options priced under $3 trade in five-cent increments (i.e., $2.50, $2.55, $2.60) and options priced above $3 in ten-cent intervals (i.e., $3.40, $3.50, $3.60). In examples where we calculated theoretical prices to illustrate a point, we narrowed the pricing increments to a penny (i.e., $3.17 or $5.14), especially where rounding these prices would have obscured the small changes we were trying to illustrate. In most instances where we calculated theoretical prices, we used the options pricing software available on-line on the website of the Chicago Board Options Exchange (www.cboe.com under the Trading Tools tab). Readers will find this pricing tool to be adequate for most everyday situations. (And in the spirit of Regulation FD, we note that we do act as an occasional consultant to the CBOE.)

Most of our examples make no references to two real-life issues: trading fees and taxes. We are fully aware of the impact these can have, but illustrations such as "you buy one call option on your favorite stock" would not make any economic sense if transaction fees were included. The bad news is that trading options usually requires buying or selling more than one contract. The good news is that commissions at certain firms are significantly lower than they were a decade or two ago, and that the breakpoint (the number of contracts at which transaction costs become negligible) has moved significantly lower. As an example, assume commissions of $25 per trade plus $2 per option, a rate that is neither the lowest available nor the highest. Buying one option at $2 (a value of $200) would generate trading fees of $27, or 13.5% of the option's value. Increase the size of the trade to five options and the commission rises to $35, which now represents 3.5% of the total option value. On 10 contracts, fees are $45, and only 2.3% of the options' value. You get the picture.

As far as taxes, we have made some brief comments in Chapter 10. The long and short of it is that options are securities, so traders and investors will end up with capital gains or losses if they use options.

It would be futile to try to acknowledge everyone who has furthered our understanding of options during the past two decades. Nonetheless, we would like to specifically thank Bernard and Denis, who took a chance on a rookie with very little option know-how; Guy and Robin, who helped us develop our presentation skills; Bill and Larry, who gave us free rein and let us develop as an option strategist; and Curtis, who created a position for us when we decided that after so many years in the educational field, it was time to get our hands dirty again.

We also want to thank the staff of The Options Institute at the Chicago Board Options Exchange who compiled all the data required for our historical analyses.

Two people reviewed the first draft of this manuscript. Marty Kearney, with whom we collaborated on our *Understanding LEAPS* book, provided comments that helped us clarify some of the more technical points, and detected inaccuracies. Lynda Walker, who made time in her very busy schedule, tried to curb our run-on sentences and made numerous suggestions to clarify the presentation of the strategies.

Finally, Stephen Isaacs, our editor, and Craig Bolt, our project editor, answered our numerous questions, kept us on schedule, and guided us through the process of producing a book.

To these and all those who contributed to this book, many thanks.

For any remaining errors, of omission or commission, we take full responsibility.

1

OPTIONS 101: BASIC TERMS, DEFINITIONS, AND STRATEGIES

The Basics

It is not necessary to understand the internal workings of an automatic transmission in order to drive a car equipped with one. It is, however, important to know the function of the steering wheel and the difference between the gas and brake pedals. Much the same can be said for investing and trading with options: there is no need to calculate second derivatives, but a firm grasp of the fundamentals is essential. Consider this chapter to be your basic driver's education. And for those who like to take the transmission apart, we refer you to Chapter 9.

Puts and Calls

Let's start with a formal definition of options. An option gives its buyer the right to purchase or to sell a security at a set price until a fixed future date. For this right the buyer pays what is referred to as the option's premium.

There are two types of options—puts and calls. Although we will move on to options on indices and other securities later, this chapter focuses on equity options.

Take this example of a call option: a DuPont (ticker symbol DD) January 45 call trading at a price of $3.30. Here is the shorthand form for this option:

DD Jan 45 call @ 3.30

This call option gives the buyer the right to purchase shares of the underlying stock, DD, at $45; this, 45, is the exercise, or strike, price of the option. This is a January option, which means that the right to purchase DD at $45 will expire some time in January. The last day on which this right can be exercised will be the third Friday in January. The third Friday applies to all expiration months, so the third week of each month is known in options circles as expiration week. After this date the option is worthless. Finally, $3.30 is the price the buyer pays to purchase the option. This is also known as the option's premium and is always quoted on a per share basis. So $3.30 means $3.30 per share, and since each option contract gives its buyer the right to purchase 100 shares of the underlying stock, the cost of purchasing this call would be $330.

Our shorthand can be summarized as follows:

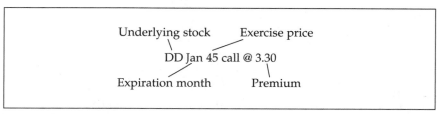

Figure 1.1

Now let's look at a put option on Sears (S): S Nov 40 put @ 1.85. This put option gives its buyer the right to sell 100 shares of S at a price of $40. This right may be exercised up to and including the third Friday in November. The cost of acquiring this right is $185 per option contract.

Note that options grant their buyers rights, but there are no obligations associated with these rights. A call buyer has the right to purchase shares only if he decides to do so. If it makes no economic sense to invoke this right, the call buyer need not do so. Also, for equity options, this right to purchase or to sell may be invoked on any business day from the day the option is purchased until the third Friday of the expiration month. This unrestricted exercise feature is commonly referred to as an *American-style option*. Options with restricted exercise features are discussed in Chapter 7 in the section on index options.

The Other Side of the Option

For every buyer there is a seller. For every option purchased one must be "sold," and for every investor who obtains a right, another investor must assume an obligation. We used quotation marks around the word "sold" because we prefer to say that options are *granted*, or *written*, rather than sold. In our earlier call option example, there must be a counterpart to the buyer of the DD January 45 call, someone who "sold" the option. It could be a trader who had purchased the option and then decided to liquidate her position for whatever reason. Very often, though, the seller did not purchase the option from someone else and has no position in any DD options. He is, in fact, *writing* the option. That is, he is taking the opposite side of the trade.

The buyer of the call obtains the right to purchase 100 shares of DD at $45 until the third Friday in January, and the writer of that option assumes the obligation to sell 100 shares of DD at that price if the buyer decides to invoke his right. This obligation is called a *contingent obligation* because the writer does not know if he will ever have to meet the obligation. The final decision is in the hands of the option buyer.

Options Created out of Thin Air

Although this may look like a headline from your favorite tabloid, it is accurate. When an investor purchases shares of a corporation, he does so from another investor who has decided to sell her shares. Buying 1,000 shares of stock on the New York Stock Exchange does not change the number of outstanding shares. Not so for options.

Consider this scenario. A stranger comes to your door and says, "I would like to buy your house, and I'm willing to pay significantly above market value. But since I am not 100 percent ready to close the deal, I would like you to grant me an option whereby I will be able to buy your house in six months at an agreed-upon price. I am willing to pay you $5,000 for this option." You talk this over with your significant other and decide that if this stranger is willing to buy your house, he can have it at the agreed price and you will gladly move to another neighborhood. If he does not buy the house, then the $5,000 he gave you will go a long way in repairing the leaking roof. You grant the stranger an option on your dwelling.

There is now one option outstanding on your house. It was created when someone who wanted to purchase an option was able to come to terms with someone who was willing to grant it. The same goes for equity and index options. When two individuals come to an agreement, options are created. One minute there are no options outstanding on Advanced BioGizmo, the next you have purchased 10 contracts from another individual who was more than willing to grant these to you. Ten options have been created.

Since the terms of listed equity options (strike price, expiration date, number of shares per contract) are all standardized, only one variable remains to be negotiated when creating options: the price paid by the buyer to the grantor. This makes the negotiation of listed options somewhat easier than agreeing on an option on your house (where one must decide if the lawnmower is included, if the closing date can be contingent on financing, etc., etc.).

Vocabulary and Definitions

To a large extent, understanding options hinges on understanding their specialized vocabulary. The following key terms cover the basics of options trading.

Underlying value. Every option is an option on something: two tickets to the big game, a piece of real estate, shares of Monsanto. This book focuses on options on equities, which have as their underlying value 100 shares of the said stock per option contract, options on exchange-traded funds (which represent part ownership in a basket of stock that usually reflects the composition of a well-known index), and index options whose underlying value, an index, is not a security of any type but simply a number. The special features of index options will be discussed in Chapter 7.

Last trading day. For equity options, the third Friday of the expiration month. This is option traders' last chance to initiate or liquidate positions in expiring options. By the time investors get back to their offices on the following Monday all of the current month's options will have expired.

Expiration date. All options have a known, finite, life that ends on their expiration date, which is defined as the Saturday following the third Friday of the month. This is often confused with the last trading day. There is very little options traders can do on expiration Saturday except buy groceries and watch Michigan football. This "extra" day harks back to the time when all of the back-office procedures were done manually and brokerage firms needed to balance their books and correct any errors that may have occurred on Friday. The week preceding expiration Saturday is known as expiration week. Some think of stocks as having no expiration date. We prefer to think of stocks as having an unknown expiration date: sometimes they expire worthless, sometime they disappear in exchange for a fixed dollar amount, but most of the time they just keep on going.

Expiration cycles. At any one time there will be four different expiration months listed for trading on any one optionable stock. (There may be two additional ones if LEAPS® are available; see LEAPS entry.) The four months available will vary depending on which of the three expiration cycles the option class belongs to. The three different cycles are known as the January, the February, and the March cycles. The January cycle consists of January, April, July, and October. The February cycle consists of February, May, August, and November. The March cycle consists of March, June, September, and December. No matter which cycle an option class belongs to, the next two available expiration months will be listed. Then the next two expiration months from the appropriate cycle will also be listed. For example, Advanced Micro Devices (AMD) trades on the January cycle. If we are in early April, the following four expiration months would be listed for AMD: April and May (the next two available expirations), and July and October (the next two months of the January cycle). After the April expiration the May options would continue trading. June options would then be listed (June would now be the second available expiration month), and the July and October options would also continue trading. The easiest way to find out to which expiration cycle a stock belongs is to pull up an option chain and see what's listed for trading.

Exercise price (also known as *strike price*). The price at which the buyer of an option obtains the right to buy or sell the underlying security. For equity options, strike prices are set at $2.50 intervals from $5 (the lowest strike price listed) to $25, and at $5 intervals above $25.

Option type, series, and class. There are two types of options: puts and calls. Options with the same expiration and strike price make up a series (for example, the December 65s). A class comprises all of the options on one underlying stock or index (all of its series); for example, all Intel options or all options on the Standard & Poor's 500® Index.

LEAPS. An acronym for Long-term Equity AnticiPation Securities.SM Long-term options. In addition to the four short-term expiration months, some stocks have two additional longer-term options known as LEAPS. All equity LEAPS expire in January and will have terms from 9 to 32 months.

Long and short. Words with two different meanings. When referring to option positions or stocks, long signifies an option, or a stock has been purchased: I am long the June 50 calls (I have bought these), or I am long shares of IBM. Short refers to options that have been written: I am short the January 95 puts (I have written these) or to a stock that has been sold short: I am short shares of GM. When referring to the overall market (or a particular stock), long or short indicates whether a position is bullish or bearish: "I am long the market" (I have a position that will be profitable if the market goes up) or "I am short the market." Note that one can be long the market (bullish) by being short some options.

Holder. The buyer of an option. Someone with a long option position.

Bid-ask. When posting option quotes, professional traders (known as market makers or specialists) must give a two-sided market: a price at which they are willing to purchase the option (the bid) and a price at which they are willing to sell the option (the ask, or the offer). A buyer who purchases on option at the asked price is said to take out (or lift) the offer. A seller who accepts the posted bid is said to hit the bid. The bid-ask spread refers to the difference between these two prices, as in: "The spread on that option is too wide."

Option chain. A listing of all the options on a specific security, usually presented in two columns, the left one listing calls, the right one puts. This information used to be found only on brokers' quote terminals but is now widely available on the Internet. "Pull up the chain on Microsoft."

Option premium. The price of an option, paid by the buyer, received by the writer. Quoted on a per share basis, an option's premium is composed of intrinsic and time value.

Intrinsic and time value. Intrinsic value is the amount by which an option is in-the-money. This is also known as the exercise value. For example, a General Electric (GE) 40 call trading at $4.40 when GE is trading at $43 has $3 of intrinsic value; the difference between an option's premium and its intrinsic value is its time value; the GE 40 call has $1.40 of time value. Time value is said to decay as the expiration date approaches and to disappear at expiration. Options very rarely trade below their intrinsic value as this would create an easy arbitrage opportunity: if the GE 40 call is trading at $2.90, buy it, exercise it, and immediately sell GE at $43. Total cost to purchase the stock would be $42.90 ($2.90 to buy the option, $40 payable upon exercise), resulting in a profit of $0.10. An option's intrinsic value is never negative. If GE is trading at $43 and the 45 call at $2.70, the call has no intrinsic value and its premium is composed exclusively of time value.

In-the-money, at-the-money, and out-of-the-money. If an option has some intrinsic value, it is said to be in-the-money. If United Technologies (UTX) is trading at $64, the September 60 call is in-the-money by $4 (it lets its holder buy the stock $4 below the current price), and the October 70 put is in-the-money by $6 (it lets its holder sell the stock $6 above its current price). Options are at-the-money when the price of the underlying stock is equal to the option's strike price: if MBIA Corp. (MBI) is $55, then both the February 55 call and the March 55 put are at-the-money. Calls with an exercise price higher than the price of the stock, and puts with a strike price lower than the current stock level, are out-of-the-money: if ICN Pharmaceuticals (ICN) is $27, the April 30 call (and all calls with higher strike prices) are out-of-the-money; the June 25 put (and all puts with lower exercise prices) are also out-of-the-money. One often hears references to the amount by which options are in- or out-of-the-money: "I just purchased a put that's $7 in-the-money," or "I'm going to write a call that's at least $5 out-of-the-money."

Exercise. To invoke the rights conferred by an option. Only buyers of options may exercise these. For example, an investor who purchased a Chevron Texaco (CVX) 90 call option (granting her the right to buy 100 shares of CVX at $90) may decide she wants to purchase this stock and add it to her portfolio. She contacts her broker and instructs him to exercise her call option. When an option is exercised, it settles three business days later (the same as purchases and sales made on the various stock exchanges), at which point she would have to pay $9,000 and would then receive 100 shares of CVX. Logic dictates that only in-the-money options should be exercised, but in actual practice at-the-money options are occasionally exercised as well.

To be assigned. If the writer of an option is assigned, he must fulfill the obligation he assumed when he wrote the option. Someone who writes an Intel (INTC) 30 put, for example, could be assigned on this contract and forced to purchase 100 shares of INTC at $30. When an investor is assigned, he is usually notified by his broker. At that point it is too late to change his mind. He must purchase the underlying stock or, if he has written a call option, he must sell the stock under option. An assignment occurs when an investor with a long position decides to exercise her option. She advises her broker, who exercises the option by notifying The Options Clearing Corporation (OCC).

The OCC sends an assignment notice to one of its member firms (selected on a random basis), and the firm assigns one of its clients, either randomly or on a first-in, first-out basis.

Trading volume. As with stocks, the exchanges report the trading volume for each option series. Note that this is always reported in contracts, not the number of underlying shares (100 per contract).

Open interest. The number of options contracts that have been opened and are still left open at the end of the trading day. When a new option series is first listed, the open interest will be zero and will remain so until the first trade occurs. If an investor purchases 20 of this new series and still holds these 20 options at the end of the trading day, the open interest will then be 20 (assuming no other trades took place). Open interest is calculated only after each trading session and is not updated during the trading day. Some traders look at this number as an indirect indicator of option liquidity: if the open interest is large, there must be a high level of interest in this option and it should be fairly liquid. But you will see instances where open interest is high and trading volume low or nonexistent. This could happen if an institution took a huge position some time ago (creating high open interest) but trading has since dried up.

Uncovered (naked) option. Refers to a short option position where the writer cannot immediately meet the obligation assumed. For example, if the writer of a call option (the obligation to sell a stock) is assigned and the writer does not own the underlying stock, he would have to purchase the stock in the open market in order to deliver it, or borrow shares to establish a short position. Uncovered options must be margined.

Margin. Another word of multiple uses. For stocks: an investor can buy a stock on margin; that is, using funds borrowed from his broker to help finance the purchase. The margin requirement is the minimum amount the investor must provide, usually expressed as a percentage. "You can purchase this stock on 50% margin." When purchasing options, the buyer must pay the full amount: long options are not marginable. For short option positions: some short option positions must be margined, i.e., the writer must have funds or securities in her account to demonstrate that she can meet the obligation she has assumed. Cash or securities (stocks, bonds, mutual funds) are acceptable as margin.

Margin call. A demand by a broker to provide additional funds to margin a position. If an investor purchased a stock using the minimum amount of margin required and the value of the stock drops, the brokerage firm may make a margin call. If received early enough in the morning, it becomes synonymous with a wake-up call.

Options Pricing: The Basics

You may have heard of the Black-Scholes option pricing model, or of binomials used to estimate the value of an option. This chapter gives just a general idea of the variables that impact option prices without getting into the mathematics involved. We will come back to this subject in more detail in Chapters 4 and 9.

No matter how complicated an option pricing equation, one usually finds only five inputs to the formula. These are:

- Stock price. As the price of the stock moves up and down, the value of an option will change. An option that was out-of-the-money can become at-the-money or in-the-money, potentially making it more valuable. A rule of thumb is that higher stock prices increase the value of calls and decrease the value of puts, while lower stock prices have the opposite effect.

- Exercise price. On a given stock, and with the same time until expiration, a 40 call will always be worth more than a 45 call. This makes sense since the right to purchase a stock at $40 has got to be worth more than the right to purchase the same stock at $45. The only exception is if two options are so far out-of-the-money that they are equally worthless (think of a 120 and a 125 call when the underlying stock is trading at $30; both of these options will likely have no value). Puts with higher strike prices will be more valuable than those with lower exercise prices.

- Time until expiration. It stands to reason that a two-month option will be worth more than a one-month option, all other variables being equal. More time increases the probability that an out-of-the-money option will become in-the-money; traders and investors are usually willing to pay up for a longer term to expiration.

■ Volatility. Think of the most boring utility and of the riskiest technology stocks you ever purchased. This gives you an idea of what volatility is all about. Now think which of those two is more likely to go up by $10 over a set period of time. And now you understand why options on high-tech stocks trade at higher premiums than those on utility shares.

■ Interest rates and dividends. This is the least important variable. The interest rate used in option pricing is usually the risk-free rate (i.e., that of Treasury bills). This lets option traders take into account the time value of money (a dollar today is worth more than a dollar tomorrow) and the opportunity cost of owning a stock (the money used to purchase shares could otherwise be earning interest). Dividends reduce the cost of carrying a stock (I am not earning 4% on the cash I spent to buy these shares, but I am getting a 1% dividend).

The Four Basic Options Strategies

Since there are two types of options, puts and calls, and since an option can either be bought or written, we obtain four basic option strategies: buying calls, buying puts, writing calls, and writing puts. These represent the building blocks that will be used in various combinations to create more complex strategies.

Buying Call Options

Purchasing call options is the most basic bullish option strategy. Since investors tend to make their first option trade during bull markets, it is also the point of entry to the world of options for many people. The basic mechanics of this strategy are best illustrated through an example.

Start with Avon Products (AVP), trading at $50.60. A trader is bullish on these shares, expecting them to rise nicely over the next few months. Of course, the most basic bullish investment strategy would be to simply buy 100 AVP shares. An alternative is to purchase one call option—for example, the July 50 call, a four-month option offered at $3.20. This would give the trader the right to purchase 100 shares of AVP at $50 until and including the third Friday of July. Is one strategy better than the other? Let's compare them from different angles.

Risk. The stock buyer assumes a substantial amount of risk. In theory, a new technological development by one of Avon's competitors could make all current makeup products obsolete and send AVP spiraling down as sales evaporate. The option buyer has only $320 at risk ($3.20 per share × 100 shares), the cost of the option purchased. The call buyer has a lower dollar risk than the stock owner.

Upside potential. Owning shares of AVP theoretically offers unlimited upside potential. Since we have yet to observe an actual stock rising ad infinitum, let's be more realistic and say that stock ownership offers significant upside potential. The call buyer, by virtue of his right to purchase shares of AVP, will be able to capture this upside by transforming his option position into a stock position. This one looks like a tie.

Breakeven point. The stock buyer's breakeven point is the price paid for the shares. If in four months, or four years, AVP is still trading at $50.60, the stockholder breaks even (although he does incur an opportunity cost because his money could have been earning interest income in a risk-free instrument). The call buyer has a breakeven of $53.20 at option expiration. This is calculated by adding the cost of the option ($3.20) to its strike price (50). If the stock remains unchanged over the next four months, the option buyer will end up with a loss. He faces a somewhat stiffer head wind. Better to own shares.

Time constraints. For the buyer of a four-month call option to make money the stock will have to increase in price some time over the life of the option. If it does not, the call either will expire worthless or may be sold for less than its purchase price. The stock buyer is in no hurry, although the sooner the stock rises, the better. But time is definitely against the option buyer.

Dividends, annual meetings, and corporate literature.
The yield on AVP is 1.5%, and over the next four months the stockholder will be entitled to one of the quarterly dividends. Stockholders also have the right to attend the annual meeting (free coffee and maybe free samples), to vote their shares, and to receive copies of annual and quarterly reports. The option buyer is not entitled to any of these privileges.

Profitability at option expiration.
To compare the profitability of the long stock and long call positions at option expiration, refer to Table 1.1, which illustrates the dollar per share gains or losses for various AVP prices. This is just another tool in our comparison.

A few comments on the table below are in order. The profit and loss on the stock position assumes a purchase cost of $50.60. The value of the call at expiration will be its intrinsic value. For instance, if AVP is trading at $56, the 50 call will be worth $6, or its in-the-money amount. Since it was purchased for $3.20, selling the call at $6 will leave the trader with a $2.80 profit. The numbers from this table are presented in another form in Figure 1.2, in what is com-

Table 1.1

AVP Price at Expiration	Profit/(Loss) on Stock	Value of 50 Call	Cost of 50 Call	Profit/(Loss) on Call
$44	($6.60)	$0	($3.20)	($3.20)
$47	($3.60)	$0	($3.20)	($3.20)
$50	($0.60)	$0	($3.20)	($3.20)
$53	$2.40	$3	($3.20)	($0.20)
$56	$5.40	$6	($3.20)	$2.80
$59	$8.40	$9	($3.20)	$5.80
$62	$11.40	$12	($3.20)	$8.80

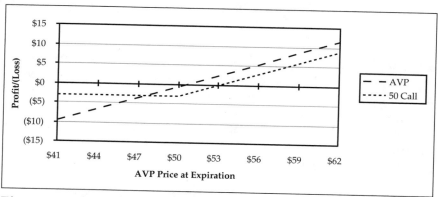

Figure 1.2 Long AVP vs. Long 50 Call

monly known as a profit-and-loss diagram, a payoff diagram, or a hockey stick diagram.

Figure 1.2 clearly illustrates the lower dollar risk of the long call position, along with its higher breakeven point. And there lies the major trade-off that all call buyers must accept: the lower risk comes at the cost of a higher breakeven. It should not come as a surprise that neither the long stock nor the long call position is better. If one were better than the other, there would be no need for the "worse" one.

In fact, investors will face this type of trade-off with any option strategy: there will be pluses and minuses when compared to a straight stock position. And as we will see in later chapters, there are also trade-offs among the various option strategies: the six-month option, for example, does give us twice as long as the three-month one, but the breakeven is further away from the current stock price.

The buyer of a call option will at some point have to take one of three follow-up actions: sell the option, exercise it, or let it expire. The buyer of our AVP July 50 call could sell this option at any point in time after buying it, just as a stock can be sold after it has been purchased. If the price of the option has risen to the point where a trader wants to take his profit, he simply sells his long position. This is referred to as a closing sale because the trader is liquidating an existing position. After the sale is executed, he will no longer have a position in this option.

The trader's second alternative is to exercise the option. He would do so only if he wanted to own the underlying shares. Most calls are exercised on or very close to their last trading day since there is very little incentive to exercise a call option early. If it is May and a trader owns an AVP July 50 call, he has the right to purchase 100 shares of AVP today at $50. But he will have the same right tomorrow, so why spend the money today when the purchase can be deferred? The $50 can be left in a bank or money market account to earn interest overnight. Of course tomorrow the same reasoning will apply: why pay now, when we can pay later? And so on until the option is about to expire and the investor who truly wants to own the shares must then exercise. Note that if the call is exercised, the effective purchase price of the stock will be $53.20, the call's premium plus the option's strike price, which is the breakeven point calculated above.

The last alternative is to let the call expire worthless. If the forecast of a higher AVP price has proven to be off the mark and by option expiration the stock is trading at $48, $46, or $36, the call will be worthless (and will therefore be impossible to sell) and it will make no economic sense to exercise it. Would you pay $50 for a stock now worth $44? No, and if you still wanted to own shares of AVP you would simply go out and purchase them at $44. So the last choice is to take no action and see the option expire worthless.

This section has looked at the purchase of a call option at only two points in time: the day the position was initiated and at expiration. In Chapter 3 we will return to this strategy and look at its performance in the intervening dates.

Buying Put Options

If purchasing a call option is the most basic bullish option strategy, then buying a put has to be classified as the most basic bearish option strategy. And if the most basic bullish investment strategy is buying a stock, its bearish equivalent is shorting a stock. And so, before we look at purchasing puts, a quick note on shorting stocks.

Assume a trader is convinced that shares of FedEx (FDX) will decline over the next few months, either because of an economic slowdown or because of a dubious claim that someone is on the brink of developing a machine that will be able to send small objects over great distances using existing phone lines. This trader borrows

500 shares from her broker and places an order to sell the shares short. Her order is filled at $60.11. (Note that borrowing the stock of companies with a relatively high number of outstanding shares is usually not a problem as most brokers will have access to these. Borrowing shares of a lightly traded small cap stock may be much more difficult.) If FDX drops to $50, our trader will purchase 500 shares at that price and return these to her broker, generating a $10.11 profit. The short seller essentially reverses the traditional order of buying and selling: instead of buying a stock at $50, waiting for it to go up, and selling it at $60, she first sells the (borrowed) shares, waits for the stock to go down, and then buys in the shares at $50. Of course, if a trader shorts FDX, there is always the possibility that the price will start rising, to $65, $70, or higher. The trader is now in a difficult situation: she sold shares at $60.11 and will have to buy them back at a higher price, creating a trading loss. And since there is theoretically no ceiling to the price of FDX or any other stock, the losses can escalate as the stock hits new highs. Short sellers need nerves of steel and/or a bottomless bank account. Most of us don't fit that profile.

An alternative to selling shares short is to purchase a put option. With FDX trading at $60.11, the May 60 put was offered at $2.90. Purchasing this two-month option gives its holder the right to sell shares (which she does not currently own) at $60 until the option's expiration date. Look at a long put position as the right to short stock, even though this right is rarely invoked. We can now compare a short stock position in FDX to a long put position.

Risk. The put buyer cannot lose more than the $2.90 premium paid. As noted, the risk of a short stock position is theoretically unlimited, although it is more accurate to say the risk is substantial. Advantage put buyer.

Profit potential. A virtual tie, as for every dollar FDX drops, the short stock generates $1 in profit and the put's intrinsic value increases by $1.

Capital required. Shorting a stock actually generates cash as the proceeds from the short sale are credited to the trader's account. But additional funds are required to margin the position, usually

50% of the value of the shorted stock. And if the stock starts climbing, additional margin may be required. Unlike a long stock position, which can be paid for in full up front, there is always the possibility that a short stock position will require additional funds. The put buyer pays the $2.90 and no more. A plus for the put buyer.

Breakeven point. The short stock position starts generating profits as soon as FDX drops below $60.11. For the put buyer to make money at option expiration the stock has to be below $57.10. The downside breakeven on a long put position is calculated by subtracting the premium ($2.90) from the put's exercise price (60). The short stock position has the higher breakeven, which is a net advantage.

Time constraints. A trader could maintain a short stock position ad infinitum, provided he pays all the dividends declared and has the capital required to maintain the position in rising markets. The put buyer has only until the option's expiration date.

Dividends. A trader who shorts a stock becomes liable for any dividends paid. This is a minor issue with FDX, which only pays a $0.05 quarterly dividend. But if a trader maintains a short position in FDX over the next ex-dividend date, she would have to pay this $0.05 dividend to the broker from whom the shares were borrowed. This is to compensate the broker who would otherwise still be long the shares and entitled to this dividend. Put buyers have no dividend liabilities, so a small plus in their favor.

Suitability. Obtaining approval at your brokerage firm to short stocks may be a long tedious process involving numerous forms and various financial requirements such as account size, net worth, and maybe others. Getting approved for buying puts is usually straightforward, this being one of the strategies brokerage firms allow to newcomers to the options market. Advantage put buyer.

Profitability at expiration. To complete the comparison, Table 1.2 calculates the profitability of both strategies for various FDX prices at option expiration.

Table 1.2

FDX Price at Expiration	Profit/(Loss) on Short Stock	Value of 60 Put	Cost of 60 Put	Profit/(Loss) on Put
$48	$12.11	$12	($2.90)	$9.10
$51	$9.11	$9	($2.90)	$6.10
$54	$6.11	$6	($2.90)	$3.10
$57	$3.11	$3	($2.90)	$0.10
$60	$0.11	$0	($2.90)	($2.90)
$63	($2.89)	$0	($2.90)	($2.90)
$66	($5.89)	$0	($2.90)	($2.90)
$69	($8.89)	$0	($2.90)	($2.90)

The table above assumes FDX was shorted at $60.11 and the May 60 put was purchased for $2.90. One can observe that as the price of FDX drops the put value at expiration increases, generating higher and higher profits. On the upside, the put buyer's risk is limited to the premium paid, whereas the losses on the short stock will continue to increase as FDX hits new highs. These numbers are presented in a different form in Figure 1.3.

Once again the trade-offs between a position in options and one in the underlying stock are clearly seen: higher breakeven for the

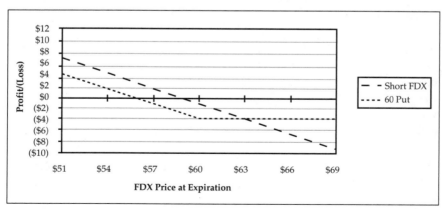

Figure 1.3 Short FDX vs. Long 60 Put

short stock position (this is a positive for a bearish strategy) versus limited risk for the long put position.

As with call options, the put buyer will have to take one of three courses of action at some point before option expiration: sell the long option, exercise it, or let it expire worthless. If at expiration FDX has increased in price, the put will be worthless and logic dictates that the trader let it expire worthless. On the other hand, if the stock has dropped to the trader's target price at or prior to expiration, she may want to take profits by selling her option. The third avenue will be taken by very few traders in very limited circumstances: exercising this put would create a short position in FDX stock and would be done only by those traders who have a short account and who wish to maintain a bearish position past the option expiration date. Most traders sitting on a profitable trade will be happy simply to liquidate their long option position.

Investors who want to take a long equity position have two basic strategies: purchase the stock or buy a call option. Traders looking to take a short position in a stock will for the most part be limited to the purchase of put options. This may in the end be all for the better: stock buyers at times look to establish longer-term positions where the time-limiting nature of options may eliminate these as a viable alternative. Traders looking to go short a stock rarely do so within a multiyear time horizon. Their focus is usually on the short- to mid-term, where options work best and where their limited risk aspect may actually permit sticking with a bearish position for a longer period of time. Too many traders who short stocks cover their positions at the first hint of a rally, not wanting to get caught in a major up move, just to see the stock head south days after they cut their losses. Options may actually give these traders added staying power.

Writing Options: Covered and Uncovered

Whenever an option is written, an obligation is assumed. If the option writer is in a position to fully meet this obligation, the option will be considered covered. Otherwise, it will be treated as uncovered, or naked.

The writer of a call option has assumed the obligation to sell shares of the underlying stock. The short option position will be covered if the writer owns sufficient shares of stock to deliver if she is assigned. An investor who is required to sell shares she owns does not face a problem (although she may not be happy with the selling price), but an investor who does not own the shares will have to scramble and purchase them, which may be an expensive proposition.

The writer of a put has assumed the obligation to purchase a stock. If obligated to buy shares, an investor must pay, i.e., must deliver cash. So a short put option is considered covered if the investor has sufficient cash set aside for the eventual purchase of these shares. (Not everyone in the industry agrees with our use of the expression *covered put*; some prefer the phrase *cash-secured put*.)

Because of the substantial risks associated with uncovered short options, we will limit our discussion to covered options in this first chapter, where our goal is to establish a firm foundation.

Writing Covered Calls

The writer of a call option assumes the obligation to sell shares of the underlying stock; the call is covered if the writer owns sufficient shares of stock to deliver in the event of an assignment. Calls can be written on shares held in a portfolio, or they can be written simultaneously with a stock purchase. The latter strategy is known as a buy/write. Both of these call writing strategies are explained in greater detail in Chapter 2.

To understand the basics of covered calls let's start with the following example:

Dell Computers (DELL):	$25.92
May 27½ call:	$1.30
May 30 call:	$0.55
May 32½ call:	$0.20

An investor holding DELL shares decides to write the May 27½ calls against his stock position. (May options have nine weeks until expiration). When an investor writes an option, the premium is credited to his account on the next business day. If the option is covered, as it is in our example, the investor is free to withdraw these funds or reinvest them elsewhere. So the immediate impact of writing covered calls is that it generates positive cash flow. The longer-term impact is that the investor may be forced to sell his shares at the option's exercise price, $27.50 in our example. We may appear to be stating the obvious, but no investor should write covered calls unless he or she is comfortable selling the shares under option at the strike price. Why would anyone commit to selling a stock at a price that seems inadequate? So let's compare the results of this strategy to those obtained by another investor who holds shares of DELL but does not write calls against them.

Risk. Both the stockholder and the covered writer are long shares and have to bear the full downside risk of the stock position. The covered writer gets paid $1.30 per share when writing the call, so one could rightfully claim that his overall risk has been reduced by this amount. In our example the option premium represents 5% of the stock price, so the covered writer ends up with 95% of the risk of the stock owner. Slight advantage to the covered writer.

Profit potential. This issue is more complex than it may appear. Looking strictly at the absolute upside potential, the stockholder is the obvious winner. If DELL goes to $30, $35, and $40 she sees her profits increasing with every up-tick in the stock price. The covered writer has agreed to sell his shares at $27.50 and so will participate in the stock appreciation only up to that point.

But under less bullish assumptions, the covered writer comes out ahead financially. Start with an unchanged stock price scenario: in nine weeks DELL is still trading in the neighborhood of $26. The stockholder has neither made nor lost any money, but the covered call writer sees the option expire worthless and gets to keep the option premium of $1.30. He ends up holding his DELL shares, but is ahead of the stock owner by $1.30. Even in moderately bullish scenarios, the covered writer comes out ahead: with DELL at $27 the calls still expire worthless and the covered writer remains ahead by $1.30. At $28 the short calls will be assigned and the shares sold at $27.50, so the covered writer has a $0.50 opportunity loss, but the $1.30 option premium keeps him ahead on an overall basis. The verdict: mixed, as the two strategies' profitability will be a function of the stock price at option expiration.

Table 1.3

DELL Price at Expiration	Profit/(Loss) on Long Stock	Profit/(Loss) on Stock for Covered Write	Option Premium	Profit/(Loss) on Covered Write
$20	($5.92)	($5.92)	$1.30	($4.62)
$22.50	($3.42)	($3.42)	$1.30	($2.12)
$25	($0.92)	($0.92)	$1.30	$0.38
$27.50	$1.58	$1.58	$1.30	$2.88
$30	$4.08	$1.58	$1.30	$2.88
$32.50	$6.58	$1.58	$1.30	$2.88

Dividends. Since the stockholder and the covered writer are both full-fledged stock owners, they both receive dividends, company financial statements, and other goodies. A tie.

Table 1.3 gives a detailed picture of the performance of the covered write strategy relative to a long stock position for various DELL prices at option expiration.

A few comments are in order. First, on the downside, the covered writer's total losses are lower by $1.30 when compared to the stock owner's. On the upside, the covered writer's total profit keeps pace with the long stock position up to a stock price of $28.80, which represents the call's exercise price plus the option premium received. Table 1.3 also shows the profit on the stock for covered write reaching its maximum of $1.58 at the option's strike price of $27.50. This is simply because it is assumed that if the stock rises above this price the short call position will be assigned, the shares will be sold at $27.50, and the profit on the stock will thus be limited to $1.58. These numbers are presented in another form in Figure 1.4.

We can now clearly see the range over which the covered calls work best: from $24.62 (the downside breakeven) to $28.80 (above which price owning unhedged shares is more profitable). And this gives us a clear indication as to when investors should consider writing covered calls: if the underlying stock is expected to move strongly, either to the upside or to the downside, avoid writing covered calls. But when a stock is expected to remain within a relatively

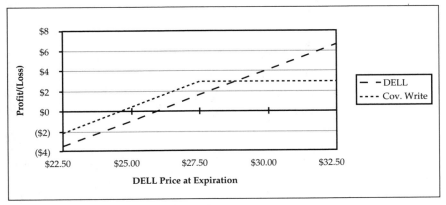

Figure 1.4 Long DELL vs. Covered Write

tight range around its current price, the strategy becomes very interesting. Chapter 2 analyzes this strategy in depth.

Writing Covered Puts

The writer of a put option assumes the obligation to purchase shares of the stock under option at the exercise price until the expiration date. If the investor has sufficient cash set aside to fully pay for the stock should she be assigned, the put is covered (or *cash-secured*, as noted earlier).

Sometimes investors are looking to add shares of a particular stock to their portfolio and are willing to pay the going market price. They then simply instruct their broker to buy this equity. At other times, they are looking to purchase a stock but are not willing to pay the current price. They would rather wait for the stock to come down to a level where it represents a better buying opportunity. They can either monitor the price of the stock and pounce if it gets down to their target price, or they can place an open order instructing their broker to buy the shares at a stated price. In either case they run the risk of the stock "running away" from them; that is, its going up significantly before they have had a chance to take a long position.

An alternative strategy to the waiting game or the open order is to write a put option. Look at the following quotes:

Caterpillar (CAT): $59.49
May 55 put: $1.10

An investor would like to add CAT to her portfolio but is unwilling to pay $59.49. She decides to write the May 55 put instead of placing an open order to purchase shares at $55. The May options have nine weeks until they expire. Let's compare her decision to write puts to the open order alternative.

Risk. The ultimate risk is stock ownership: both the put writer and the investor who places an open order to buy the stock at $55 could end up as stock owners and would thereby have the full downside risk of the stock. In our example, the investor who places the open order would have $55 at risk (the cost of the stock). With just $53.90 at risk (the $55 cost of the stock less the $1.10 option premium received), the put writer has a slight advantage.

Stock never gets down to target price. If CAT does not drift down to $55 by option expiration, neither investor will end up owning the stock. The difference is that the investor who placed the open order will have nothing to show for his efforts, while the put writer will keep the $1.10 option premium for writing the put. The put writer is in fact being paid to wait, and when the put expires worthless, she may have the opportunity to write a CAT July 55 put and capture additional option premium. A net advantage to the put writer.

Cost of changing one's mind. The investor who places an open order can change her mind at any time, at no cost, so long as she does this before CAT hits $55. Changing her mind could mean deciding not to purchase the stock after all, or moving her buying target up or down. The put writer's situation is a bit more complex as she may be able to change her mind even after CAT has dipped below the $55 strike price. The put writer can cancel her obligation to buy CAT by covering the puts she wrote; i.e., by buying back the May 55 puts. If CAT has risen or remained unchanged, she will probably be able to buy back the puts for less than the premium she obtained when writing them, generating a small profit. If, on the other hand, CAT has fallen below $55 and the puts have not yet been assigned, our investor will still have a chance to cover her puts, but she may be doing so at a loss if the options are trading above the $1.10 premium she received. So a mixed verdict: no cost to the investor who placed the open order and who acts in due time, but for the put writer a little more time to act (as it is extremely unlikely that the options would be assigned as soon as CAT hits $55) but the possibility that covering the short put position will result in a loss.

Stock at target price only briefly. If CAT pulls back from its current price and drops to, say, $54.50, where it trades for a few days, and then rallies back to the $60 area, an investor who placed an open order will have purchased the shares at $55 as she was waiting in the queue bidding $55. The put writer will probably not be assigned on her short put, especially if CAT makes only a brief trip below $55. The investor with the open order only needs CAT to trade down to $54.99 to purchase her shares; the put writer will either need CAT to be below $55 at expiration (in which case it is virtually certain she will be assigned on her puts) or for the stock to drop significantly below the option's strike price in order to get assigned early. A slight advantage goes to the investor with the open order.

Table 1.4 calculates the put writer's profit and loss for various CAT prices at option expiration.

Before we comment on some of the numbers in Table 1.4, let's review the three alternatives open to the writer of a put option.

Table 1.4

CAT Price at Option Expiration	Change in CAT Price from $59.49	Value of 55 Put	Premium Received from Writing 55 Put	Profit/(Loss) on 55 Put
$65	$5.51	$0	$1.10	$1.10
$60	$0.51	$0	$1.10	$1.10
$55	($4.49)	$0	$1.10	$1.10
$50	($9.49)	($5.00)	$1.10	($3.90)
$45	($14.49)	($10.00)	$1.10	($8.90)

- If the option is out-of-the-money, the simplest choice is to let this option expire worthless. In our example, this outcome would require CAT to be trading above $55 at expiration.

- The put writer may decide to cancel her obligation by covering (buying back) the written option. If the option is trading below $1.10 when it is covered, the trade results in a profit; otherwise, a loss would have to be absorbed.

- Wait for the option to be assigned. If CAT is trading below $55 and the expiration date is fast approaching, the investor who sticks to her game plan of buying CAT at $55 does nothing and waits to be advised by her broker that she has been assigned on her short put position and is therefore now a CAT shareholder.

Given these three alternatives, the numbers in Table 1.4 can be interpreted as follows: if CAT ends up above $55 at option expiration, the put writer will pocket $1.10 as the option expires worthless. If CAT drifts down below $55 and the decision is made to cover the put, the loss realized is that given in the far-right-hand column. But if the put writer decides to wait for assignment and purchase the stock, the losses calculated in the far-right-hand column would only represent unrealized losses on the stock purchased at $55 but with a cost basis of $53.90. In this last instance the investor would own the shares and would be at risk of any further decline in the price of CAT but would also be in a position to benefit from any rally in the price of the stock. If this investor wrote the put in order to purchase CAT on a pullback in its price, we have to assume that her outlook for the longer term is that at $55, CAT represents good value and that she is comfortable holding these shares, even though they may now be below her purchase price.

Figure 1.5 gives a visual representation of the strategy's potential profit and loss, keeping in mind that if the stock is purchased on assignment, the losses are unrealized.

As a reference point, Figure 1.5 also illustrates the profit and loss of a long stock position taken at a $59.49 price. Not illustrated is the result of placing an open order to purchase CAT at $55; the profit and loss on such an order would depend on whether or not CAT traded down to $55 over the next nine weeks.

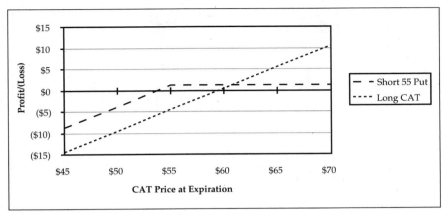

Figure 1.5 Long CAT vs. Short 55 Put

The Building Blocks

The four strategies described here represent all the building blocks necessary to create any option position. The following chapters will look at these strategies on their own and in conjunction with one another in more complex positions such as spreads and straddles.

2

BASIC
INVESTMENT
STRATEGIES

MOST OPTION STRATEGISTS use the expressions *covered write* and *buy/write* interchangeably to refer to the same option strategy. We beg to differ. Although both strategies involve a long stock position and the writing of call options, we view the covered write and the buy/write as two distinct strategies to be used in different investment environments.

For investors who have never traded listed options, the covered write is probably the best place to get their feet wet; we will make it this chapter's starting point as well. For most brokerage firms, covered writing is a "Level 1" strategy, which means it is relatively easy to get approval for it and it may represent the first step in getting experience to move on to more complex strategies.

Covered Writing

As explained in Chapter 1, a covered write combines a long stock position with written call options. The first question we need to answer is when would an investor initiate a covered write.

Entering into the Strategy

Say you own 500 shares of Harley-Davidson (HDI) that you purchased a little while ago and that are now trading at $50.01. The stock has moved up nicely since you purchased it, and although you are not ready to pull the trigger you would certainly become a seller on a rally to the $55 area. A couple of clicks of your mouse and you find the following quotes on HDI call options:

July 55 calls (4 weeks):	$0.55–$0.65
August 55 calls (8 weeks):	$1.15–$1.30
November 55 calls (21 weeks):	$2.60–$2.75

If you are looking to sell your shares at $55 you could always enter an open order with your brokerage firm instructing them to sell your shares when they reach this target price. Or you could consider writing five HDI call options. You would be assuming the obligation to sell your 500 shares at $55, a price you are comfortable with. Should you write the July calls, the August, the November, or look at the even longer-dated options? November looks like a long time away. July is just around the corner, but $0.55 on 500 shares represents $275 before transaction costs, not what you consider a significant amount. The August calls look interesting: $1.15 per share translates into $575 before fees, not a negligible amount, and you are comfortable holding your shares over the next eight weeks. Instead of placing an open order to sell your shares at $55, you write five of the August 55 calls.

Possible Outcomes

The best thing that can happen to you (meaning the outcome that generates the highest profit) is for HDI to rally somewhere north of $55 by the August expiration date, the call options to be assigned, and for you to sell your shares at your target price of $55. Of course, an investor who writes options receives a premium, which he gets to keep. This amount would be credited to his account on the business day following the trade (one-day settlement), and since there is no margin required on this option position, the cash can be withdrawn or reinvested. Another way to look at it is that if the calls are assigned and you do end up delivering your shares at $55, your effective selling price would be $56.15—$55 from the sale of the stock and $1.15 from writing the options.

The second possibility is for HDI to rally but not reach $55. It could be anywhere in the $51 to $54 range at August expiration, in which case the calls you wrote would expire worthless and you would keep the option premium. In addition, you could either sell your shares, write another five 55 calls (expiring in September or October), or revise your target price. In any case, you would still pocket the $1.15 per share you received when you initiated the option position.

Finally, HDI could drop in price by August expiration. At this point it will be necessary to revise your original target price of $55. Is this still realistic? Do you still want to hold the shares? Is $50 a more realistic exit point? If you answered yes to the last question, then writing September or October 50 calls may make the most sense. In any case, you still keep the $1.15 option premium.

And what if, should HDI rally past $55, you decide to reconsider your target price of $55? We deal with this topic later in the chapter, in the section titled "Rolling Strategies."

Covered Writing Against Losing Positions

It's easy to set a selling target on a stock that was purchased at a lower price. But what if you bought shares of AOL Time Warner (AOL) in the $30 to $31 range and the stock in now $27.66? Does it make sense to write covered calls?

To answer this question, forget about options. You bought AOL, the stock is down, and you are reevaluating this investment. If you come to the conclusion that it is best to cut your losses and reinvest the funds somewhere else, then covered writing may be a strategic alternative. For instance the two-month 30 calls are trading at $0.80. If you write these and the stock rebounds to $30, you could get out even or with a slight profit. But the option's premium of $0.80 may be a small consolation if the stock continues its southbound journey and ends up in the $20 range.

If you are a disciplined investor, you have sold stocks at a loss. Writing covered calls against a losing stock position can ease the pain. Some investors refuse to write calls under these circumstances because they don't want to lock in a loss. But whenever you sell a stock at a price below its cost basis, you are also locking in a loss.

Another way to deal with losing stock positions is the repair strategy outlined in Chapter 5.

The Naked Covered Writer

Although the expression appears to be an oxymoron, we have encountered many naked covered writers. These are investors who, to continue with the same example, may hold shares of HDI and have no intention of selling them. They look at the July 55 calls and conclude: "This stock will never get to $55 over the next four weeks, so I'll write the July 55 calls. It's not a lot of money, but it's free money."

Naked covered writers are effectively writing uncovered call options. It's not that they don't hold the underlying security they might be forced to deliver, but that they have no intention of making good on their obligation. They may as well not own the shares, but then they would run into problems with their brokerage firm's compliance department. So they use stocks they own to margin their uncovered option positions.

We all know what happens at some point. Within two weeks, HDI rallies to $56 or $57 and the naked covered writer is forced to cover his short option position. He pays $2 or $3 for options he wrote at $0.55. If you recognize yourself here, it's time to own up. Maybe you have been going to cocktail parties telling everyone that you have been "trading options" by writing some covered calls. Except that you never, or rarely, let a stock get called away. When your short calls go in-the-money, you cover them so you won't have to sell your shares. This is probably a very good indication that covered writing is not for you. Maybe you don't have the temperament or the risk profile of a covered writer. As long as you recognize it, this should not be a problem. There are plenty of other options strategies out there (eight additional chapters follow this one), and one or two may be better suited to your investing style.

Covered Writing Conclusion

We view covered writing primarily as a strategy to help you set selling targets. For a lot of investors, writing covered calls increases their discipline: they are forced to decide today at what price they will sell a stock they own. They will need enough discipline not to turn into a naked covered writer.

Another take on covered writing is that it can be a profitable alternative to entering open sell orders on stocks in a portfolio. There is no cost to entering an open sell order, but there is also no benefit to the investor if the underlying stock never reaches the order's selling price. Writing a covered call can be viewed as "getting paid" to wait, for the option premium is kept whether the stock reaches the option's strike price or not. The downside of the covered write is that an open order can be canceled at any time at no cost. The covered writer who changes his mind can cover his short option position, but if the stock has rallied sufficiently, buying back these calls may result in a trading loss on the option position.

The Buy/Write

We view the buy/write as a package: an investor buys a stock and writes call options simultaneously—a trade that is easily placed at most brokerage houses. If the covered write is a strategy used to sell stock at target prices, the buy/write is initiated with the aim of earning a specified rate of return on the overall strategy.

Assume, for example, that an investor is looking to establish a buy/write on Microsoft (MSFT) trading at $64.05. The following short-term options are listed for trading:

February 65 call (3 weeks):	$1.35–$1.45
February 70 call (3 weeks):	$0.15–$0.25
February 75 call (3 weeks):	$0.00–$0.10
March 65 call (7 weeks):	$2.45–$2.55
March 70 call (7 weeks):	$0.75–$0.80
March 75 call (7 weeks):	$0.20–$0.25

Our investor selects the March 65 calls (we'll discuss option selection below), buys 400 shares of MSFT, and writes four of the selected calls at $2.45. There are two returns that should interest investors initiating buy/writes: the static and the if-called returns.

Static Return

The static return answers the question What will my return be if the price of the underlying stock remains unchanged? It is calculated as follows:

$$\frac{\$2.45}{\$64.05 - \$2.45} = 3.98\%$$

It is also customary to annualize this return, especially when comparing buy/writes using options with varying terms to expiration. This is done as follows:

$$\frac{3.98\% \times 52 \text{ weeks}}{7 \text{ weeks}} = 29.5\%$$

A more refined calculation of this return would take into account transaction fees and dividends (if any) that would be received. Remember to include dividends as part of your return on investment if the ex-date (and not the payable date) falls between the day the position is initiated and the options' expiration date.

Some may argue that we are double-counting the option premium in the above calculation because it appears in both the numerator (representing the profit earned) and the denominator (where it reduces the initial investment). To understand where we are coming from, assume an investor initiates a buy/write in an account that is initially empty. She purchases the shares at $64.05 and receives $2.45 for writing the call. She obviously has to pay for the stock, but the option premium can be used to partially pay for these shares. So she needs to deposit only $61.60 per share in her account to fully pay for the position. This is her initial investment and the denominator in our equation. If the price of the shares remains unchanged, the options expire worthless and she is left with the shares worth $64.05—a profit of $2.45 and equal to the option premium; this is the numerator in our equation.

If-Called Return

The if-called return represents the best-case scenario. This return will be earned only if the underlying stock rises above the options' exercise price, the options are assigned, and the shares are sold at $65. Its calculation is similar to the static return calculation, but it also includes the stock's appreciation from its purchase price ($64.05) to its potential selling price ($65). This represents the maximum return the strategy can generate.

$$\frac{\$2.45 + \$0.95}{\$64.05 - \$2.45} = 5.52\%$$

Once again, it is customary to annualize this last return.

$$\frac{5.52\% \times 52 \text{ weeks}}{7 \text{ weeks}} = 41\%$$

There are two assumptions behind this last eye-popping number. The first is that MSFT will rise above $65 and the shares held will be called away. The second is that buy/writes with similar if-called returns will also generate their maximum potential returns. So take the 41% with a grain of salt and don't expect that kind of return consistently with this strategy.

Expiration and Strike Price Selection

The preceding example quoted six available option series, which was only a fraction of all the options listed. April and July expirations were also available, as were two series of LEAPS expiring in roughly 12 and 24 months. The strike prices also stretched from $25 to $110 for some of the short-term options and from $30 to $180 for the LEAPS. Where does one begin in selecting expiration and strike?

First, a lot of options can be eliminated simply because they are so far in- or out-of-the-money. Looking at the February options we listed, the 70 call was bid at $0.15, and there was no bid on the 75 call (and those with higher strikes). The February 65 call was $1.35 bid; calculating the annualized returns with this call we get 37% for static and 63% for if-called. The numbers look better than those obtained with the March 65 call, but transaction fees will represent a greater percentage of the option premium and the final numbers could end up being close to equal, especially the static return.

Moving to the March options we note the 75 calls bid at $0.20 (not worth it in dollar terms) and the 70 calls at $0.75. What about this last one? Here are the returns:

$$\text{Static:} \quad \frac{\$0.75}{\$64.05 - \$0.75} = 1.18\% \text{ or } 8.8\% \text{ annualized}$$

$$\text{If-called:} \quad \frac{\$0.75 + \$5.95}{\$64.05 - \$0.75} = 10.6\% \text{ or } 78\% \text{ annualized}$$

By comparing the returns from the March 65 and 70 calls we can focus in on one of the key decisions relating to the buy/write. The 65 call has a higher static return, 29.5% annualized, than the 70 call (8.8% ann.). On the other hand, the 70 call has a higher if-called return of 78% annualized versus 41% for the 65 call. The trade-off comes down to higher static return (obtained with at-the-money options) or higher if-called returns (generated by writing out-of-the-money calls). Keep in mind that a buy/write has a higher probability of earning its static return than of earning its if-called return. Also notice that as one writes calls that are further and further out-of-the-money, more and more of the strategy's total potential return comes from stock appreciation and not from the premium received from writing the options. The potential if-called return of the March 65 call was $2.45 from the options' premium and $0.95 from stock appreciation; for the March 70 call, there was $0.75 of option premium and a full $5.95 of stock appreciation. The more out-of-the-money the call written, the more the overall position starts looking like a straight long stock position.

There is no one correct answer, but when establishing a buy/write, keep the following in mind:

- Shorter-term options will produce higher annualized static returns; be wary of returns generated by options that have less than one month until expiration. These numbers are not realistic because it is impossible to repeat a two-week buy/write 24 times in one calendar year.

- There is a relatively low probability of realizing the if-called return of shorter-term options. Remember, this requires the stock to move up to or above the option's strike price by the expiration date.

- The further out-of-the-money the written call, the more the position behaves like a pure equity position. If you are so bullish on a $50 stock that you are only willing to write the 60 strike, maybe you should simply forget about the option. The small premium received will probably not generate a significant static return and is probably an inadequate payment for the upside you are giving up.

Breakeven and Downside Protection

In addition to the two returns calculated above, investors usually refer to a third number: the strategy's breakeven. Our MSFT buy/write had us purchasing shares at $64.05 and writing the March 65 calls at $2.45. Our net outlay was $61.60, which represents the strategy's breakeven point. A $61.60 stock price at option expiration would have us losing $2.45 on the stock but realizing a gain of $2.45 on the options expiring worthless. We would be breaking even because even though the gain on the option is a taxable event, the unrealized loss on the stock isn't (unless we immediately sell the stock).

Downside protection simply tells us how far below the current stock price our breakeven point is. A $61.60 breakeven gives us 3.8% downside protection.

In-the-Money Buy/Writes

Is there any argument in favor of an in-the-money buy/write? For instance, one could purchase Procter & Gamble (PG) at $81.88 and write a six-week 80 call at $3.40. Since the call is in-the-money, the static return will be the same as the if-called return (if the stock remains unchanged, the call will be assigned). The profit potential is limited to $1.52 (the $3.40 of option premium less the loss on the stock purchased at $81.88 and sold at $80), a 1.94% return, or 16.8% annualized. This is a more conservative strategy as its maximum profit will be attained even if the price of the stock drops, as long as it does not go below $80.

What about moving even further in-the-money and writing the six-week 75 call for $7.30? The profit potential is now down to $0.42—a return of 0.56%, or 4.8% annualized. This is probably too low a return as it was calculated before transaction costs were taken into account.

Turning to a more volatile stock, we find Amazon.com (AMZN) trading at $14.05, the 11-week 12½ call at $2.75 and the 11-week 10 call at $4.50. Crunching the numbers we find that the 12½ call yields a profit of $1.20, or 10.6% (50% annualized), and the 10 call a $0.45 profit, or 4.7% (22% annualized). If the 22% annualized rate of return that would be realized even if AMZN dropped $4 (a full 28% of its current price) sounds very appealing, please read the next section on stock selection and turn to the section on taxes in Chapter 10. This last point would be moot if the position were initiated in a tax-deferred account.

Stock Selection

You have a certificate of deposit that is coming due and, given the low interest rates, you decide to enter the equity markets via a buy/write. You have narrowed your search to two candidates, and when you calculate the potential returns with two-month options you obtain the following:

Bills Pills: Static return: 1.5%   If-called return: 3.1%
    (9% ann.)   (18.6% ann.)
Bobs Lobs: Static return: 2.2%   If-called return: 4.5%
    (13.2% ann.)   (27% ann.)

Looks like a no-brainer: Bobs has a higher static and a higher if-called return. Why bother with Bills? But wait. Selecting your buy/writes strictly on the basis of returns is a recipe for disaster. Bobs is providing higher returns because the options are trading with higher premiums. But high option premiums usually reflect higher risk. If you build a buy/write portfolio based on the highest returns available, you will end up owning a collection of extremely high-risk stocks. Is this what you are trying to accomplish?

Most investors view the buy/write as a risk reduction technique, so it is doubtful that those attracted to the strategy would want to fill their portfolio with today's most volatile issues that may turn out to be in tomorrow's equity obituaries. The most important point to remember is that a buy/write involves purchasing a stock. If you were not doing a buy/write, would you still want this stock in your portfolio? If the answer is no, you should not include it in your buy/write program.

Selecting stocks for buy/writes. If you are a straight stock buyer, you must be able to identify stocks that will go up in price in order to make profitable trades. However, if you are initiating buy/writes you need only identify stocks that will remain unchanged or go up for the strategy to be profitable. The good news for investors who use options is that the stocks that remain unchanged or go up (the buy/write candidates) outnumber the stocks that go up (the long stock candidates).

Rolling Strategies

These follow-up strategies are as applicable to covered writes as they are to buy/writes although their primary appeal will be to investors using buy/writes.

Rolling Out

A few months ago you initiated a buy/write, purchasing Johnson & Johnson (JNJ) and writing the March 65 calls. It is now Wednesday before option expiration and JNJ has rallied to $66. Assuming the stock remains unchanged over the next 48 hours, you will be assigned on your calls and forced to deliver your shares. Should you let well enough alone, or should you take action and see if you can milk this position for another month? Consider the following markets:

JNJ:	$66
March 65 call:	$1.00–$1.10
April 65 call:	$2.10–$2.20

The March option has 3 days until expiration, and the April option has 31 days. A straight rollout consists in buying the 65 call (at $1.10) to cover the current short option and simultaneously writing the April 65 call (at $2.10), a roll that can presently be executed for a $1 credit. Your obligation to sell your shares of JNJ at $65 would be extended another four weeks and you would net $1 in the process. Does this trade make any sense?

We start our analysis by assuming nothing is done, in which case the calls will be assigned, you will be forced to sell your shares, and you will end up with $65 in cash. You will probably start looking for a new investment opportunity for this sum. If you decide to roll out your short call position, you would be earning $1 over the next four weeks. Your return would therefore be: $1 ÷ $65 = 1.54%, which can be annualized as follows: 1.54% × (365 / 28) = 20.0%.

Some comments on the numbers used, and those not used, in our analysis. We use $1 because this is the extra return rolling out will generate. If JNJ went ex-dividend between the March and April expirations, we would add the dividend amount to the net option premium because it would increase our return. We use $65 as the denominator in calculating our return for the simple reason that if we do nothing this is the amount of cash we will have to reinvest. By rolling out we generate an extra dollar on $65—not on the current stock price of $66 (as far as we are concerned it doesn't matter by how much JNJ is above $65 since any price above our option's exercise price will result in assignment). The number of days used to annualize our rate of return is 28, which represents the length of the strategy's extension, not the 31 days until the April options expire since we are locked into the strategy for the next three days.

Two numbers that did not enter into our analysis are the original cost of the stock and the premium received from writing the March 65 calls. Accountants refer to these as *sunk costs*. There is nothing we can do to change our cost basis on the shares, and whatever we received from writing the March call was credited to our account some time ago and has probably been reinvested. Yes, we may be covering the March call at a price that is higher than the premium originally received, thereby creating a "loss" on this individual option, but it is necessary to look at the bigger picture. If the March call was originally written for $0.60, covering it at $1.10 will create a $0.50 loss, but the effective selling price of our JNJ shares will have been raised from $65.60 (the 65 strike price plus the March option premium of $0.60) to $66.60 (the 65 strike price plus the March premium of $0.60 plus the $1.00 credit generated by rolling out). The "loss" on the March option will be compensated by a higher "profit" on the sale of the stock, assuming the April calls are eventually assigned.

Rolling our short March 65 calls to April is not without risks. We would not be earning a 20% annualized rate of return if this were a slam dunk. We will be holding the shares an additional month, during which time they could decline substantially. Our original buy/write presumed that we were comfortable holding shares of JNJ, and our rolling out the option position is based on the same assumption.

In our example, JNJ was only $1 above the short calls' exercise price. As the underlying stock moves further and further above the calls' strike price, the less attractive rolling out becomes. We can estimate the net credit of the March to April rollout to be $0.70 with JNJ at $67, $0.40 at $68, and $0.20 at $69. At some point, an investor will decide to let the stock go—i.e., wait for assignment and reinvest the cash obtained somewhere else, or look at an alternative strategy such as rolling up and out, the topic of our next section.

Rolling Up and Out

Let's look at the situation of an investor who wrote covered calls on her shares of General Dynamics (GD). She wrote the May 90s when the stock was trading around $87 and is now looking at the following situation on the Wednesday before May expiration:

GD:	$94
May 90 call:	$4.00–$4.10
June 90 call:	$5.60–$5.70
June 95 call:	$2.90–$3.00
July 95 call:	$4.20–$4.30

Rolling from the May 90s to the June 90s would generate a $1.50 credit, an excellent rate of return. Although our investor originally thought that selling her shares at $90 would represent a fair price, she is now wondering if she could raise her exit point.

She considers rolling her May 90 calls up (to a higher strike price) and out (to a further expiration date) to the June 95 calls, but she realizes that paying $4.10 to cover her May option and writing the June 95s for $2.90 would leave her out of pocket $1.20. Looking slightly further out, she notices the July 95 calls at $4.20; she could pay $4.10 to cover her May option, write the July 95 call at $4.20, get credited a dime (and use it to cover her transaction costs), not be out a penny, and have raised her GD selling price from $90 to $95.

This textbook illustration of rolling up and out highlights the conditions necessary for the trade to make economic sense. First, GD is a somewhat more volatile stock than JNJ, and covered writers will quickly learn that it is difficult to roll up and out with low-volatility stocks. Second, to be executed for even money (or a slight credit), the roll necessitated moving from an expiring option to one expiring two months later, not the next available month. One of the reasons a lot of investors are attracted to covered writing is the positive cash flow the strategy generates. But if a covered writer is forever rolling up and out for debits, the raison d'être of the strategy is nullified.

By rolling up and out, our investor obtains an additional $5 of potential profit from her covered write. But note the importance of the word *potential*. GD is currently at $94, and the additional $5 will be realized only if the stock is trading at or above $95 in two months. Moreover, by moving her expiration date from May to July she must hold her shares an additional two months, during which time she has to bear the full downside risk of this equity position. But under the right circumstances, which we view as keeping the time commitment relatively short and being able to roll for even money or a credit, rolling up and out definitely should have a place in the covered writer's arsenal.

Rolling Down

A few months ago an investor purchased shares of Liz Claiborne (LIZ) in the low 30s and wrote the 35 calls as part of his covered writing program. The stock has since retreated to $28 and the short calls expired worthless this past Saturday. This investor would like to continue writing call options against his stock position, but a quick look at LIZ option quotes has revealed the four-month 35 call to be $0.10 bid. Writing options for a dime makes very little sense, and he is now wondering if he should consider writing a lower strike price call, such as the 30s, effectively rolling down.

But wait, someone tells him, if you paid in the low 30s for the stock and write the 30 calls, you are committing yourself to selling your shares below their cost, effectively locking in a loss. Why would anyone want to lock in a losing position?

This is a recurring question, and we like to answer it with a question we asked a few pages back: do you ever sell stocks at a loss? Disciplined investors will tell you that it is imperative to sell losers: if you sell only your winning positions and keep all of your stocks that have gone underwater, sooner or later you will end up with a portfolio made up entirely of your mistakes. Getting rid of your errors is the only way to keep moving forward.

With those not so original comments in mind, let's take another look at LIZ. Our investor purchased shares in the low 30s and the stock is at $28, so the question becomes should he jettison the stock at the current price, or should he write the 30 calls hoping to sell the shares on a rally to $30? We have no objections to writing calls with a strike price below the cost of the underlying stock. We view the disciplined covered writer as one who sticks to the game plan and one who also knows that absorbing losses is part of investing.

In our LIZ example the decision should be based primarily on our investor's revised outlook for the stock. If the drop to $28 is seen as the start of a downtrend, the shares should probably be sold immediately. If it is seen as a mere correction within a bull market, then writing the 30 calls will generate some immediate cash flow, in addition to setting a selling target where one's losses will be cut. Psychologically, this may not be the easiest position to establish, but taking a loss rarely is.

Buying Protective Puts

Conceptually, the purchase of protective puts could be the most easily understood option strategy. An investor holds shares, is nervous about an upcoming earnings announcement, and purchases put options as a form of insurance. For example, an investor holds 800 shares of Cisco Systems (CSCO) trading at $18.60 in the first week of February. The earnings are due the following week, and the February 17½ puts (which expire one week after the earnings news) are quoted $0.55 to $0.60. This investor has seen the results of companies coming in a penny or two below street estimates but hesitates to sell the stock because he sees good potential longer term. He buys eight of the February puts and sleeps well that night, knowing that no matter how bad the earnings might be, he has the right to sell his shares at $17.50 and has therefore limited his downside risk.

The problem with purchasing puts as insurance is that in retrospect it is always the wrong decision. If CSCO beats the street and the stock rallies, you may hear our investor grumble that he just wasted his money. If the stock gets clocked on bad news, he will change his refrain, saying that he should have sold the stock and not bothered with these options. But can't this same argument be made whenever one purchases insurance? If the car isn't wrecked or the house doesn't burn down, hasn't the money been wasted? Well, not quite. In fact, the insurance offered protection and, in most situations, insurance buyers would rather not have to make a claim.

Investors also have a difficult time getting their mind around the fact that the best thing that can happen to them when they buy protective puts is for them to expire worthless. For the investor who owns CSCO and who has purchased the February puts, the optimal outcome is for the corporation to blow away the estimates and for the stock to rally to a new high.

Strike and Expiration Decisions

The two decisions the buyer of protective puts has to make are the same ones before the insurance buyer: for how long a term and for what level of protection.

In our CSCO example, short-term options were perfect for the situation. If the concern had been that inventories would be building up to needlessly high levels over the next three months, then purchasing three- or four-month options would have made sense. The option's term should correspond to the period during which insurance is desired.

The second decision relates to the level at which the coverage will kick in. With insurance this is known as the deductible; with options it's the strike price. Back to CSCO. The nervous investor purchased eight of the 17½ puts at $0.60 each. At the same time, the 15 puts were offered at $0.15. If all he had wanted was disaster insurance, then paying $0.15 per share would have done the job, as he would have traded a lower insurance cost for a higher deductible. (A couple of years ago we realized that no matter which deductible you choose for your car insurance, it will turn out to be the wrong one. We had an accident-free year, after which we thought a higher deductible and lower premium would have done just fine. When a colleague's son wrapped his dad's car around a tree, the man realized he should have paid more for the lower deductible policy. We both bought insurance with the wrong deductible!)

When to Insure

If you are like most of us, when the fire insurance on your home is about to expire you renew your policy. And you probably do the same with your car insurance policy. Should you also insure your stocks and automatically renew this insurance when it comes due?

We don't think so. If an investor is uncomfortable holding stocks for the longer term without them being insured, then it is probably safe to say that this investor's risk tolerance does not stretch to holding equities. Buy bonds.

Protective puts should be used as short-term hedges in front of earnings reports or other announcements, or to lock in a profit while waiting for a short-term capital gain to turn into a long-term one, or to help carry a position from one tax year to the next. But before purchasing puts as part of your tax planning, see Chapter 10.

Purchasing Call Options

To some, buying calls is a speculative trade, a strategy that investors should avoid. It's true that most calls are bought as a trade, with the purchaser having no intention of ever owning the underlying security. But there are two situations where an investor looking to add a stock to her portfolio may be well served by buying call options.

Long Cash/Long Call Strategy

Take the case of an investor who has become long-term bullish on the shares of Bristol-Myers Squibb (BMY). She has between $25,000 and $30,000 to invest, enough to purchase 600 shares of the stock at $45.01. The stock has come down in price to a level she finds very attractive, but she does have some shorter-term worries, such as the next earnings report and some pending regulatory issues.

She could wait, but then if all the stars line up and the stock rebounds quickly, she could also miss taking part in the initial phase of that stock's rally. A look at the BMY June options (with 20 weeks until expiration) reveals the following:

BMY:	$45.01
June 40 call:	$6.00–$6.50
June 45 call:	$2.90–$3.10
June 50 call:	$1.00–$1.15

One possible solution to her dilemma is to purchase six BMY call options. This has the advantage of locking in the price at which she could eventually purchase the shares, and it permits her to sit on the fence for the next couple of months to see how the earnings and other announcements turn out. She would also be risking a relatively small percentage of the capital she has to invest, leaving the balance in her money market account.

She chooses the June expiration because she believes that by that time the dust will have settled. Her problem is choosing a strike price: 40, 45, or 50. This decision is a balancing act between the amount at risk and the effective purchase price of the stock upon exercise. For example, purchasing the 40 call results in an eventual stock purchase price of $46.50 (the $6.50 option premium plus the $40 paid when the call is exercised), a relatively small premium over the current price of $45.01. But the 40 call also leaves $6.50 per share at risk: if BMY is below $40 at the June expiration, these calls will expire worthless.

The 50 call, on the other hand, results in only $1.15 being at risk but creates an effective purchase price of $51.15. There is no one correct answer as to which call our investor should purchase. If she is fairly confident the stock is now reaching bottom, she may be comfortable risking $6.50 per share to lock in an attractive purchase price. And this still represents a fraction of the amount she would have at risk if she purchased the stock outright. If her risk tolerance isn't so high, she may be more at ease risking $1.15 and accepting a higher entry point. She might reason that if the stock rallies back above $50 this would be a positive signal, and she would at that point be willing to pay a higher acquisition cost.

She should also consider that middle road, the June 45 call. By risking $3.10 she would be locking in a $48.10 effective buying price, a compromise solution.

Choosing among various option series always involves trade-offs. For this investor it will be between the amount at risk and the eventual buying price. The option series purchased will be chosen based on the tug-of-war between the investor's fear and greed, although you will note that we did not consider options that were more than one strike price in- or out-of-the-money. Options that are two or more strike prices away from the stock's price are usually not relevant. If they are too far in-the-money, the increased risk does not justify the small reduction in effective buying price obtained. If they are too far out-of-the-money, the odds of their ever being exercised are virtually nil.

One point to keep in mind during the option selection process is that the investor's goal is to eventually own BMY shares. That ultimate goal should be the driving factor in choosing the strike price.

Buy Call/Start Saving Strategy

The preceding example assumed that the investor had the funds necessary to purchase the shares she wanted, but that's not always the case. Take the situation of another investor who would like to add 1,000 shares of Unocal (UCL) to his portfolio. With the stock trading at $38.86 such an investment would require about $40,000, but our investor has immediate access to only $10,000.

His first alternative would be to purchase roughly one-quarter of the 1,000 shares he wants to own with his current cash, start saving, and add to his position as funds become available. One of the risks of such a plan is that if UCL starts to rally, his 1,000 shares could end up costing him more than $40,000.

Turning to options, and more specifically to LEAPS, this investor finds the 20-month UCL 30 call to be quoted at $10.40–$10.90. Purchasing 10 of these LEAPS would lock in an effective purchase price of $40.90 (the 30 strike price plus the $10.90 LEAPS premium), would have an initial cost of $10,900 (slightly more than the cash available), and would give our investor 20 months to save up the $30,000 necessary to exercise the LEAPS calls.

Assuming the savings are deposited into a money market account yielding 3%, and assuming monthly compounding, our investor would have to save $1,463 every month. With a 4% yield, the monthly savings required would be $1,451. Under the 3% assumption, the adjusted cost of the stock would be $40.16 per share ($10,900 to purchase the LEAPS, plus 20 monthly installments of $1,463 totaling $29,260 for a grand total of $40,160). Note that the difference between the $40.16 cost in this paragraph and the $40.90 obtained in the previous paragraph represents the interest income earned.

This buy calls/start saving strategy has two major advantages for an investor in this situation. First, the cost of the full 1,000 shares is locked in when the position is initiated: $10.90 per share needs to be invested immediately and another $30 at option expiration in 20 months. The investor will get the immediate upside appreciation of a full 1,000-share position, although he will not get ancillary benefits such as dividends and shareholders' rights such as voting. Second, call buying is by definition a limited risk strategy. If our investor's forecast for UCL was off base and this stock is trading below $30 in 20 months, our investor's risk will be limited to the option premium paid. Granted, in this example, the option premium paid represents a substantial percentage of the stock price, 28% to be precise. Which then begs the question: is it possible for the price of a stock to fall by more than 28% over a 20-month period? Only those investors who spent the first two years of the new millennium on Mars will answer in the negative.

Entering into the buy call/start saving strategy does not mean a decision is taken today and no further action is required during the next 20 months. Someone who purchases these LEAPS calls should view his holding as he would a 1,000-share position. If there are developments that would cause him to sell his shares, then he should probably sell his calls. If the stock hits his target price before expiration and he would be selling the shares, he should also sell his calls. This investor has created a position that looks like and feels like 1,000 shares; it should be treated as such.

Should our investor hold his long LEAPS for the full 20 months, he will then have to come to a final decision. Should he sell the

LEAPS or exercise them? Assuming UCL is above $30 and the calls are not worthless, his sell or exercise decision should be based on his reassessed outlook for UCL. Is this a stock he still wants to add to his portfolio, or has he found a more attractive investment alternative? In either case, he will have the funds available to take action.

Yes, this strategy does imply a fair amount of discipline, as it requires establishing a regular savings plan. But no more discipline than is required to participate in an automatic withdrawal plan that funnels a monthly contribution to a mutual fund.

Writing Equity Put Options

This strategy encompasses the best and the worst of options. If you have not heard any horror stories about put writers, you probably don't go to cocktail parties. Everybody knows somebody, or at least somebody who knows somebody, who was writing put options and. . . . The magnitude of the final disaster probably grows with every retelling, but it remains a disaster nonetheless. Yet other investors write equity puts year in and year out, love the strategy, and are comfortable knowing they will not end up as a topic of cocktail party conversation. Why these two extremes?

Writing Puts Without and with Leverage

A put writer assumes the obligation of purchasing a stock at a specified price. The risk of this strategy is easy to quantify: the put writer could become a stock owner and would have to bear the full risk of stock ownership. If an investor is comfortable owning stocks, should she be less comfortable writing puts?

Take two people, both with roughly $20,000 to invest, and both looking to add Disney (DIS) to their portfolio. DIS is trading at $20.66 and Mr. Barrel instructs his broker to purchase 1,000 shares at the market. Mr. Lock decides not to purchase DIS outright, but to assume the obligation to purchase 1,000 shares at $20. So he writes 10 November 20 puts at $0.70. The options expire in six weeks.

If the stock never dips to $20, Mr. Lock will never be assigned on his puts. Should the options expire worthless, his return will be $0.70 on an investment of $20. That's a yield of 3.5%, or 30% annualized. But did Mr. Lock make an investment of $20? Writing a put entails assuming an obligation, but it does not require investing any cash in the traditional sense of the word. Yes, his broker will require him to post sufficient margin, but this would not be a problem if the $20,000 he has to invest is in his brokerage account, or if he holds sufficient securities to margin the trade.

This is where the psychology of the trade is as, if not more, important than its pure mechanics. We would like to see Mr. Lock segregate $20,000, if not physically, then at least mentally, and reserve this sum to purchase DIS if he is so obligated. When some put writers see this sum sitting in their account, they consider it to be idle and decide to invest it somewhere else. This cash is not idle. It is earning a 30% annualized rate of return in addition to the interest paid on the account's cash balances.

If history is any guide, here is how Mr. Lock gets into trouble. He writes 10 November puts at $0.70 and they expire worthless. "That was easy," he says. And he sells 10 more, maybe the January 20 puts. These also expire worthless. "Too bad I didn't write more," he concludes, and writes 15 of the March puts. They expire, and he writes 20 of the May puts, then 30 of the July. But his winning streak finally comes to an end. The stock heads south and before he knows it his broker is on the phone telling him he is the proud owner of 3,000 shares of DIS, for which he just paid $20.

Of course this happens when the stock is down, and maybe when the overall market is slumping. Mr. Lock gets nervous—or worse, gets a margin call—and liquidates part or all of his position as the stock is hitting a new 52-week low. He is now perfect material for cocktail party conversation.

The problem with put writing is not put writing. It's the extent to which the option position is leveraged. When Mr. Lock wrote 10 puts and had $20,000 in cash, his puts were cash-secured. He had all of the funds required to pay for the stock. When he wrote 15 contracts he had $20,000 to pay for $30,000 worth of stock; a slightly leveraged position, but one with which a lot of investors would be comfortable. By the time he got to 30 options he had $20,000 backing up a $60,000 obligation. It is easy to blame options for the mess some investors get into, but often the real culprit is overleveraging.

Put writers should be aware of the risks of early assignment. See Chapter 4.

Rolling Short Put Positions

We noted earlier that covered writers have a number of rolling alternatives available to them as their short options approach expiration. Put writers should also consider rolling out some of their positions.

Consider an investor who a little while back wrote the Computer Associates (CA) April 20 puts for $1.25. Her goal was straightforward: she liked CA but was not willing to pay the current price of $22. By writing the 20 puts she took on the obligation of buying shares at $20, and by receiving $1.25 in option premium she reduced her potential purchase price to $18.75, a buying target with which she was comfortable. One week before expiration Friday, CA has drifted down and she finds the following quotes:

CA:	$19.05
April 20 put:	$1.40–$1.45
May 20 put:	$2.30–$2.40

If CA remains unchanged during the next week and if our investor does not cover her puts, she will be assigned and end up owning CA at an adjusted price of $18.75. But she could also roll out her April options to May for an $0.85 credit (cover the April at $1.45, write the May at $2.30). Adding this $0.85 to her original premium of $1.25 totals $2.10, effectively bringing her potential purchase cost to below $18, an interesting proposition. If she rolls out to May and CA rallies sharply over the next five weeks, she could see the May options expire worthless and not be assigned (and thus not have a position in CA), which would leave her with a $2.10 profit for her efforts.

Rolling out can be analyzed from two perspectives. An investor can look at the lower purchasing level the rolling strategy establishes. In the previous example, it reduced an effective buying price of $18.75 to $17.90, although the probability of owning the stock was somewhat diminished by pushing out the expiration date. Rolling can also be analyzed from the perspective of a return on cash. Assume that our investor has $20 per share set aside in a money market fund to pay for the CA shares she is looking to purchase. By rolling her position out an additional four weeks she is earning $0.85 on this $20 a 4.2% return that annualizes to 55%. This is a great rate of return, but it is also a message from the options market as to its perception of the high risk inherent in CA shares.

Other Rolling Strategies

Rolling down (to a lower strike price) and out (to a deferred expiration date) is rarely done with puts. There are few circumstances in which this trade can be done for even money or a small credit. And since put writers are usually looking either to purchase the underlying stock or to capture some option time premium, doing so for a debit makes little sense. To be done for even money or better, rolling down and out will require one or more of the following conditions to be met:

■ The underlying stock is relatively volatile.

■ The price of the stock is relatively high. Rolling down and out from an $80 strike to a 75 is much easier than from a $30 strike to a 25 because it represents a smaller percentage reduction in the option's strike.

■ The short position will have to be rolled out to one of the deferred expirations (a two- or three-month put may have to be written instead of a one-month option).

Rolling up and out is technically not a roll, but a decision to move to a higher strike price, usually after the options initially written have expired. Assume that CA had rallied to the $24 area after our investor wrote her April puts. At the April expiration she would see her short puts expire worthless, and if she were still interested in adding these shares to her portfolio she would now have to decide if she wanted to raise her buying price to $22.50, one option strike price higher than her first series. Stock investors will recognize this as a version of "chasing a stock up"—something we prefer to avoid. When a stock we are looking to purchase gets away from us, we remind ourselves that it's not the only fish in the sea and that there may be other interesting opportunities elsewhere.

Finally, when should investors roll out their short put positions? Looking back to the CA example, we see the April 20 put offered at $1.45 with the stock at $19.05. This put is in-the-money by $0.95, so purchasing it at $1.45 means paying $0.50 in time premium, a half-dollar that will disappear over the next week, assuming an unchanged CA price. Our investor may feel it is a bit early to roll out her position because the April put will probably lose its time premium more rapidly than the May put over the next few trading days and the spread between the two options should widen, assuming an unchanged stock price. Our only note of caution is that puts have a tendency to be assigned early more frequently than calls. We prefer to be a little early in rolling out our short puts rather than too late.

Systematic Option Writing

Many investors alternate put writing with covered call writing. They write puts on stocks they would like to add to their portfolio; some puts expire worthless, others are assigned. When assigned, they start writing covered calls against the shares held; when the calls are assigned, they deliver the stock and resume put writing.

With $100,000 an investor could write puts on 10 different equities, and by keeping the total value of the stock that would have to be purchased if all puts were assigned to $100,000, this investor would never have to purchase stocks on margin.

The appeal of allocating part of a portfolio to an option writing program is that this strategy will generally outperform equities in flat markets, will still be profitable in bull markets, and be somewhat less painful in bear markets. It's simply another way to diversify one's investments.

BASIC TRADING STRATEGIES

Buying Calls

When traders become interested in the options market, the first strategy they generally use is purchasing call options. This often leads to their first frustration with the options market and, too often, their first loss.

That buying calls is traders' entry point into the world of options should not be too surprising. Most investors first take interest in equities during a bull market: the news is positive, friends are making money, and it all looks so easy. Traders turn to options in those same bull markets. They are already making money on their stocks, they've heard about options, and buying calls is presented as the most basic bullish option strategy. If a bull market is good for stock owners, it must be great for call holders.

Selecting Calls Based on Price

The call buyer, whether a first-time trader or a crusty old vet, is often overwhelmed by the large number of options listed on any one security. A typical stock will have six expiration dates available (four short-term options plus two long-term LEAPS) and a minimum of three strike prices, more often five or six strikes, giving a total of 18 to 36 different options from which to choose. Confronted with this selection, many options traders select a series based on the one variable that is immediately apparent to them—price.

The April 35 calls at $3.40 look expensive, especially when compared to the April 40 calls at $1.05. The May 40 calls are $2, but the 45s can be purchased for only $0.35. And buying the lower-priced options lets the trader purchase a greater number of contracts. The last time you owned a stock that went up nicely, you could not help repeating to yourself, "Should have bought more." You are not about to make the same mistake with options. By purchasing the lower-priced options you can buy more with the same trading capital, and it would be foolish not to do so.

Looking Beyond an Option's Price

Unfortunately, too many options traders are guided by price. There are two basic assumptions underlying an option trade, and both should be used in the selection process. The first assumption is that for a given position a trader will be willing to risk a fixed dollar amount. In other words: "I have $2,500 to allocate to this one position and to risk," not "I am looking to purchase calls on 400 shares no matter what they cost." We view traders as allocating blocks of their trading capital to each of their positions.

The second assumption is that a trader is looking to maximize his return on capital on any one trade. Don't laugh; this obvious point is ignored more often than traders are willing to admit. To illustrate the point, look at the following selected options on Minnesota Mining & Manufacturing (MMM):

MMM: $115.50
April 105 call: $11.90–$12.30

April 110 call:	$8.20–8.50
April 115 call:	$5.10–$5.20
April 120 call:	$2.70–$2.90
April 125 call:	$1.20–$1.30

The April options have 60 days until expiration, and a trader who is bullish on MMM is wondering which of these calls to purchase. Traders looking only at option premiums are often drawn to the lower-priced options because they can buy more. For example, a trader who decides to risk $3,000 on his MMM position could purchase only 2 of the 105 calls but would have sufficient funds to buy 23 of the 125 calls. At cocktail parties, it sounds better if he can claim to have bought "a 20 lot" rather than just two options. But let's be more thorough and analyze this situation from the perspective of return on investment.

Let's start with the purchase of the at-the-money 115 calls. The return on this option at expiration will obviously be a function of how MMM performs over the next 60 days. Table 3.1 calculates the return on trading capital obtained if the 115 calls are purchased for various MMM prices at option expiration.

Table 3.1

MMM Price at Option Expiration	Value of 115 Call at Expiration	Cost of 115 Call	Profit/(Loss)	Return on Trading Capital
$112.50	$0	$5.20	($5.20)	(100%)
$115.00	$0	$5.20	($5.20)	(100%)
$117.50	$2.50	$5.20	($2.70)	(52%)
$120.00	$5	$5.20	($0.20)	(4%)
$122.50	$7.50	$5.20	$2.30	44%
$125.00	$10	$5.20	$4.80	92%
$127.50	$12.50	$5.20	$7.30	140%
$130.00	$15	$5.20	$9.80	188%

Table 3.2

MMM Price at Option Expiration	Value of 105 Call at Expiration	Cost of 105 Call	Profit/(Loss)	Return on Trading Capital
$102.50	$0	$12.30	($12.30)	(100%)
$105.00	$0	$12.30	($12.30)	(100%)
$107.50	$2.50	$12.30	($9.80)	(80%)
$110.00	$5	$12.30	($7.30)	(59%)
$112.50	$7.50	$12.30	($4.80)	(39%)
$115.00	$10	$12.30	($2.30)	(19%)
$117.50	$12.50	$12.30	$0.20	2%
$120.00	$15	$12.30	$2.70	22%
$122.50	$17.50	$12.30	$5.20	42%
$125.00	$20	$12.30	$7.70	62%

Table 3.3

MMM Price at Option Expiration	Value of 125 Call at Expiration	Cost of 125 Call	Profit/(Loss)	Return on Trading Capital
$122.50	$0	$1.30	($1.30)	(100%)
$125.00	$0	$1.30	($1.30)	(100%)
$127.50	$2.50	$1.30	$1.20	92%
$130.00	$5	$1.30	$3.70	285%
$132.50	$7.50	$1.30	$6.20	477%
$135.00	$10	$1.30	$8.70	669%
$137.50	$12.50	$1.30	$11.20	862%
$140.00	$15	$1.30	$13.70	1054%

The same type of analysis can be performed for all call options, but we will limit ourselves to two additional series: the in-the-money 105 call in Table 3.2 and the out-of-the-money 125 call in Table 3.3.

Yes, some of those returns on the 125 call are eye-popping, but before jumping to conclusions let's look at this from another angle. Which option offers the better return on trading capital if MMM rallies to $120? $125? $130? By referring back to the three tables you will find that the answers are the 105 call, the 115 call, and the 125 call.

The conclusion is that no one option will offer the best return on trading capital; there is only one best option for a given price of MMM at option expiration. Table 3.4 expands on the previous three tables and in the right-hand column identifies the "best" option for a given stock price at expiration.

Table 3.4

	Return on 105 Call	Return on 115 Call	Return on 125 Call	"Best" Option
$102.50	(100%)	(100%)	(100%)	None
$105.00	(100%)	(100%)	(100%)	None
$107.50	(80%)	(100%)	(100%)	105 C
$110.00	(59%)	(100%)	(100%)	105 C
$112.50	(39%)	(100%)	(100%)	105 C
$115.00	(19%)	(100%)	(100%)	105 C
$117.50	2%	(52%)	(100%)	105 C
$120.00	22%	(4%)	(100%)	105 C
$122.50	42%	44%	(100%)	115 C
$125.00	63%	92%	(100%)	115 C
$127.50	83%	140%	92%	115 C
$130.00	103%	188%	285%	125 C
$132.50	124%	237%	477%	125 C
$135.00	144%	285%	669%	125 C

Some of the conclusions we can draw from this last table come as no surprise:

- No one option works best under all outcomes.
- The higher the call's strike price, the higher its breakeven point, and the higher the price to which the underlying must rise for this option to be profitable.
- If the price of the underlying stock goes down by a sufficient amount, all of the options will expire worthless.

The key consideration in selecting which option to purchase turns out to be not the price of the option, but the trader's forecast for the price of the underlying stock. With MMM at $115.50 the 105 call was the best option for a rally to slightly above $120; from that point to somewhere around $128 the 115 call offered the better return on trading capital; and above $128 the 125 call looks like the better choice. The trader who has just decided to purchase some calls on MMM must ask: Where do I expect this stock to be trading in 60 days? Is $130 a realistic target? Do I want to err on the side of caution?

This last question is an important one. Comparing the 115 and the 125 calls, we have a breakeven of $120.20 for the first option and $126.30 for the second one. It is obviously easier to earn a positive return by purchasing the 115 call. But what about those home runs one can hit with the 125 call? What if the stock goes to $130 or $135? At those higher prices the 115 call, even if its returns are significantly lower than those of the 125 call, are still quite attractive. Erring on the side of caution (by purchasing fewer calls with a lower strike price instead of a greater number with a higher exercise price) may not produce as many home runs but will certainly generate more singles and doubles.

The example here was simplified. We ignored the 110 and 120 calls in addition to strikes below 105 and above 125 that were listed for trading at the time we created this example. But even with a more complete analysis our conclusions would remain the same.

The MMM example can be easily replicated for any call buying situation because the options' values at expiration will be equal to their intrinsic value and the returns on trading capital a cinch to calculate. But what if our trader is purchasing calls on MMM with the expectation that the stock will move up over the next two to four weeks? He will be more interested in how the returns on trading capital look sometime before expiration, an exercise that requires making an assumption as to how the options will be priced at that point in time.

Using a technique from economics class, we will start by assuming that the options' volatility estimate will remain constant over the life of the options. We will relax this assumption a little later. The question now is, which option will provide the higher return on trading capital if MMM hits its target price prior to option expiration? To find the answer we start with Table 3.5 which, based on an unchanged volatility assumption, calculates the value and the return for the 115 call for various stock prices and different times to expiration.

Table 3.5 Value of 115 Call/Return on Trading Capital

	60 Days	50 Days	40 Days	30 Days	20 Days	10 Days	Expiration
$112.50	$3.70/ (29%)	$3.27/ (37%)	$2.80/ (46%)	$2.27/ (56%)	$1.65/ (68%)	$0.94/ (82%)	$0/ (100%)
$115.00	$4.85/ (7%)	$4.41/ (15%)	$3.94/ (24%)	$3.40/ (35%)	$2.76/ (47%)	$1.94/ (63%)	$0/ (100%)
$117.50	$6.36/ 22%	$5.92/ 14%	$5.43/ 4%	$4.88/ (6%)	$4.24/ (18%)	$3.50/ (33%)	$2.50/ (52%)
$120.00	$7.95/ 53%	$7.55/ 45%	$7.11/ 37%	$6.62/ 27%	$6.04/ 16%	$5.45/ 5%	$5/ (4%)
$122.50	$9.78/ 88%	$9.38/ 80%	$8.96/ 72%	$8.57/ 65%	$8.11/ 56%	$7.69/ 48%	$7.50/ 44%
$125.00	$11.72/ 125%	$11.40/ 119%	$11.05/ 113%	$10.69/ 106%	$10.36/ 99%	$10.10/ 94%	$10/ 92%
$127.50	$13.82/ 166%	$13.50/ 160%	$13.24/ 155%	$12.96/ 149%	$12.73/ 145%	$12.57/ 142%	$12.50/ 140%
$130.00	$16.02/ 208%	$15.78/ 203%	$15.52/ 198%	$15.33/ 195%	$15.16/ 192%	$15.06/ 190%	$15/ 188%

The above exercise can be repeated for the 105 and 125 calls, a process we will spare you. But the results from Table 3.5 can be combined with the equivalent results for these two other calls and the "best" option for each square in the grid selected. This was done and compiled in Table 3.6.

Although it analyzes the returns from only three options, Table 3.6 presents all of the potentials and pitfalls of the different option series. If your price target on MMM is $120, which option should you purchase? If the stock hits $120 within 10 days of your establishing your position, the 125 calls offer the highest return on trading capital. If reaching this target takes from 20 to 30 days, the 115 call is the most efficient vehicle, and any longer makes the 105 call the trader's choice. This is a roundabout way of saying that there are two variables that must be taken into account when selecting which option to purchase: the target price of the underlying stock and when it is expected to reach this price.

Table 3.6 Highest Return on Trading Capital/Call Option

	60 Days	50 Days	40 Days	30 Days	20 Days	10 Days	Expiration
$112.50	(23%)/ 105	(26%)/ 105	(29%)/ 105	(32%)/ 105	(35%)/ 105	(38%)/ 105	(39%)/ 105
$115.00	(6%)/ 105	(9%)/ 105	(12%)/ 105	(14%)/ 105	(16%)/ 105	(18%)/ 105	(19%)/ 105
$117.50	32%/ 125	14%/ 115	7%/ 105	5%/ 105	3%/ 105	2%/ 105	2%/ 105
$120.00	94%/ 125	66%/ 125	37%/ 115	27%/ 115	23%/ 105	22%/ 105	22%/ 105
$122.50	172%/ 125	141%/ 125	105%/ 125	66%/ 125	56%/ 115	48%/ 115	44%/ 115
$125.00	261%/ 125	228%/ 125	192%/ 125	152%/ 125	105%/ 125	94%/ 115	92%/ 115
$127.50	377%/ 125	344%/ 125	308%/ 125	267%/ 125	219%/ 125	165%/ 125	140%/ 115
$130.00	500%/ 125	471%/ 125	438%/ 125	402%/ 125	359%/ 125	315%/ 125	285%/ 125

This table also lets us see how different options behave. Start with the out-of-the-money 125 call. On a quick run-up in the price of the stock, this is the option to own: it has the highest return on a move to $117.50 on the initial trade date, and to $120 within 10 days. But as expiration nears, MMM has to rise to higher and higher levels to make this the option of choice. Conclusion: out-of-the-money options perform best only if the underlying stock rises soon after the trade date or if the stock rises by a substantial amount.

As for the in-the-money 105 call, it holds its own if the price of the stock remains unchanged or drops slightly. This is easy to understand since most of its premium is intrinsic value that will not decay over time. Of course, should MMM fall below 105 it will perform no better than the other two options because it will also expire worthless. This in-the-money option performs best in slowly or moderately rising markets.

An Option's Sweet Spot

We first developed the notion of an option's sweet spot in the LEAPS book we coauthored with Marty Kearney. Look at the area in Table 3.6 where the at-the-money 115 call offers the highest return on trading capital. This is what we named the option's sweet spot—that area in the price and time continuum where it outperforms all other options. By refining the numbers and calculating the breakeven points more precisely we come up with Figure 3.1, which illustrates the 115 call's sweet spot.

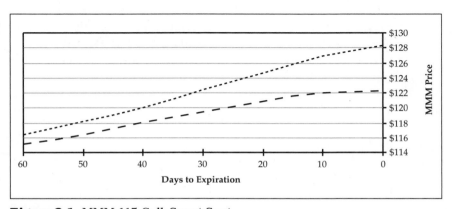

Figure 3.1 MMM 115 Call: Sweet Spot

Calculating multiple options' sweet spots before every call purchase is bound to drive even the most avid option trader into muni bonds. We certainly would not advise trying to re-create this exercise. But at-the-money calls will have sweet spots similar in shape to this one, which can therefore be used as a template. Remember that this sweet spot was created by comparing the 115 at-the-money call to both the 105 and 125 calls. If we had used the 110 and 120 calls in our analysis the sweet spot would be somewhat narrower.

Out-of-the money options will have a sweet spot above the one depicted in Figure 3.1, and its general shape can be inferred by looking at the numbers in Table 3.6. The sweet spot for in-the-money options will lie below that of the at-the-money options. Think of these as a reality check: you are about to purchase the MMM March 125 calls. Is it realistic to expect this stock to trade in this option's sweet spot some time before or at expiration? If not, choosing an option with a lower strike price (and therefore a lower sweet spot) may be a more conservative way to take a position in this stock.

Relaxing the Volatility Assumption

We have not yet discussed the full impact of changes in volatility on option pricing, so you may want to return to this section after reading Chapters 4 and 9. But we want to address the question of what happens to an option's sweet spot if the option's volatility estimate changes.

When a stock rallies, a change in volatility is likely to be one where the estimate is reduced (this is discussed in more detail in Chapter 9). So the trader is bound to ask, "If the stock goes up as I expect, and the option's volatility estimate declines, how will this change the call's sweet spot?" To view the result, make the unrealistic assumption that the option's volatility estimate drops to zero. What shape would the sweet spot then take? This is an easy question because at expiration the option's volatility is zero. (Remember, at expiration an option will be trading at its intrinsic value and volatility will not come into the equation.) So, if volatility drops to zero 30 days before expiration, the option's sweet spot at that point in time would be defined by the same boundaries as the ones it has at expiration. In other words, the sweet spot would shift upwards. Assuming that an option's volatility estimate will fall to zero is unrealistic, but it helps us visualize the impact of a reduction in volatility—an upward shift in the option's sweet spot. This is a point of importance to the buyers of out-of-the-money calls, whose options have become somewhat less attractive. Note that an option's sweet spot cannot shift any higher than its boundaries at expiration, as these represent the sweet spot's upper limits.

An Option's Profitability Boundary

It is important to remember that an option's sweet spot may include an area where losses are realized. Since the sweet spot establishes only that area where an option outperforms other options (outperform means either a higher return or a lower loss), it may also be of interest to look at the option's profitability boundary. This boundary is better understood through an illustration. Figure 3.2 gives us the boundaries of the three MMM calls from our example.

The boundaries tell us how much the underlying stock has to increase in value for the option buyer to break even at any given date. Obviously, options buyers want the price of the stock to be above the boundary of the call they have purchased. Once again we have assumed that the options' volatility will remain constant until expiration.

It is often said that call buyers are fighting an uphill battle. Our boundary graph clearly illustrates how steep the slope is for selected options. An option's profitability boundary should be used as a

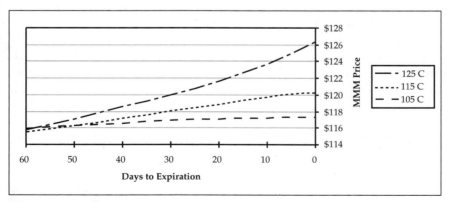

Figure 3.2 MMM Calls: Profitability Boundaries

quick reality check. How probable is it that this particular stock will be trading above its boundary prior to expiration? More important, how probable is it that it will be trading above its boundary by an amount sufficient to generate an adequate profit?

Note that if the volatility used to price these options increases, the options' boundaries will be pushed down, which is good. The reverse happens if the volatility estimate is reduced. The only point in the graph that will not change is the option's boundary at expiration, since at that point in time an option's value will not be impacted by volatility but will be equal to its intrinsic value.

Choosing the Option's Expiration Date

Those who are hoping to find an analysis as elaborate as the one presented earlier for strike price selection are bound to be disappointed. The question here is, by which date do you expect this stock to reach your target price? We would recommend answering this question before looking at the stock's option quotes. It is impossible to ignore the fact that the September options are less expensive than the Octobers, and the August calls even less pricey than the Septembers. So even though it may be late July, many traders opt for the August contracts based on price alone.

Selecting options' expiration dates based on price will always lead to buying the shorter-dated options and will too often lead to a trader running out of time—being right about the stock, being right about the direction, but being out of the market when the stock finally moves because the April calls expired two weeks ago.

If you expect a stock to move over the next 30 days, it would appear that a one-month option fits the bill. But if you purchase a two-month option you are giving yourself some additional leeway, and there is no need to hang on to your two-month option until expiration. If after 30 days the stock has performed as expected, sell it and take your profits.

The trade-off in buying more time is best illustrated by an example. Take a look at the 28- and 56-day options on Quick Pop Stock (QPS).

QPS: $45
28-day 45 call: $1.76
56-day 45 call: $2.51

Table 3.7

QPS in 28 days	Expiring Option	Return on Trading Capital	Option with 28 Days Remaining	Return on Trading Capital
$45	$0	(100%)	$1.76	(30%)
$47.50	$2.50	42%	$3.37	34%
$50	$5	184%	$5.37	114%
$52.50	$7.50	326%	$7.67	206%
$55	$10	468%	$10.10	302%

Let's look at what happens to each of these options when QPS is up by various amounts in 28 days. Table 3.7 assumes that the volatility used in pricing these options remains unchanged.

By "buying more time," i.e., purchasing the 56-day option, losses are reduced if QPS remains unchanged or rises only slightly, but some upside potential is lost as well because the return on capital is higher with the shorter-term option when QPS rallies sufficiently. And here one sees the major trade-off between shorter- and longer-dated options: shorter-term options provide more leverage if the underlying stock performs as expected but result in relatively larger losses if the stock remains unchanged or rises only slightly. We generally argue in favor of buying more time, as we prefer to give up a little if we are correct in our forecast in order to obtain additional staying power.

When to Sell Long Calls

Many investors say, "I know when to buy calls, but I never can figure out when to sell them." We offer a two-part answer.

The sale of a long call position could be triggered by an option target price. For example, you purchased a call at $3 with a $6 goal. If the option goes to $6, sell it. An alternative to this simple target is to sell the option if it reaches $6 or if it drops to $1. The latter includes a stop loss mechanism that should be part of disciplined trading.

The second, and perhaps preferable, method for triggering the sale of long calls is to set target prices for the underlying stock and not the option. If you purchase a call when a stock is trading at $44 and your forecast is that it will rise to $49, sell your option when the stock reaches this level, even though it may not be trading at the price you had anticipated. There is no reason to hold on to a call position once the underlying has reached your forecasted price. A more complete approach would be to sell your long calls if the stock reached $49, or if it dropped to $39.

With either method, you should also consider selling half of your position if the underlying stock reaches your upside target (and set a second target for the other half) while exiting the whole position if the downside sell point is reached. This is a form of the age-old technique of letting your profits run but cutting your losses.

Finally, if you purchased a two-month option when you were expecting the underlying stock to make a move over the next month, and if your plan was to sell the option one month before expiration, then stick to your guns. Sell the call after one month, even if it means taking a loss.

Buying Puts

Buying puts is the mirror image of buying calls. Put buyers expect the price of a stock to fall over a short or extended period of time. Most of the foregoing discussion on selecting strike prices and expiration dates for call options applies to puts as well.

Shorting Stocks

Before the advent of options, a trader who believed that the shares of Such & Such (SNS) were about to head south had but one avenue open to her: short shares of SNS. As we saw in Chapter 1, in shorting a stock a trader sells shares she does not own in the hope that their price will drop so she can purchase them later at a lower price. This trader is reversing the normal order of the two stock trades. Instead of buying a stock, waiting for it to go up, and then selling it, the trader sells the stock short, waits for it to go down, and then buys it. Sell high, buy low instead of buy low, sell high.

How can a trader sell shares she does not own? She simply borrows these from her broker. (Brokers are more than willing to lend stock because they usually charge a borrowing fee.) For instance, a trader borrows 500 shares of SNS and sells these short at $44. If her forecast is correct and SNS drops to $34, she can then cover her position by purchasing SNS at $34 and returning these shares to her broker. Her profit is $10 per share.

Of course there is always the possibility that SNS will misbehave and start rallying. At some point this trader will want to cut her losses and cover her position. If she buys back 500 SNS at $50, she would have a loss of $6 per share (buying at $50 and selling at $44, not in that order).

There are two types of problems associated with shorting stocks. The first type is financial. A broker will not let a trader short stock without her margining her position; that is, depositing cash or securities in her account to guarantee potential losses on the trade. If the price of the shorted stock starts to rise, the broker will increase the margin required as the unrealized losses start accruing. In theory, since there is no limit as to how high the price of a stock can rise, the losses on a short stock position could be unlimited. In addition to the initial and maybe additional margin, a short seller could face a buy-in. This happens if the broker is no longer able to lend stock to the trader. A buy-in could occur when too many investors ask for their stock certificates or, more likely, simply want to sell the shares they rightfully own. A third more minor cost is the dividend liability. If a trader is short SNS on the day it goes ex-dividend, she must pay this dividend to her broker, who in turn pays the investor from whom he borrowed the shares.

The second order of problems with a short stock position is psychological. Maintaining a short position is nerve-wracking. The stock goes up a dollar and you start worrying. It goes up another dollar and you wonder if you should cover, and so on until you can't sleep at night. On average, retail investors maintain their short stock positions for only short periods of time, usually not long enough for their forecast to come to reality. That's why a lot of bears have turned to put options.

Buying Puts: An Example

A trader has turned bearish on the shares of American International Group (AIG) and expects these to tumble over the next three months. An Internet search produces the following quotes:

AIG:	$71.12
May 55 put:	$0.40–$0.55
May 60 put:	$0.85–$1.00
May 65 put:	$1.85–$1.95
May 70 put:	$3.40–$3.60
May 75 put:	$5.90–$6.10

Note that the May options have 86 days until expiration. Our trader is willing to risk $2,000 on a bearish trade. He looks at the 60 puts, thinking: "If I purchase these, I am only risking $1 a share. This isn't a lot of money, so maybe I should purchase 20 contracts." Wrong reasoning. If he is thinking in terms of $1 a share, why not reduce the risk to $0.50 per share and try to purchase 40 of the 55 puts at $0.50? We prefer to think of the dollar amount that is being committed to the trade. This trader is not risking $1 or $0.50 a share, but $2,000, and his aim should be to earn the highest return possible on this amount.

We turn to Table 3.8 to find out how to best position ourselves for a fall in the price of AIG.

From this table we can calculate the expiration date price range over which each option generates the highest returns. This is summarized in Table 3.9.

Table 3.9 shows that if AIG rallies above $75 buying puts is not a good idea because all the puts expire worthless. On any pullback down to $62.80 (which represents an 11.7% drop in the price of AIG)

Table 3.8

AIG Price	55 Put Value	55 Put Return	60 Put Value	60 Put Return	65 Put Value	65 Put Return	70 Put Value	70 Put Return	75 Put Value	75 Put Return
$50	$5	809%	$10	900%	$15	669%	$20	456%	$25	310%
$55	$0	(100%)	$5	400%	$10	413%	$15	317%	$20	228%
$60	$0	(100%)	$0	(100%)	$5	156%	$10	178%	$15	146%
$65	$0	(100%)	$0	(100%)	$0	(100%)	$5	39%	$10	64%
$70	$0	(100%)	$0	(100%)	$0	(100%)	$0	(100%)	$5	(18%)
$75	$0	(100%)	$0	(100%)	$0	(100%)	$0	(100%)	$0	(100%)

Table 3.9

	From	To
75 Put	$74.95	$62.80
70 Put	$62.80	$59.20
65 Put	$59.15	$54.75
60 Put	$54.75	$48.90
55 Put	$48.85	$0.00

the 75 puts generate the highest returns. For the "it's just a dollar" 60 put to top the chart AIG needs to fall to at least $54.75, or a 23% drop. It boils down to how much of a bear our investor is in this particular instance.

When looking at the data in Table 3.9, remember that because an option has a relatively narrow range over which it offers the highest return does not mean it is not profitable outside of that range. For example, the 70 put (which most traders would classify as at-the-money) is the best option from $62.80 down to $59.20, a range of only $3.60. If a trader buys this put and the stock moves significantly below $59.20, this purchase will remain very profitable, although not as profitable as a 65 or a 60 put. One last calculation that the put buyer should make is that of the puts' downside breakeven. How far down does AIG have to go before the trader gets his money back? Breakeven at expiration is simply the option's strike price less the premium paid. Table 3.10 summarizes these for AIG.

Table 3.10

Put Option	Premium	Downside Breakeven
May 55	$0.55	$54.45
May 60	$1.00	$59.00
May 65	$1.95	$63.05
May 70	$3.60	$66.40
May 75	$6.10	$68.90

We believe that choosing which put option to purchase with the help of tables such as the three developed in this section will reduce the tendency too many option traders have of buying more low-priced options rather than fewer higher-priced ones. Remember that the aim is not to impress your peers by trading large quantities of options, but to dazzle them with the profits you are generating.

Puts' Sweet Spot

Like call options, each put option has its sweet spot. We see no need to repeat the calls' full analysis, but the most important points should be underscored:

- Out-of-the-money puts are suitable only if the price of the underlying stock drops soon after the position is initiated or if it falls by a significant amount by the expiration date.

- In-the-money puts will hold more of their values if the stock remains unchanged or if it declines by a relatively small percentage.

- At-the-money options have a sweet spot that is initially narrow, but it widens as the expiration date approaches.

Puts' Profitability Boundary

As with calls, we can illustrate the profitability boundary of the different options from our example. This is presented in Figure 3.3.

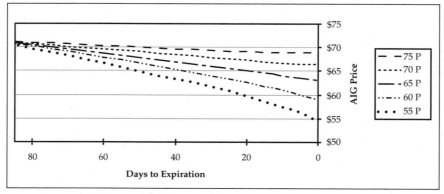

Figure 3.3 AIG Puts: Profitability Boundaries

Referring to the boundaries graph, the put buyer can ask himself how likely it is that AIG will trade below the boundary by an amount sufficient to generate a good trading profit. Although calculating profitability boundaries before every put purchase would be ideal, it may not be practical. But a trader can draw a quick and dirty profitability boundary by following these three easy steps:

1. Set the initial point of the boundary (on the date the position is established) at the then-current stock price.
2. Set the boundary's end point, on the expiration date, at the put's breakeven level (equal to the put's strike price less the premium paid).
3. Draw the boundary not as a straight line, but following the general shape illustrated in Figure 3.3. For this last step it is important to notice that the shape of the boundary will be determined by how far the put is out-of-the-money or if it is in- or at-the-money. The further out-of-the-money the put is, the more curved the profitability boundary will be.

Choosing an Expiration Date

What type of bearish scenario are you envisioning? Are you expecting a quick pullback next week after the earnings announcement or do you think this stock is about to start a long slide reminiscent of some of the dot-bomb debacles? Although we will discuss option pricing in more detail in a later chapter, the following theoretical put prices may help in choosing an expiration date. We have assumed a stock price of $100, a 40% volatility, a 3% risk-free interest rate, and no dividends.

Let's start with the at-the-money 100 puts. A trader is bearish over the short term. Should she purchase the one-month options at $4.43 or the two-month options at $6.20? You can see that a strong argument can be made for purchasing more time. Whereas the first month costs $4.43, the second month can be purchased for an additional $1.77. It has the look of "buy one, get the second one at half price." Even if this trader expects to be out of her position in 30 days, the two-month option may be a more conservative way of trading. If the price of the stock remains unchanged, the buyer of the one-month put would see the option expire worthless and lose 100% of

Table 3.11

Time to Expiration	100 Put	90 Put
1 month	$4.43	$1.03
2 months	$6.20	$2.29
3 months	$7.56	$3.43
6 months	$10.48	$5.86
1 year	$14.38	$9.60
2 years	$19.40	$14.40

the amount risked on the trade. The buyer of the two-month option would see the value of the option drop from $6.20 to $4.43 (as the two-month option becomes a one-month option), a loss of 29% of the amount risked. If a trader purchases a two-month option when her time frame is 30 days, she must show enough discipline to get out of the position after one month.

For readers who are looking for things to avoid, we have observed that some traders are reluctant to sell options they have purchased prior to their expiration date. Their argument is that they are selling something valuable, or they fear a conspiracy in which the underlying stock will start moving the minute their sale order is executed. We think they should adopt the attitude that getting a dollar today may be better than getting a nickel on expiration Friday.

Repeat the one-month/two-month option exercise with three- and six-month options and with one- and two-year options. The same relationships hold, and once again we find ourselves arguing in favor of buying more time.

Buying Out-of-the-Money Puts

What about the out-of-the-money 90 puts? The relationship among the various premiums is different from the one between the at-the-moneys. The one-, two-, and three-month options are roughly priced at a dollar per month. Which of these should a bear purchase, since there are no savings in buying the longer-dated options?

As in many other scenarios, the answer will depend on how the underlying stock behaves. If a trader buys a one-month put at $1.03

and one month later the stock is unchanged, he could purchase another one-month put at $1.03. The result will be roughly the same as if he had purchased the two-month put at $2.29. But what if the stock rallies 10% during the first month and our trader is still bearish? If the trader purchased the one-month put, he will now have the opportunity to buy another one-month option. If he decides to remain with options that are 10% out-of-the-money, he will be able to raise the put's strike price to $100. The higher the stock rises during the first month, the higher the trader can reset the put's exercise price.

The third possible outcome is for the stock to fall in price. With the stock price anywhere below $89, the put purchase will have been profitable. But if the stock falls to, say, $95 or $91, the trader will have a difficult decision to make if, after 30 days, he wants to remain long put options. The 90 strike puts will expire worthless. The 90 puts expiring one month later will be closer to being at-the-money and will probably be trading at a premium substantially above $1. If the trader only wants to purchase options that are 10% out-of-the-money, he will have to select puts with an 85 or 80 strike price, setting a lower and lower breakeven point.

Another practice to avoid is buying the target price—selecting options with a strike price equal to one's target price on a stock. Say a trader is looking for a stock to drop to $90, so he purchases the 90 puts. If the stock reaches the $90 target at expiration, the put option will be worth . . . not a penny. For the buy-the-target-price strategy to work, the stock will have to hit the target price very quickly so that the put option (which will then be an at-the-money option) will be priced with a fair amount of time premium (which will dwindle down to zero by the option's expiration date).

4

OPTIONS 401: OPTION PRICING, VOLATILITY, AND A FIRST GREEK LETTER

Understanding the mechanics of option pricing and the various meanings of volatility can help a trader shape appropriate options strategies. This chapter takes us beyond the theoretical notions discussed earlier and lays the foundation for the strategies presented in the next four chapters.

Option Pricing: Beyond the Basics

The basics of option pricing were discussed in Chapter 1. Now let's explore the five pricing variables in more detail.

Stock Price

Table 4.1 gives the theoretical prices for 50-day at-the-money call options for stocks at various prices. A 30% volatility has been assumed with a 4% risk-free interest rate and no dividends.

The higher the stock price, the higher the option price. The relationship is linear: the call on the $40 stock costs twice as much as the one on the $20 stock. This should not come as a surprise. Purchasing two of the at-the-money calls on the $20 stock would cost $186 and would give the buyer the right to acquire $4,000 worth of shares at their current market price. Purchasing one of the at-the-money calls on the $40 stock would also cost $186 and give the buyer the right to acquire $4,000 worth of shares at their current price.

Another way to view these prices is in terms of puts and insurance. Assuming the same volatility, insuring an $80 stock should cost twice as much as insuring a $40 stock. How does this relationship hold up with options that are in- or out-of-the-money? Table 4.2 looks at some 70-day call prices for three stocks, all based on a 30% volatility assumption, 4% risk-free rate, and no dividend.

First note that the strike prices are in- and out-of-the-money by the same percentage (10%) for all stocks. Then look at the out-of-the-money options: the relationship stands, except for some small

Table 4.1

Stock Price	At-the-Money Call Price
$20	$0.93
$40	$1.86
$60	$2.79
$80	$3.72
$100	$4.66

Table 4.2

Stock Price	Option Series	Option Price	Option Series	Option Price
$50	45 call	$6.01	55 call	$1.02
$100	90 call	$12.03	110 call	$2.03
$150	135 call	$18.04	165 call	$3.05

rounding discrepancies. The same goes for the in-the-money options. Note that the 45 call, which is 10% in-the-money, has a premium of $6.01, representing $5 of intrinsic value and $1.01 of time premium. The 90 call, also 10% in-the-money, is worth $12.03, which represents $10 of intrinsic value and $2.03 of time premium. It's logical, to within a penny.

Exercise Price

Since strike prices are fixed, there doesn't appear to be much to say except that calls with lower strikes will be more valuable than calls with higher strikes, and that puts with higher strikes will be more valuable than puts with lower strikes.

In fact, there are two circumstances under which the strike price of an option will be adjusted. The first is a stock split. Take your plain vanilla 2-for-1 split of a stock trading at $100; the holder of 100 shares will receive an additional 100 shares, the stock will trade at $50 ex-distribution, and the total value of the holding will remain unchanged at $10,000. What happens to the trader who was holding a June 100 call on this stock? That option will be adjusted twofold: the strike price will be halved to $50, and the number of contracts held will be doubled. So the holder's right to purchase 100 shares at $100 will become the right to purchase 200 shares at $50. This same adjustment will be made for all x-for-1 stock splits.

The treatment is somewhat different when the split is not of the x-for-1 type, but a 3-for-2 split, a 5-for-4, or some other odd combination. Take a $60 stock that is going to split 3 for 2. The holder of 100 shares will end up with 150 shares trading at $40. The holder of one October 60 call will see the strike price adjusted to $40 but will not end up with 1.5 contracts because there is no such thing as listed fractional options. The number of shares per contract will therefore be increased to 150, so the trader ends up with one October 40 call that covers 150 shares. This also means that the premium multiplier is changed to 150. If he sells this option (post-split) at $2, his account will be credited $300 ($2 × 150). Options that have more or fewer than 100 shares as underlying usually trade under an adjusted ticker symbol, such IBZ for adjusted IBM options or GMZ for GM.

In the rare cases of reverse stock splits, even those of the 1-for-x, variety, the strike price will be adjusted upward, and the number of shares covered by each contract will be reduced accordingly. So the holder of a February 10 put of a stock that consolidates on a 1-for-5 basis would end up with one February 50 put covering 20 shares.

The second event that will trigger an adjustment in strike prices is a corporation's paying of a dividend equal to 10% or more of its stock price. Take a company whose stock is trading at $80 and that declares a special cash dividend of $10. When the stock goes ex-dividend, all option strike prices (puts and calls) will be reduced by the dividend amount of $10.

Spin-offs do not usually result in any strike price adjustments. If Big Brother Corp. spins off its Little Guy Subsidiary on the basis of one Little Guy share for every seven Big Brother held, then the 50 call, which used to be the right to purchase 100 shares of Big Brother, becomes the right to purchase 100 shares of Big Brother and 14 shares of Little Guy for the aggregate exercise price of $5,000. A small cash adjustment will be made for the fractional share of Little Guy not obtained upon exercise of this call. The options covering both Big Brother and Little Guy will also trade under an adjusted ticker symbol.

Interest Rates and Dividends

Have you ever noticed that for a given stock the at-the-money calls usually trade at a higher premium than the at-the-money puts? Some people say that it's because more investors are bullish than bearish, so the demand for calls is greater, which pushes up prices. Some claim that over the longer term the market has always gone up and calls are justifiably more expensive. And others say that the price of a stock can only go down 100%, while its upside is unlimited, and this asymmetry leads to higher call prices. All of these

Table 4.3

	Risk-Free Interest Rate					
	0%	2%	4%	6%	8%	10%
Call Premium	1.67	1.74	1.81	1.89	1.97	2.05
Put Premium	1.67	1.60	1.55	1.49	1.44	1.39

explanations may make intuitive sense, but they explain nothing about the relative prices of puts and calls.

To understand what is happening, let's look at one of our theoretical stocks, Boring Boring (YAWN), currently at $60. YAWN pays no dividends, and its options are trading at a 20% implied volatility. Using our options pricing software we can calculate the theoretical value of the 45-day YAWN at-the-money puts and calls for various interest rate assumptions, as shown in Table 4.3.

Only Japan has (nearly) tested the 0% risk-free interest rate assumption. Nevertheless, the result we obtain is interesting: under that assumption, the calls' and puts' premiums are identical. Furthermore, as we use higher and higher interest rate assumptions, the call premium increases while the put premium decreases.

The difference between the put and call premiums reflects the time value of money. Assume you own a call option on YAWN, the stock has moved up above the option's strike price, and your intention is to exercise this call because you want to take possession of the stock. Equity options are American-style, so you could exercise your call even though it may still have four weeks left until expiration. But why would you exercise early? Why spend the money now when you can spend it later, keeping it in an interest-bearing account in the interim? Call options let you defer purchasing the stock, and the higher the interest rate, the more valuable this feature becomes, as your cash earns more interest sitting on the sidelines. The calls' premiums reflect this.

Higher interest rates make call options more valuable. Why do they reduce the value of puts? The fact is, higher interest rates widen the difference between put and call prices (remember that under the 0% interest rate assumption, the put and the call were valued at the same price). We will return to this idea in Chapter 9.

Table 4.4

| | Time Until Expiration | | | |
	45 Days	90 Days	135 Days	180 Days
Call Premium	1.81	2.65	3.33	3.92
Put Premium	1.55	2.11	2.53	2.86
Difference	0.26	0.54	0.80	1.06

Table 4.4 is a further illustration of this phenomenon. The longer the time to expiration, the more valuable the call becomes relative to the put.

What about the impact of dividends? The call holder can earn interest on the cash until the option is about to expire; but he forgoes any dividend paid. This reduces the advantage of the long call position. The higher the stock's yield, the lower the advantage gained by deferring the purchase of the stock. Dividends effectively lower the stock's cost of carry. If you purchase shares when the risk-free interest rate is 4%, the money used to purchase the stock is not earning the 4% return it could otherwise earn. This is your cost of carry. If the stock yields 1%, you are forgoing the 4% interest income but collecting the 1% dividend. Your cost of carry has dropped to 3%. And there are instances where a stock's cost of carry is negative: think high-yielding utility stocks in a low interest rate environment.

The lesson to be learned from this section is not to jump to conclusions. An analysis that once appeared in a reputable financial publication noted that put premiums had become more expensive relative to call premiums over the past 12 months. The author concluded that investors were becoming more bearish and paying up for puts. The reality was that during this period interest rates had been falling, so the author was measuring not a shift in sentiment, but simply how option prices react to a changing interest rate environment.

Time to Expiration

Options are often referred to as "wasting" or "decaying" assets; although these terms carry a negative connotation that may not reflect the complete picture, the fact remains that tomorrow an

Table 4.5

	Time to Expiration (Months)											
Interest Rate	1	2	3	4	5	6	7	8	9	10	11	12
0%	1.70	2.40	2.96	3.41	3.81	4.18	4.51	4.82	5.12	5.39	5.65	5.90
4%	1.78	2.56	3.20	3.73	4.20	4.65	5.06	5.44	5.81	6.16	6.49	6.82

option will be worth less than it's worth today, all else being equal. If all other things were continuously equal, options would be worthless. This section stops everything but the clock and looks at the impact the passage of time has on options' premiums.

We all understand instinctively why a two-month option should be worth more than a one-month option with identical terms. More time means a greater probability that the underlying will move by a substantial amount. But we must now quantify this instinctual knowledge. Table 4.5 calculates the theoretical value of a call option assuming a 30% volatility, a $50 stock price, a $50 exercise price, and no dividends. The values have been calculated using two different interest rate assumptions.

The 4% interest rate assumption gives us real-life premiums, while the 0% scenario permits us to focus on a more theoretical relationship. Under the latter scenario, note that the one-month call is priced at $1.70 and the four-month is at $3.41; that's a 1-to-2 ratio except for rounding. Comparing the one-month to the nine-month call we get a 1-to-3 ratio. And the ratio between the two- and one-month options (2.40 ÷ 1.70) turns out to be 1.4, which happens to be the square root of two. The relationship, it turns out, is a function of the square root of time. Given the value of the one-month option and a calculator with a square root function, it is child's play to fill in the grid.

This relationship is only approximate in real life, where interest rates are rarely 0%, but it remains useful. For those who are more visual, this time decay is illustrated in Figure 4.1.

Figure 4.1 is the classic illustration of an option's time decay. For the option buyer it contains two pieces of bad news: options lose value over time, and this time decay accelerates as the expiration

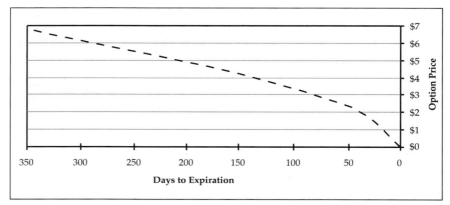

Figure 4.1 Time Decay: At-the-Money Call

date approaches. But note that the acceleration occurs only in the last two months prior to expiration; before then the time decay is very close to linear.

The assumptions behind Figure 4.1 were a $50 stock and a $50 strike—in other words, an at-the-money option. If we move in- or out-of-the-money, the options start behaving in a different way. Figure 4.2 traces two out-of-the-money options' values over time: one a 55 call (10% out-of-the-money) and the other a 60 call (20% out-of-the-money).

It would be difficult for time decay to be any more linear than what is illustrated in Figure 4.2. The two options simply become worthless at a different point in time, when the option pricing model estimates that given the time to expiration and the amount by which the call is out-of-the-money, the probability of the stock reaching the option's strike price is virtually nil.

Finally, in-the-money options will behave much like the out-of-the-money options, except that their values will converge on their intrinsic amount, not on zero. For instance, the 12-month 45 call (10% in-the-money) is valued at $9.54, which represents $5 of intrinsic value and $4.54 of time premium. The 12-month 55 call was priced at $4.79. The $4.54 of time premium in the 45 call will decay in a fashion very similar to the $4.79 of time premium of the 55 call, converging on a $5 final value (the call's intrinsic value) instead of becoming worthless.

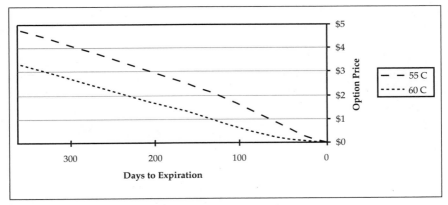

Figure 4.2 Time Decay: Out-of-the-Money Calls

The foregoing analysis was based on options trading at a 30% volatility. The relationships hold for higher-volatility stocks, as is clearly shown in Table 4.6.

Under the 0% interest rate assumption, the 2-to-1 price ratio between the four- and one-month options holds for the three volatilities illustrated. Under the more realistic 4% interest rate assumption, the theoretical relationship is close for all, and actually closest for the 60% volatility. With the higher volatilities the interest rate component makes up a smaller and smaller part of the options' total prices, and the relationship converges toward the 2-to-1 obtained under the 0% interest rate scenario. It could be said that under higher-volatility assumptions, the volatility component overwhelms the interest rate component of the option's price.

To close this section, a few words about puts. We saw earlier that higher interest rates result in lower put prices. Under a 0% interest

Table 4.6

Interest Rate	30% Volatility		45% Volatility		60% Volatility	
	1-month	4-month	1-month	4-month	1-month	4-month
0%	1.70	3.41	2.55	5.11	3.40	6.80
4%	1.78	3.73	2.67	5.41	3.53	7.09

assumption the one-month at-the-money put (using our $50 stock and a 30% volatility assumption) is valued at $1.70, while the four-month put is at $3.41. Raise the interest rate to 4% and the one-month put is $1.63, while the four-month is $3.14. Once again, as the interest rate is increased the theoretical relationship diverges from the theoretical 2-to-1 ratio, but not by an amount that would matter to most investors and traders. Puts will lose their time premium in a fashion very close to that illustrated in the foregoing call time decay tables and graphs.

Volatility

Most traders and investors have an instinctive understanding of volatility if only because they can feel its effects on their stomach. But this gut understanding needs to be sharpened to gauge the role of volatility in option pricing. Before delving into the different meanings of the word *volatility*, let's examine its impact on option pricing. You may want to return to this discussion after reading the next section.

The convention is to measure volatility on a yearly basis. When you purchase a 13-week Treasury bill yielding 3.8%, the rate you are quoted is an annualized rate, even though this instrument will be long gone before the end of the year. The same applies to volatility. A stock's volatility over 60 trading days may be given as 32%, or 22-day options may be trading with an implied volatility of 44%. It should be understood that both of these volatility numbers have been annualized, even though the time frame in question is much shorter.

We all agree that the higher a stock's volatility, the more expensive its options. We try to quantify this in Table 4.7, where theoret-

Table 4.7

| Interest Rate | Volatility | | | | | | |
	10%	20%	30%	40%	50%	60%	100%
0%	1.98	3.95	5.92	7.89	9.85	11.81	19.55
4%	2.50	4.45	6.40	8.36	10.31	12.25	19.95

ical option prices are calculated for a conveniently priced $100 stock. We start by looking at the 91-day at-the-money calls under two interest rate scenarios.

Looking at the prices calculated under the 0% interest rate assumption, we find a fairly linear relationship. Except for rounding errors, the price calculated with 20% volatility is double that calculated with 10% volatility, that with 30% is three times, and so on. This should not come as a surprise if volatility is held to be a measure of risk. A stock with twice the volatility has twice the risk, so the at-the-money options cost twice as much.

Looking at the option prices under the 4% interest rate assumption, we find the relationship to be close to linear but somewhat distorted by the interest rate component. For example, the 40% volatility option is valued at $8.36, not $8.90, which is what one would expect based on the $4.45 value of the 20% volatility option. Note that the higher the volatility used, the less important the interest rate component becomes relative to the total option value since the interest rate component remains relatively constant (at about $0.50) over the whole range of volatility estimates.

Table 4.8 is our first look at out-of-the-money options. We look at the same $100 stock but calculate prices for the 91-day 110 calls.

The relationship for this out-of-the-money call is not as straightforward as our previous example. But start with the 50% volatility assumption and notice what happens as it increases: the call price goes up around $2 for every 10% increase in volatility. So above 50% the relationship is linear. Starting with a very low volatility of 10% gives us a nearly worthless call; by increasing the volatility the option's value slowly builds until the option's price starts increasing linearly. The way to think about this is that for 50% or higher volatility, the 110 call is close to being an at-the-money option. Yes,

Table 4.8

Interest Rate	Volatility									
	10%	20%	30%	40%	50%	60%	70%	80%	90%	100%
0%	0.05	0.96	2.51	4.32	6.12	8.11	10.16	12.19	14.22	16.23
4%	0.09	1.15	2.78	4.63	6.46	8.47	10.52	12.56	14.58	16.59

Table 4.9

Interest Rate	Volatility									
	10%	**20%**	**30%**	**40%**	**50%**	**60%**	**70%**	**80%**	**90%**	**100%**
0%	0.00	0.13	0.89	2.17	3.61	5.49	7.36	9.22	11.07	12.91
4%	0.00	0.17	1.02	2.37	3.85	5.76	7.65	9.52	11.38	13.23

it is $10 out-of-the-money, but the more volatile the stock the less significant $10 becomes. This phenomenon is further illustrated in Table 4.9, where we repeat the exercise for the 120 call, which is even further out-of-the-money.

The option prices become linear at volatilities above 70%. The explanation is the same as above. If one is dealing with a 70% volatility stock, $20 is not a big deal, and the 120 call, even though it is out-of-the-money by 20%, is behaving as though it were at-the-money.

It has been said that changes in volatility have the greatest percentage impact on the price of out-of-the-money options. This is easily illustrated by rearranging some of the data from the previous three tables as we have in Table 4.10, where we examine the impact of volatility rising from 30% to 40% for different strike prices when the underlying stock is trading at $100.

But remember that the higher the volatility, the more loosely the terms *at-the-money* and *out-of-the-money* need to be applied.

The impact of volatility changes on in-the-money options will be similar to the impact on the out-of-the-moneys if one only takes into

Table 4.10

	Call Prices		$ Change	% Change
	30% Volatility	**40% Volatility**		
100 Call	6.40	8.36	1.96	30.6%
110 Call	2.78	4.63	1.85	66.5%
120 Call	1.02	2.37	1.35	132.4%

account the options' time premium. For instance, the 110 call was valued at $2.78 using 30% volatility and 4% interest rates. Under the same assumptions the 90 call could be estimated to be worth $12.78; that includes $10 of intrinsic value and a symmetrical amount of time premium at $2.78. Running the actual numbers would give you a $12.66 option value, close enough for most traders.

Volatility or Volatilities

Volatility is probably the most common word in the language of options. Unfortunately, its exact meaning is often left unexplored. This section looks at the different meanings this word can take and their appropriate uses.

Historical Volatility

As its name implies, historical volatility looks at the past and tells us how volatile a stock (or an index) has been over a given time frame. There is little room for argument here. A stock has traded the way it has traded, and that's the end of the story. You can't argue with the past.

The only place where there is room for debate is in deciding which period represents the stock's history. Options traders live in the here and now; looking at how volatile a stock was five years ago is of little relevance to today's marketplace. Should one look at the last week, the last month, the last quarter, or the last year? There is, of course, no right answer, but our preference is to look at two time periods—a longer one (maybe a year) and a shorter one (maybe a month, or even a week if there has been anything out of the ordinary). By comparing the two periods we can see if the stock is currently more or less volatile than its average. It should be noted that for the more established stocks (read blue chips if you will) historical volatility tends to be relatively constant.

To learn how to crunch the numbers, see the relevant section in Chapter 9. Let's assume you calculated IBM's historical volatility over the last three months to have been 32%. What does this number tell you? The answer, 32%, is actually the standard deviation of the stock's returns. If you hark back to your statistics class you will

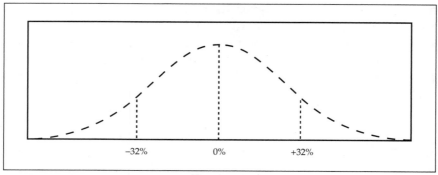

Figure 4.3 Expected Returns in One Year

remember that standard deviation is associated with the so-called bell curve (also known as a normal or Gaussian distribution), and roughly two-thirds of observations are expected to fall within plus or minus one standard deviation. Figure 4.3 will provide the necessary flashback.

A 32% volatility tells us that if—and this is a big if—the stock's volatility remains what it has been in the past, one year from now there is a 68% probability that the return on this stock will fall between −32% and +32%. It also tells us there is a 95% probability that the stock's return will fall somewhere between −64% and +64% (i.e., plus or minus two standard deviations).

What if your time frame is shorter than one year? Can a stock's historical volatility be of any help? Absolutely: a yearly volatility number can easily be adjusted to a shorter time frame. For example, you can convert annualized volatility to quarterly volatility by multiplying the yearly number by the square root of the fraction of a year the time period in question represents. So, to convert to a three-month time frame (a quarter of a year), multiply by the square root of one-quarter, which is one-half. So 32% annualized volatility becomes 16% over a three-month period. This tells us that there is a 68% probability that the stock's return over the next three months will fall somewhere between −16% and +16%. To convert to a monthly number, multiply by the square root of one-twelfth (1 ÷ 3.46) to obtain a monthly volatility of 9.2%. To convert to daily volatility, multiply by the square root of $1 \div 256$ ($1 \div 16$) to obtain a daily volatility of 2%. In this last example 256 represents the approximate number of trading days in a year. Of course, this assumes that the future will resemble the past.

Future Volatility

How volatile will a stock actually be over the next three months? Unfortunately, we do not know this today, and when we do know it, in three-months' time, it will be historical volatility, not future volatility. It would be nice to know future volatility, but if we did we would not be writing about it in an options strategy book.

Implied Volatility

Of the five variables that are used in option pricing equations (stock price, exercise price, time to expiration, interest rate, and volatility) four are empirically verifiable. You can check the stock price on the NYSE or Nasdaq; the exercise price is fixed and will not change during the life of the option; you can count the numbers of days until expiration on a calendar or your fingers; the risk-free interest rate is a well-known quantity you can look up in the newspaper. That leaves one unknown—volatility.

But for listed options there is another known quantity, and that is the option's premium. If you want to know how much a DaimlerChrysler August 40 call is worth, you can try to calculate this yourself, or you can simply look at what price this option is trading on one of the exchanges. There is no need to reinvent the wheel.

This leaves us in a situation where we know the answer (the option's premium) and four out of the five variables that are used in finding this answer. In high school, we confronted these types of problems known as "solving for x." We can solve for x using the option premium and the four observable variables; this is how to calculate implied volatility.

Implied volatility is the number that, when plugged into an option pricing equation, gives as the answer the option's current price. In other words, it is the volatility number the market is using to price this option. Implied volatility will be revisited in Chapter 9.

Forecasted Volatility

Implied volatility can be viewed as the market's volatility forecast. Of course, anyone can forecast future volatility. Just remember that a forecast is only a best guess and therefore contains an element of subjectivity.

Option Pricing Volatility

One of the inputs to the Black-Scholes model and other option pricing equations is volatility. Which of the four volatilities described above should be used as a variable? To determine the "fair" price of an option we should use future volatility. The price of the option will then fully reflect the stock's risk. The only problem is, no one knows what future volatility will be.

Since the future is unknown, traders must use their own forecast. This may be based on historical volatility (under the assumption that the future will resemble the past), implied volatility (under the assumption that the marketplace knows best and who are we to argue with professional traders), or various other methods (which may include chicken entrails, astrology charts, or that deep feeling in one's gut).

Overvalued and Undervalued Options

We have all heard the terms *overvalued* and *undervalued* options. Such expressions assume a comparison is being made between the current price of an option and a benchmark. It could also be said that a comparison is being made between the option's implied volatility (a measure of the option's current price) and someone's forecasted volatility (used to establish the benchmark).

It is important to understand that when a claim is made that the January 70 puts are undervalued this simply means that someone's (the setter of the benchmark) forecasted volatility is higher than the option's implied volatility. Some service providers claim they scan the options market looking for overvalued and undervalued options. When you hear this, just remember that it's the service provider's opinion (i.e., its forecasted volatility) versus the market's opinion (i.e., the option's implied volatility).

Real-World Volatilities

We have discussed the various meanings of volatility somewhat abstractly, but now let's look at the real world. What should we expect when calculating implied volatilities? What's the range of numbers that can realistically be seen in the marketplace? We have done a limited survey of equity options and offer our results in Table 4.11. Keep in mind that this is one sampling done at one point in time and that these numbers will change over time.

One fact should not be too surprising—the order in which these stocks fell: relatively sedate consumer stocks and utilities at the low end, the more mature technology stocks in the middle, and the

Table 4.11

Stock	Option Implied Volatility
Johnson & Johnson	16%
Procter & Gamble	20%
TXU Corp.	22%
Verizon Communications	22%
General Electric	27%
International Business Machines	28%
Microsoft	30%
Amgen	31%
Intel	36%
AOL Time Warner	41%
Cisco Systems	49%
Genzyme	53%
Siebel Systems	61%
Broadcom	71%
Amazon.com	72%
PMC-Sierra	73%
JDS Uniphase	75%
I2 Technologies	94%

newer up-and-coming (or down-and-going?) equities at the high end. If nothing else, when you see implied volatility of 40% on a stock about which you don't know anything, you now have a reference point. It could be an interesting exercise to recalculate the implied volatilities for these same stocks and see how the market has reassessed their relative risk. Yes, implied volatility can be volatile. As an example, International Business Machines used to have one of the most constant implied volatilities (ranging from the mid- to high-20s); the stock then decided to go from $160 to the low $50s in a relatively short period of time and all of a sudden its options' implied volatility rose to the low- to mid-40s.

Note that we quote our volatility numbers without fractions. Some computer programs will spit out 40.52% as an option's implied volatility. The numbers to the right of the decimal point are pure rubbish. Write down 41% as the implied volatility and move on.

The Greeks: Delta

Alphabet Soup Stock (ABCDE) is trading at $50. Some of its call options are shown in Table 4.12.

If ABCDE rises in price by $1 over the course of the trading day (which means the options will still have 45 days until expiration), by how much do you expect each of the various options to increase in price? We can easily recalculate the values of these options with ABCDE at $51, as shown in Table 4.13.

As ABCDE went from $50 to $51, call prices increased. This much we expected. The options' prices also increased at different rates, which should not come as a surprise to those who have dabbled in

Table 4.12 ABCDE @ $50

45-day 45 Call	$5.81
45-day 50 Call	$2.55
45-day 55 Call	$0.86

Table 4.13 ABCDE @ $51

	Call Price	Change in Price
45-day 45 Call	$6.66	$0.85
45-day 50 Call	$3.16	$0.61
45-day 55 Call	$1.15	$0.29

the market. This change in an option's price is known as the option's *delta*. If you are about to purchase a call on ABCDE, or on any other stock for that matter, is this a piece of information you would like to have? In all likelihood yes, to either help in selecting an option (choosing the one with a higher delta to capture a greater percentage of the stock's move, for example), or to set expectations (when the 55 call only increases by $0.30 when the underlying goes up $1 you should not be surprised).

If you want to know the delta of an option, there is no need to repeat the above exercise. Most option pricing software (including the program used to calculate the preceding prices, which can be found under the Trading Tools tab at www.cboe.com) will give you deltas along with price. When we calculated the prices for Table 4.12, we also obtained the deltas shown in Table 4.14.

Why the discrepancy between the deltas we calculated and those given by the option pricing software? Because delta is only valid for an infinitesimal change in the price of the stock, something that is impossible to observe, even with stocks trading in pennies. A more interesting observation is that deltas change. All of the calls have higher deltas at $51 than they had at $50. The industry lingo is that the calls are "picking up deltas" as the price of the stock increases.

Table 4.14

	Delta (ABCDE @ $50)	Delta (ABCDE @ $51)
45-day 45 Call	0.83	.87
45-day 50 Call	0.54	.60
45-day 55 Call	0.25	.30

But let's get practical and examine what this means for options traders and investors. First, in many instances there is no need to use pricing software to estimate an option's delta, keeping in mind the following guidelines:

■ At-the-money call options will have deltas of approximately 0.50, no matter the time to expiration or the stock's volatility.

■ Out-of-the-money options will have deltas lower than 0.50, and the further out-of-the-money an option is, the closer its delta will be to 0.00.

■ In-the-money options will have deltas greater than 0.50, and the further in-the-money the option, the closer delta will approach 1.00, the highest value delta can take.

A quick note on put options. Since delta is the expected price change in the value of an option, when the price of the underlying goes up, puts will have negative deltas. The delta of at-the-money puts will be approximately −0.50. Deltas of out-of-the money puts will be greater than −0.50 and will approach 0.00 as the puts move further and further out-of-the-money. In-the-money puts will have deltas lower than −0.50 and tending toward −1.00 as the puts go further and further in-the-money.

We have already noted that deltas change as the price of the stock moves up and down. This is represented in Figure 4.4, which depicts the deltas of the 45-day 50 call for various stock prices; also included are the deltas of the same option when it has only 15 days remaining until expiration.

Figure 4.4 illustrates two points. First, deltas go from 0.00 (when the option is far out-of-the-money) to 1.00 (when it is deep in-the-money), but they do not do so in a linear fashion. Delta changes relatively slowly at first, then more rapidly as it becomes an at-the-money option, and finally more slowly once again. Second, we can observe the impact the passage of time has on deltas. The delta remains relatively close to 0.50 when the stock is trading around $50 (and the option is at-the-money); it tends toward 0.00 when the stock is below $50 (and the option is out-of-the-money); and it moves toward 1.00 when the underlying is above $50 (and the call is in-the-money).

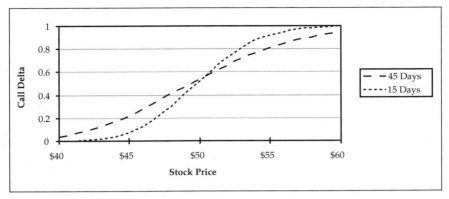

Figure 4.4 Deltas: 50 Call

At expiration, a call's delta will either be 0.00 (if the option is out-of-the-money and about to become worthless) or 1.00 (if it is in-the-money and about to turn into the underlying stock). This last comment may need some clarification. If a call is in-the-money immediately prior to expiration, we say it is about to turn into stock because a long call position that is exercised becomes a long position in the underlying stock. And stock has a delta of 1.00, since if a stock goes up $1.00, then, by definition, the value of this stock has gone up $1.00. As an in-the-money option approaches expiration, it starts behaving more and more like the stock it is about to become, and its delta tends toward the delta of the stock, 1.00.

What does all this mean for the options trader? If you are going to purchase a call, you should know its delta because that will tell you how your option will behave if the price of the underlying moves in the anticipated direction. You should also be aware that if you purchased an out-of-the-money call, for each day that goes by, that option's delta will be slightly lower (the option is losing deltas). This is not good because your call is becoming less sensitive to moves in the price of the underlying. Conversely, an in-the-money call will be picking up deltas on a daily basis, a definite positive. But do not confuse picking up deltas and losing deltas with changes in the value of an option. An option can pick up deltas and fall in value even if the price of the underlying remains unchanged. Remember what we said earlier in this chapter about how options lose value over time.

Table 4.15

Strike Price	Calls Quantity	Calls Delta	Puts Quantity	Puts Delta
45	+17	0.83	−22	−0.17
50	−32	0.54	−32	−0.46
55	+37	0.25	+19	−0.76

Delta and Complex Positions

One characteristic of deltas is that they are additive—one option's delta can be added to that of another. Take a market maker in ABCDE options. Over the course of a trading day she has bought and sold various option series and is now long and short the puts and calls shown in Table 4.15.

This market maker is long some calls and puts, but she is also short some calls and puts. What does her overall position look like? Should she be bullish, bearish, or indifferent? How can she protect herself if she does not like the overall position? Table 4.16 calculates this trader's net delta. This is done by simply multiplying the number of contracts by each option's delta, paying close attention to the plus and minus signs. Remember, puts have negative deltas, and a short position generates a minus sign.

So this trader's net delta is +608 for the calls and +402 for the puts for a total net delta of +1010 (we multiplied the deltas by 100 because there are 100 shares underlying each option). This tells us

Table 4.16

	Calls Quantity	Calls Delta	Calls Q × Delta	Puts Quantity	Puts Delta	Puts Q × Delta
45	+17	0.83	1411	−22	−0.17	374
50	−32	0.54	−1728	−32	−0.46	1472
55	+37	0.25	925	+19	−0.76	−1444
	Total Call Deltas		608	**Total Put Deltas**		402

that if ABCDE goes up $1, this trader's option position will go up approximately $1,010 in value. This also tells us that if ABCDE goes down $1 the options will lose $1,010 in value. This is where we can start thinking of delta in terms of stock equivalent. If the option position gains $1,010 on a $1 rise in the price of the stock and generates an equal loss on a $1 drop, it is fair to say that the option position is behaving like 1,010 shares of stock. Holding 1,010 shares of stock would generate the same gains and losses as this option position, at least initially.

If this market maker is risk averse, which most are, how can she hedge herself? Being long the equivalent of 1,010 shares, her hedge would be to sell short 1,010 shares of ABCDE. The resulting stock and options position would offset one another: if the stock rises $1, the options produce a $1,010 gain and the short stock a $1,010 loss; on a $1 drop of ABCDE the options lose $1,010 which is offset by a comparable gain in the short stock position. The fancy term used to describe this technique is *delta hedging*, and a position where the options' and the stock's deltas add up to approximately zero is referred to as *delta neutral*.

As noted, deltas change as the price of the stock moves around. So the hedge created by this market maker is not perfect, as the options' deltas will change at different rates and the stock's delta will remain constant. See Chapter 9.

This is all very good for professional traders, but what about the value for your average options trader? Calculating a position's net delta can provide useful information when using strategies that involve as few as two options, such as bull call spreads, discussed in Chapter 6. For instance, a trader who purchases a call with a 0.61 delta and writes a different call with a delta of 0.40 has a net position delta of 0.21. This would tell him by how much ($0.20) his spread can be expected to change in value for a $1 move in the price of the underlying stock.

Impact of Volatility

What impact does a stock's volatility have on its options' deltas? A higher volatility will have an effect similar to having a longer dated option, as illustrated in Figure 4.4. The logic is straightforward: more time or a higher volatility gives the underlying stock a chance to make a major move. Although Figure 4.4 illustrates deltas for two different time frames it could also depict the deltas for a lower-volatility stock (equivalent to the 15-day option) and of a higher-volatility stock (represented by the 45-day option).

Although deltas are always fractional and expressed in hundredths, traders often refer to an option with 77 deltas, or they talk about being short 600 deltas. This is traders' lingo—the decimal points are dropped and fractions are treated as whole numbers.

The Risks of Early Assignment

All equity options are American-style options, meaning that their holder may exercise them on any business day up to and including the third Friday of the expiration month. The converse is that writers of equity options run the risk of being assigned early on any stock option they write. Is it possible to quantify the risk of early assignment?

Early Assignment on Call Options

To gauge the risk of early assignment, it is useful to view the situation from the option buyer's perspective and to ask ourselves if there is any economic gain to be had by exercising an option early. Take the holder of an in-the-money call who intends to exercise her option and take delivery of the stock. Her call gives her the right to purchase 100 shares at $65, and since it is an American-style option, she could exercise it today, pay $6,500, and receive 100 shares of the underlying stock. But tomorrow she will have the same right to pay the same $6,500 and receive the same 100 shares. What incentive does she have to exercise early? Why spend the money today when she can wait until tomorrow and earn one day's interest on her funds in the interim? And will she want to spend the money tomorrow when she can wait another day and earn another day's interest?

Clearly, call holders have little or no reason to spend now when they can spend later, so very few calls are exercised early. The one exception is with dividend-paying stocks. The call holder who exercises her position on the day before the stock goes ex-dividend will receive the stock and the stock's dividend. So the question now becomes what makes more economic sense: spending the money now and getting the dividend, or spending the money later (i.e., at option expiration), forgoing the dividend but earning interest on the cash that will be used to purchase the stock? A logical investor will exercise when the value of the dividend is greater than the value of the interest that should be earned between the ex-dividend date and the option expiration date. Keep in mind that the dividend amount is a known quantity, and that interest rates are subject to change. Also, investors do not always act the way economics textbooks tell them to. For example, a speculator who owns an in-the-money call on a stock about to go ex-dividend might not exercise it because he has no intention of purchasing the underlying stock.

Summing up, calls are rarely exercised early and are therefore rarely assigned early, except when a dividend enters into the equation.

Early Assignment on Put Options

Once again it is best to analyze this situation from the perspective of the option holder. An investor purchased a 40 put to protect a long stock position a little while ago. The stock has tumbled to $30, and with the put still having one month to expiration this investor is now faced with a dilemma. He could exercise his put early and get $40 for his shares or wait until the expiration date. The advantage of exercising early is that he would rather have the $40 to reinvest today rather than in a month's time. But by exercising early he would no longer hold his shares, which could rally back above $40 during the next four weeks. What should he do?

The question cannot be answered as easily as it can be with the previous call example. Our investor must now weigh the advantage of getting his money early against the chance that the stock will rally above $40, in which case he could sell the stock for more than $40. Our observation is that quite a few investors elect to take the cash as soon as possible and that put options tend to get exercised early much more often than calls. This simply means that the risk of early assignment is somewhat higher with short puts than it is for short calls, and it is also more difficult to estimate when it will happen.

C H A P T E R 5

ADVANCED
INVESTMENT
STRATEGIES

Covered Straddles and Combinations

Assume that some time ago you acquired 500 shares of General Motors (GM) and 500 shares of International Paper (IP). Both stocks are trading around their purchase price and you still hold a favorable opinion of these two stocks. Without trying to fix something that isn't broken, let's ask a couple of questions about these holdings. First, would you consider selling these stocks (one or the other) at a higher price? Of course you would. The issue is how much higher? So let's rephrase the question. Would you consider selling these stocks 10% above their current price? If you expected these stocks to double or triple over the next few years, your answer would probably be no. But a 10% return over a relatively short period of time might interest you.

The second question is: would you consider adding to these positions; that is, buying additional shares, if you could purchase them 10% below their current prices? You obviously have a favorable outlook on these stocks; otherwise you would not have purchased them. And if you bought some shares around their current prices, buying more 10% below where they are trading now might appeal to you. But if you decide that you don't want more than 500 shares, that's fair enough.

Repeat this exercise with the stocks currently in your portfolio. If you find one or more for which you answered yes to both questions, there may be an option strategy that can help you méet your investment objectives. So let's assume that you own 500 shares of IP and 500 shares of GM, that you are willing to sell both of these stocks 10% above their current price, and that you would purchase an additional 500 shares 10% lower. You could sit and wait for these stocks to move up or down 10% and simply sell or buy when they reached those points. But if this were the preferred strategy we would not be bringing it up in an options strategy book, would we?

Covered Straddles

Start with GM, trading at $60.45. You are willing to sell these shares at a 10% premium, or at $66.50. The indicated option strategy for an investor who holds a stock and is looking to sell it at a higher price is to write covered calls, as seen in Chapter 2. Writing a covered call is agreeing to sell shares of a stock you own at a higher price. But you are also willing to add to your position and purchase 500 additional shares of GM at a 10% discount, or at $54.40. The indicated option strategy for an investor who is looking to acquire shares of stock at a price below today's market price is to write put options (also covered in Chapter 2). Writing put options is agreeing to purchase shares of stock at an agreed price, usually below the current level.

It now stands to reason that for the investor who answered yes to both of our questions the indicated option strategy is to write both calls and puts. This strategy is known as a *covered straddle* if the put's and the call's strike prices are the same or as a *covered combination* (often shortened to "covered combo") if the strike price of the call is higher than the strike price of the put. With GM at $60.45, the June 60 calls (with 12 weeks until expiration) could be written for $3.10 and the June 60 puts written for $3. The investor who owns GM and writes the June 60 straddle will face one of two possible outcomes at option expiration: either GM will be trading above $60 or below $60. Let's examine each outcome.

If GM is above the options' strike price of $60 at June expiration, the outcome will be similar to that of a covered write. The short calls will be in-the-money and will probably be assigned, forcing the investor to sell his shares of GM at $60. Like the covered writer, this investor will keep the premium of the written call options, $3.10 in our example. But this investor also wrote some 60 put options, which will expire worthless because the stock will be trading above $60. This second option premium ($3) also is pocketed, so the effective selling price of GM is $66.10—the 60 strike price, plus the $3.10 call premium, plus the $3 put premium. Yes, this is $0.40 short of our selling target price of $66.50, but we'll consider it acceptable for now.

The second possible outcome at June expiration is for GM to be trading below $60. Our investor is now in the position of the equity put writer: the puts are in-the-money, will probably be assigned, and shares purchased at $60. But once again, two option premiums will be collected, as the investor keeps the puts' premium and the out-of-the-money calls expire worthless. The effective buying price of the additional shares of GM is therefore $53.90—the 60 puts' exercise price, less the put premium of $3, less the call premium of $3.10. This time we did a little better than our goal of buying 10% below the current price.

Yes, there is a third possibility—the stock closing exactly at (or very close to) $60 on the options' last trading day. What would happen? It's impossible to tell. Remember that the buyers of the options decide whether or not they will exercise, and in this case there may be two individuals involved—one deciding whether or not to exercise the calls and another deciding whether or not to exercise the puts. The calls or the puts could be assigned, or both. Although we have witnessed a lot of bizarre occurrences in the world of options, we have yet to see someone being assigned on both the puts and the calls of a short straddle. However, the only way to completely remove the uncertainty is for the investor to cover the straddle (buy back both options) or to roll his position to another month (buy back both June options and write the Julys).

Covered Combinations

Our second stock was IP, trading at $43.01. Against these shares we could write the July 45 calls for $1.55 and the July 40 puts for $1.30. This strategy, where the strike prices of the puts and the calls are different, is known as a covered combination. The results will be similar to those for the covered straddle written against GM if, at option expiration, IP is above the call's strike price or below the put's strike price. In the first instance, the shares will be sold at $45 and both the call premium of $1.55 and the put premium of $1.30 will be kept, for an effective selling price of $47.85. That's more than 10% above IP's price when the strategy was initiated. Should IP end up below $40 at option expiration, additional shares of IP will be purchased at $40 and both option premiums kept, for an effective purchase price of $37.15.

But in the covered combo example, there is truly a third potential outcome: IP could be trading between $40 and $45 at option expiration. In that case, the calls would be out-of-the-money and expire worthless, and so would the puts. The investor would retain ownership of the original 500 shares of IP, and if her investment objectives are still the same, she could proceed to write another combination, say the September 40–45 combo for an additional premium of $2.25. When a second combination is written against a stock, some eye-popping numbers often appear. With IP, if the first combo is written for $2.85, and a second one for $2.25 (remember that the first combination used 16-week options, whereas the second one is assumed to use 8-week puts and calls, which explains the lower value of the second combo) the option premiums total $5.10, creating an effective selling price of $50.10 (45 plus $5.10) and an effective purchasing price of $34.90 (40 less $5.10). Very attractive indeed.

The Extent to Which the Options Are Covered

The expressions "covered straddle" and "covered combination" could be considered somewhat misleading—at least in regard to the "covered" qualification. In a covered straddle or combo, only the written call is considered covered; the put, from a risk and a margin perspective, is uncovered, or naked. Which leads to the question of how much margin is required to establish either of these strategies. If an investor writes a straddle or combo against a stock that she owns outright (i.e., she has not borrowed any funds against this stock position), then the underlying stock will, in itself, be sufficient to meet the strategy's margin requirement.

Look at it this way: the call is covered by the long stock position, so no margin is required. The short put potentially obligates the investor to purchase additional shares of a stock she already owns. Assuming no options are involved and this investor wanted to double up on a stock even though she had no cash in her account, she could purchase the additional shares on margin by borrowing the funds from her broker. The original stock and the newly purchased stock would become the collateral for the broker loan. If this investor writes a put option, she has not purchased additional shares but has taken on the obligation to buy these. If the put is assigned, she could then purchase the second lot on margin.

This is where caution is required. Although it may not be obvious, writing covered straddles and combos leverages the underlying stock position. If the underlying stock has been purchased on margin (i.e., is already leveraged), writing a covered straddle leverages an already-leveraged position. This is fine as long as everything goes according to plan. But throw a monkey wrench into this position and you have a recipe for disaster. We prefer to write straddles and combos against stocks that are clear of margin debt. See the section on risk management in Chapter 10 for further comments.

Testing for Suitability

There is a quick test to help you decide if either of these strategies is right for you, or right for a given scenario. Take Sealed Air (SEE), trading at $43.21. The seven-week options are $1.50 for the 45 call and $1.20 for the 40 put. You own 600 shares of SEE and are asked to answer the following three questions:

1. Would you be willing to sell your shares at an effective price of $47.70 seven weeks from today? Note that this represents a return of slightly more than 10% (based on the current stock price) for a relatively short period of time. If you are like most investors, you would probably agree to this selling price.

2. Would you mind earning $2.70 per share on your SEE holdings over the next seven weeks, assuming the stock stays relatively unchanged? Another no-brainer. Earning $2.70 represents a 6% return—not bad for seven weeks on a stock that is going nowhere.

3. Do you really want to buy 600 additional shares of SEE at an effective purchase price of $37.30? This is a more difficult question. If you answer no, or if you are not sure, a covered combo on SEE probably is not right for you under this scenario.

Setting Buying and Selling Targets

The two preceding examples, GM and IP, set buying and selling targets that were 10% below and above the stocks' prices. Are these realistic parameters? Based on our experience, yes. By writing straddles or combinations using one- or two-month options, the 10% targets can be set for the majority of stocks. Only those stocks with a very low volatility will require three- or four-month options. Remember that if you are using one-month options and are able to create buying and selling targets 20% or more above and below a stock's price, you should conclude that the options' market views this particular stock as very risky, as the options reflect a very high implied volatility.

What if a 10% band is judged too narrow? A wider combination, say, writing the 50 puts and the 65 calls instead of the 55–60 combo, or longer-dated options, could be used. Each of these solutions brings its own problems. Widening the distance between a combination's strike prices may result in writing options with very low premiums: the 50 puts may be trading at $0.20 and the 65 calls at

$0.30. You may not want to assume all of the risks of this option position for a mere $0.50 per share. Writing longer-dated options commits you to your obligations for a greater period of time (remembering that it is always possible to cover your short options before expiration).

Straddle or combo—which is better? From earlier chapters readers know that we hesitate to use the term "better." We prefer to look at the trade-offs. Straddles will generate more time premium, which is maximized when options are at-the-money, while combos will create relatively higher and lower effective selling and buying prices. One feature we like about combos is that occasionally the puts and the calls both expire worthless, creating an opportunity to write a second set of options. When this happens, the economics of the overall strategy become quite appealing.

Building a Stock Position

Covered straddles and combinations also can be used to build a stock position. Let's assume your goal is to purchase 2,000 shares of Starbucks (SBUX), currently trading at $24.06. You have no objection to paying the stock's asking price, but if you could accumulate the shares at a lower average cost, so much the better. One possible strategy is to purchase 1,000 shares at $24.06 and write a covered combination, say the April 25 calls at $0.65 and the April 22½ puts at $0.55. Your preferred outcome is for SBUX to close below $22.50 (but not too far below!) at option expiration. You would then purchase another 1,000 shares of SBUX at an effective price of $21.30 ($22.50 exercise price less total option premiums of $1.20) and your final position would be long 2,000 shares at an average cost of $22.68 ($24.06 on the first 1,000 shares and $21.30 effective purchase price on the put assignment).

Of course, there are two other possible outcomes:

- SBUX goes nowhere by option expiration (nowhere being defined as anywhere between $22.50 and $25), the puts and the calls expire worthless, and you pocket the $1.20 option premium. You now have two choices, assuming your goal is still to accumulate 2,000 shares. You could write another covered combo or you could buy another 1,000 shares of SBUX at the then market price, keeping in mind that you have still reduced your average purchase price by $0.60 (the $1.20 total option premium from the covered combo divided by 2 since you only wrote 10 calls and 10 puts but ended up purchasing 2,000 shares).

■ SBUX rises above $25 and you are forced to sell the 1,000 shares you own at an effective selling price of $26.20. This is obviously not a best-case scenario if you intended to hold SBUX for the longer term, but it is quite profitable nonetheless. So use this strategy only with those stocks you would not mind selling if they have a quick run-up after you have initiated your half-position.

Follow-up Action

As with other option strategies, covered straddles and combinations may at times require follow-up action. Since one of the series, the puts or the calls, will generally be out-of-the-money, there is usually a need to deal only with the in-the-money options. The exception is if the underlying stock is trading very close to a covered straddle's strike price shortly before expiration (say the Wednesday or Thursday before expiration). In this case, the indicated follow-up action is to cover the short straddle and write the next month out. For instance, if you have written an October 65 straddle against shares you own and the underlying is at $64.70 two days before option expiration, you may want to cover the October 65 straddle and write the November 65 straddle in order to capture additional time premium. The one downside to this rolling out is that it involves four options and most likely four commissions; if you are short 20 straddles and trading with a discount broker, this will probably not be an issue. If you are short two straddles and paying relatively high commissions, you may end up with very little additional time premium in your account (but with a happy broker).

As noted, follow-up action relating to covered straddles and combinations will only involve one option: either the call or the put, whichever is in-the-money. If the underlying stock has risen above the calls' strike price and no action is taken, the shares will most likely be sold upon assignment. An investor could decide to roll out the short call position and also would have to consider writing new puts. For example, a 70–75 combo was written against a stock that has risen to $78 a few days before option expiration. Do nothing and the stock will be called away (this may be the preferred outcome). But some investors will prefer to roll out the short 75 call, most likely to the next month, in order to capture additional time premium.

What about the puts? With the stock at $78, the one-month 70 puts may not be trading at a sufficiently high premium to justify writing them. The one alternative left is to write the 75 puts, transforming a 70–75 combo into a 75 straddle. This will increase the amount of time premium sold but will also raise the overall risk of the position, as the investor could be obligated to purchase shares at $75 up from the original obligation of $70.

If the underlying has dropped below the puts' exercise price, follow-up action will have the same general pattern as that in the previous paragraph. Do nothing and additional shares will be purchased (which once again may be the desired outcome). Roll out the in-the-money puts and you will capture additional time premium, and you will be left deciding whether or not to write a new series of calls, either with the same strike price as the original calls or with a lower strike price.

The Repair Strategy

Let's face it: if we purchased only stocks that went up, by now we would be sailing in the South Pacific or indulging in some offbeat hobby such as identifying neotropical caterpillars. But that's probably not the case.

Assume, for instance, that you purchased 400 shares of Clear Channel Communications (CCU) at $60. Before you knew it, CCU was going across the bottom of your television screen at $50. And there was a subtle change in your investment objectives vis-à-vis this stock: the original goal, to make some money, has now become not to lose any money. In other words, getting your money back looks like a very interesting proposition.

The last time you found yourself in this situation your brother-in-law suggested doubling up. If you were willing to buy 400 shares at $60, why not buy another 400 at $50? This brings your average cost down to $55, so a rally back to this level would let you get out of your position without any damage. You only have one problem with doubling up: it requires investing an additional $20,000. And thinking about it, you have a second problem with this technique: 800 shares will leave you with twice the downside risk that 400 shares carry. Lowering your breakeven appears to be an excellent idea, but it doubles your risk and requires substantial additional capital. No thank you.

Where Options Come In

Enter options. With CCU trading at $50.71, the April 50 calls, which have 100 days until expiration, are quoted at $4.60–$4.70, and the April 55 calls are at $2.35–$2.50. Consider the following trade, remembering that you own 400 shares: purchase four of the April 50 calls at $4.70, and simultaneously write eight of the April 55 calls at $2.35. No need to be a mathematical genius to calculate that this option position can be initiated for even money. Buying four contracts at $4.70 costs $1,880, and writing eight calls at $2.35 brings in the same amount. There is no cost to you, except for transaction fees.

But are you getting involved with uncovered calls here, writing eight contracts when you hold only 400 shares? No. All of the written calls are covered. Your 400 shares cover four of the short calls, and the four calls you have just purchased will cover the other four short options. There are no uncovered options involved here and hence no margin requirement.

So what have you accomplished? You have in fact doubled up on your stock position without having to put up any additional capital and without having increased your downside risk. The four call options you purchased give you the right to buy 400 additional shares of CCU at $50. You will obviously exercise this right only if it makes economic sense to do so. Your downside risk does not increase. If CCU continues moving down, you will continue to accrue losses on the 400 shares that you own, but the options, both those purchased and those written, will all become worthless. Since the option position was initiated for even money, if the stock does drop and renders all long and short options worthless, the options will have no impact on your overall position: they will neither help you cut your losses, nor will they increase your accruing losses.

The strategy only works if you get a little help from the stock. Assume that over the next 100 days CCU rallies to $55. In this case you have the right to purchase 400 shares at $50, bringing your average cost down to $55. Selling 800 shares at $55 would let you break even. Not bad, as you have taken your breakeven point down from $60 to $55 without having to put up an extra $20,000.

What if CCU rallies to $60? You will still have the right to purchase 400 additional shares at $50, but the options you have written will now come into play. By writing eight of the April 55 calls, you will have committed yourself to selling 800 shares at the strike price of $55. So although the repair strategy lowers your breakeven (good), it does not let you participate in any price appreciation above your breakeven point (not so good).

Table 5.1 gives the profit-and-loss profile of the overall strategy—stock and options—assuming the original 400 shares of CCU were purchased at $60.

As you look at Table 5.1, keep in mind that the cost of the long options and the premium received from the written options are not taken into account because they cancel each other out. The table has two columns for Value of Short 55 Calls because two of these were written for every 100 shares held and for every long call option.

The table summarizes the foregoing discussion: at prices of $50 and below, all options end up worthless and have no impact, positive or negative, on the overall profitability of the position. The overall breakeven point has been lowered to $55, a definite positive. But

Table 5.1 The Repair Strategy

CCU Price at Option Expiration	Profit (Loss) on CCU	Value of Long 50 Calls	Value of Short 55 Calls	Value of Short 55 Calls	Total Profit/ (Loss)
$65	$5	$15	($10)	($10)	0
$60	0	$10	($5)	($5)	0
$55	($5)	$5	0	0	0
$50	($10)	0	0	0	($10)
$45	($15)	0	0	0	($15)

above $55, the overall position can do no better than breaking even; this could be perceived as a negative, but will be addressed below.

Entering and Exiting the Position

We should address some practical considerations relative to initiating and closing out this strategy. Initiating the position is fairly straightforward as most brokers will accept an order such as: "Buy 4 CCU April 50 calls and sell 8 CCU April 55 calls for even money." This type of order ensures that both sides of the order get executed and you are not left with half a position. It also indicates you are indifferent as to the price you pay for the 50 calls, as long as the calls you are writing fully offset the cost incurred.

Exiting the repair strategy can be a little more complicated. Assume that by the options' expiration date CCU has rallied to $55 or higher and that you have decided to get out of your position completely. You will then have two choices: trade out of part of the options or exercise your long calls and wait for assignment of the written options. Your goal should be to maximize your proceeds after transaction costs, and this should dictate which route you take.

Assume, for instance, that CCU has risen to $57 or $58 on expiration week. The first way to exit the overall position is to wait until the Friday before option expiration, exercise your long calls, and wait for assignment on your short calls. You run the risk of early assignment on your short option, but this should not be an issue unless the stock's ex-dividend date is some time before expiration. (Early assignment and ex-dividend dates were discussed in Chapter 4.) The cost of exiting the position in this fashion will be the transaction costs of exercising your long calls and of being assigned on your short options.

The second alternative is to close out your long options and half your short options, by selling four April 50 calls and buying to cover four April 55 calls. The value of this spread will be close to $5. But it is highly unlikely, because of the bid-ask spread on both options, that you will be able to sell this position for the full $5. Assume the best you can do is to sell this spread for $4.90. Should you do so, or should you exercise your long calls and wait for assignment on your short options? Exercising and waiting for assignment will generate $5 before transaction costs. Would these be less than $0.10 per share?

If so, then the first technique of exercising and waiting for assignment makes more sense. On the other hand, if you can sell the spread for $4.95 less transaction costs, and this nets you more than exercising/waiting for assignment would, do so; then simply wait for the last four short calls to be assigned and deliver your original 400 shares. You will need to sharpen your pencil, taking into account all transaction costs to determine which is the better way to close out this strategy.

Exit Fear, Enter Greed

Let's try to think this strategy through in realistic terms. You bought 400 shares of CCU at $60 and the stock is now just north of $50. You read about the options' repair strategy and think it's great: no capital required, no additional downside risk, and you bring your breakeven down to $55. You call your broker and execute the trade. The stock starts to show signs of life—$52, $53—and you are feeling pretty good. Then, $54, $55—you're a genius; the stock is where you want it to be and you are about to break even. But CCU keeps going, and suddenly it's trading at $58, $59. Now the repair strategy starts looking idiotic: just as your stock is about to go above your acquisition cost (and make you some money), you are about to be forced to sell your shares at $55.

It looks like you have changed your mind and greed is taking over from fear. You want out of this option strategy but are afraid to ask how much it's going to cost you. Take another look at Table 5.1, paying attention to the value of the options if the price of CCU is $60 at expiration. Each 50 call is worth $10, and the 55 calls are worth $5. Getting out of the option position means selling the four long 50 calls at $10 (a $4,000 credit) and buying to cover the eight short 55 calls at $5 (a $4,000 debit). Guess what: you can get out of the option position at no cost, except for transaction fees.

Two points to be noted. First, with CCU at $60, the option position could be closed out for even money only very close to expiration. One week prior to expiration (keeping all the pricing variables constant) the 50 calls would be trading around $10, but the 55 calls would be closer to $5.15, implying a $0.30 per share cost of winding down the spread. Second, if CCU is higher than $60, then you have no choice but to pay up to close out the options. At $62, for example, the 50 calls would be worth $12, the 55 calls $7, for a net debit of $2 per share. In fact, the debit required to close out the position will be equal to the amount by which CCU is trading above $60 ($2 at $62, $7 at $67, etc.)

Selecting Expiration Date and Strike Prices

In our example, CCU had dropped from $60 to $50.71, a fall of slightly more than 15%. The repair strategy was initiated for even money using roughly three-month options (100 days until expiration). These are actually good parameters to keep in mind. You will find it relatively easy to repair stocks down 12% to 18%, maybe even 20%, using two-, three-, or sometimes four-month options. What about stocks down more than 20%? For instance, assume we had paid $70 for CCU; with the stock around $51, this would represent a drop of close to 28%. Can anything be done?

Yes, but the greater damage will take longer to repair. On the same day we initiated the repair strategy with the 100-day April options, some 273-day January LEAPS calls were quoted as follows: January 50 call $8.90–$9.20; January 60 call $5.00–$5.20. It would therefore have been possible to purchase four of the January 50 calls and write eight of the 60 calls for a small credit. The overall position would lower the breakeven to $60. This makes sense: the more a stock is down, the longer it will take to repair it, and the more of a bounce will be needed to reach the breakeven point. (Remember that in our first example CCU only had to rally $5 to $55 to break even, not the $10 needed here with the LEAPS.)

By using LEAPS it is possible to repair stocks down 30% and sometimes 40%. But this is the limit. Unfortunately, there is not much we can do with dot-bomb and Enron-type disasters.

Repairing High-Volatility Stocks

How much did it cost you to learn that high-flying stocks are the ones most likely to come crashing down? Well, here's a bit of good news: the more volatile stocks are also the ones that are easiest to repair.

When we created our CCU example, its options were trading with an implied volatility of 40%. Let's assume a similar stock, called

Unclear Communications (UNCL), was also trading at $50.71, but that this latter equity was more volatile and its options traded with a 60% implied volatility. We can obtain the following theoretical option prices for UNCL:

February options (37 days):   50 call: $4.25
                                55 call: $2.25
April options (100 days):   50 call: $6.75
                                55 call: $4.80

Let's assume we also acquired UNCL at $60 and are simply trying to break even on our position. With CCU we needed to go out to April to initiate the repair strategy for even money. With UNCL the same 50–55 spread can be initiated for a small credit using the February options. This is obviously a positive as a quick bounce over the next five weeks would permit us to break even. Looking further out, we can calculate the following theoretical LEAPS prices for UNCL:

January LEAPS (273 days):   50 call: $10.95
                              60 call: $7.50
                              70 call: $5.20

With CCU, the 50–60 repair strategy was initiated for a small credit of $0.80. The same spread with UNCL results in a $4.05 credit (2 × $7.50 − $10.95), and a 50–70 spread can be created for a small debit of $0.55 (2 × $5.20 − $10.95). These afford us the following two choices: the 50–60 spread creates an effective selling price of $70, to which we add the initial credit of $4.05, allowing us to repair a stock that was purchased at $74. The 50–70 spread creates an effective selling price of $90, from which we must subtract the initial debit of $0.55, letting us repair a stock that was bought at $89.

By now you should be getting the idea: the repair strategy works well with higher-volatility stocks. Of course, for the strategy to work we need some help from the underlying—it has to rally at least part way to our purchase price. If things go from bad to worse and the stock continues to drop, our options will not protect us against this downdraft. The one exception, where some downside protection is obtained, is when the repair strategy is initiated for a credit. The UNCL 50–60 spread was initiated for a $4.05 credit. If this stock continues on its downward path and all options expire worthless, this $4.05 credit is kept and helps reduce any additional accruing losses.

Investors are often interested in the repair strategy but bewildered by the number of option series listed and the even more numerous ways in which they can be combined to create various spreads. So a few words are in order about the mechanics of the repair strategy. Start with the current price of the stock. You will want to purchase the calls that are closest to being at-the-money. Then assess the damage. If the stock is down $10, you need to create a $5 spread; if it has dropped $20, you will need a $10 spread. If you are dealing with a $40 stock that you purchased for $50, you should be looking to buy the 40 calls and to write the 45 strike. In terms of expirations, start with 90-day options: the 40 calls are trading at $3.10 and the 45s at $1.35. Using these would cost you $0.40. So you look at the next available month (options with 118 days until expiration) and find the 40 calls are $3.50, while the 45s are $1.75. By using the latter options, you can initiate the position for even money.

While it is nice to initiate the repair strategy for even money, and even nicer to do so for a small credit that will pay for transaction fees, you shouldn't out of hand reject a repair spread that can only be initiated for a small debit. If you have $70 sunk into a losing equity position, putting up an additional $0.50 per share to significantly reduce your breakeven point might not be a bad idea and should not be dismissed as throwing good money after bad.

Leveraging an Equity Position

Traders, probably more than investors, have an interest in creating leverage. Still, numerous investors are looking to leverage all or part of their portfolio, which is why this strategy is included in this chapter.

Traditional Leverage: Borrowing

The old-fashioned way to create leverage is to purchase stocks with borrowed funds, commonly referred to as *buying on margin*. Quite simply, margin magnifies returns, both to the upside and to the

Table 5.2

	Buy SLB (Cash)		Buy SLB (Margin)			
SLB	Profit/ (Loss)	Return on Investment	Profit/ (Loss)	Interest Cost	Total P/(L)	Return on Investment
$67	$8	13.6%	$8	($0.15)	$7.85	26.6%
$65	$6	10.2%	$6	($0.15)	$5.85	19.8%
$63	$4	6.8%	$4	($0.15)	$3.85	13.0%
$61	$2	3.4%	$2	($0.15)	$1.85	6.3%
$59	0	0%	0	($0.15)	($0.15)	(0.5%)
$57	($2)	(3.4%)	($2)	($0.15)	($2.15)	(7.3%)
$55	($4)	(6.8%)	($4)	($0.15)	($4.15)	(14.1%)
$53	($6)	(10.2%)	($6)	($0.15)	($6.15)	(20.8%)
$51	($8)	(13.6%)	($8)	($0.15)	($8.15)	(27.6%)

downside. This is illustrated in Table 5.2, which compares purchasing shares of Schlumberger (SLB) at $59 on a fully paid basis, and buying the same amount of stock on 50% margin (which signifies that the investor puts up 50% of the stock's purchase price, borrowing the balance from her broker).

The returns on a cash basis are calculated on an initial investment of $59. For the margin purchase we assumed that the stock is held 30 days and interest on the loan is 6%. The returns for the margin purchase are calculated based on an initial investment of $29.50. As you can see, buying SLB on 50% margin nearly doubles the returns to the upside but causes twice as much damage on the downside. In theory, a 50% drop in the price of SLB would result in a 100% loss of the initial investment (not including interest expense), but it is doubtful that a brokerage firm would let an investor stay with such a position all the way down unless other securities were in the account to margin the position.

Alternative Leverage: Remove Borrowing, Add Options

The upside to leveraging a stock position is higher returns, the downside greater losses. Is there any way that one could capture the former without having to accept the latter? Let's start with some markets.

SLB: $58.92
Aug. 60 call: $4.10–$4.30
Aug. 65 call: $2.20–$2.25

Note that the August options have a little more than four months until expiration. An investor has $30,000 to commit to SLB, enough to purchase 500 shares, but because of his very bullish forecast for the next few months he is considering purchasing 1,000 shares using 50% margin. An alternative strategy would be to buy 500 shares of SLB, buy five August 60 calls, and write ten of the August 65 calls. The stock purchase would use up the $30,000, but the option position would be initiated for no cash outlay, as the cost of the 60 calls ($2,150) would be fully covered by the premium received from writing the 65 calls ($2,200).

If you read the previous section, you will recognize this strategy as the repair strategy repackaged and used to a different end. Nevertheless, it is worth looking at the numbers in depth. Table 5.3 summarizes the strategy at option expiration for various SLB prices.

Table 5.3

	Profit/(Loss) on SLB	Value of 60 Call	Value of 65 Calls	Total Profit/(Loss)	Return on Investment
$67	$8	$7	2 × ($2)	$11	18.7%
$65	$6	$5	$0	$11	18.7%
$63	$4	$3	$0	$7	11.9%
$61	$2	$1	$0	$3	5.1%
$59	0	$0	$0	0	0%
$57	($2)	$0	$0	($2)	(3.4%)
$55	($4)	$0	$0	($4)	(6.8%)
$53	($6)	$0	$0	($6)	(10.2%)
$51	($8)	$0	$0	($8)	(13.6%)

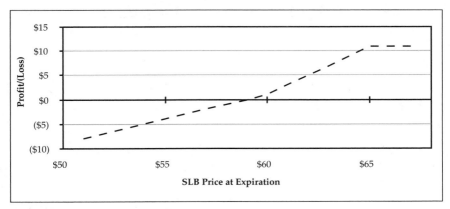

Figure 5.1 Buy SLB + Calls

In filling in Table 5.3 we took two shortcuts. We ignored the slight credit ($50) that was generated when the option position was initiated, and we rounded up the cost of SLB from $58.92 to $59. Compare the returns on investment when SLB falls below $59 to the returns on purchasing SLB on a cash basis in Table 5.2: they are the same, indicating that our strategy has the downside risk of a cash investment in 500 shares. From $60 up to $65 the returns are similar to those obtained with stock purchased on margin. The difference is that with the options there is no interest expense, but the leverage aspect of the strategy does not kick in until the stock reaches $60 (from $59 to $60 the investor only benefits from the appreciation of 500 shares). As with the repair strategy, no further gains accrue once the stock hits the short options' strike price. The per share profit and loss of this strategy is illustrated in Figure 5.1.

Notice that in Figure 5.1 the profit-and-loss line rises from $60 to $65 at an angle steeper than 45 degrees. In fact, over this range, profits increase by $2 for every $1 SLB goes up. This is the first time a line on any of our payoff diagrams has not been rising or falling on a one-for-one basis with the underlying stock.

By using options, our investor leverages his stock purchase—not by buying shares with borrowed funds, but by obtaining the right to purchase additional shares at $60, just slightly above the stock's current price. This right to double up is financed by writing covered call options whereby he agrees to sell both the 500 shares he now owns and the 500 shares he has the right to purchase at a price of $65. Obviously, an investor would enter into this strategy only if his price target for the stock was somewhere in the $65 range. Or would he?

Expanding the Strategy's Range

Take a look at the following quotes:

SLB:	$58.92
Jan. 60 call:	$6.60–$6.80
Jan. 70 call:	$3.10–$3.30

An investor who has a $70 target price on SLB could leverage his position by purchasing one of the January 60 calls and writing two of the January 70 calls for each 100-share lot he purchases. He will not be able to establish the option position for even money because the call purchased will cost $6.80 and the two calls written will generate only $6.20 in total premium. But most investors would probably be willing to pay an additional $0.60 per share (on a stock trading at $58.92) in order to leverage this stock from $60 to $70. When compared to the August options, the January calls double the range over which the stock can be leveraged. Why would anyone bother using the August options?

The reason is simple: this strategy will generate its maximum profit potential only when the options are close to expiration. Think about what happens if SLB quickly runs up to $70, the price where the strategy hits its maximum profit using the January options. For every 100 shares held the position is short two of the 70 calls. These will then be at-the-money options and probably still hold a lot of time premium. Unwinding the position would entail covering these options (i.e., paying all that time premium to buy them back), which would inevitably reduce the gain realized. To illustrate this point, Figure 5.2 estimates the per share value of the stock and options position at three points in time: at expiration (which reflects the strategy's maximum profit potential), one month before option expiration (to show how much of the strategy's gain is actually captured during the last month), and one month after the strategy was initiated (to show the impact of a quick run-up in the price of SLB—

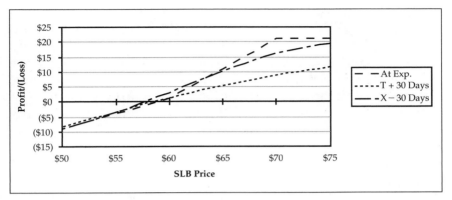

Figure 5.2 SLB + Options

remember that the strategy was initiated when the January options had a little over nine months until their expiration).

There are two costs to this strategy. The first is its limited upside potential. The second is a hidden cost. To realize the maximum profit potential for a given SLB price, an investor will have to wait until close to the expiration date. Observe in Figure 5.2 that if SLB rises to $65, $70, or $75 30 days after the position has been initiated (labeled T + 30 Days in the figure), the options do not add any leverage to the position. The profit-and-loss line climbs at a 45-degree angle, the same result that would be obtained with an unleveraged stock purchase. Note further that if SLB is trading at $70 one month before expiration (labeled X − 30 Days), our stock-plus-option strategy generates a profit of approximately $17 per share, higher than the $11 gain a straight stock purchase would yield, but less than the $21 possible with the stock plus options strategy.

The comments made in the repair strategy section about unwinding the stock and option positions and changing one's mind also apply to investors "buying one and writing two" to create leverage. On the latter topic, if an investor used the January options and if by the expiration date SLB were trading at $80, it would be possible to unwind the call positions for close to even money by selling one of the 60 calls at $20 and buying to cover two of the 70 calls at $10 each, or $20. If the stock does go to $80 and the options are unwound, the end result will be a loss of leverage. If an investor bought 500 shares at $58.92, he will still hold these shares (now at $80) and the option position will have had very little financial impact because it was initiated for a $0.60 debit and closed out for even money.

In the balance are no interest expense and the downside risk of a cash basis position, versus leverage limited to a determined range and a strategy that only realizes its maximum potential close to option expiration. Is it worth initiating such a position? We think so, especially if one is expecting a quick $5 increase in the price of a stock or has a longer-term outlook and does not object to waiting until option expiration. In this latter case, if the underlying stock runs up, the position starts behaving like a covered write, another position that generates its maximum return only at, or close to, expiration.

Also, for some investors, this may be the only way to obtain leverage in certain accounts. Some brokerage firms permit bull call spreads in tax-deferred accounts (IRAs, 401(k)s, etc.). Since our leverage strategy consists of a covered write (long 100 shares, short one call), which all brokerage firms allow in tax-deferred accounts, and a bull call spread (long one call, short a higher strike call), it may be possible to execute this strategy in what are essentially cash accounts.

Final Variation

Sometimes it is difficult to get the stars to line up. Take the case of an investor who has sufficient cash to purchase 1,000 shares of National Semiconductor (NSM) and is looking to leverage her purchase with call options. She expects NSM to rise to $35 over the next three months and pulls up the following quotes:

NSM:	$30.00
December 30 calls:	$3.10–$3.30
December 35 calls:	$1.30–$1.40

Buying 10 of the 30 calls and writing 20 of the 35 calls would result in a $0.70 per share debit—an amount our investor is unwilling to pay. She could establish the 30–35 call spread for even money if she used longer-dated options, but she is unwilling to commit herself to this position for more than three months. Is she totally out of luck?

She will have to compromise, but there is no need for her to dismiss the use of options. By fiddling with the numbers she comes up with the following: purchasing 6 of the December 30 calls would cost $1,980, and writing 16 of the December 35 calls would generate $2,080, netting her a $100 credit, sufficient to pay for her transaction costs. Her final position would be long 1,000 shares, with the right to acquire 600 additional shares at $30 and the potential obligation to sell 1,600 shares at $35.

Our investor was unable to double up using options while remaining within her trading parameters. But she was able to enter into a position for even money where she would earn $1.60 for every dollar that NSM rose above $30 until it reached $35. She leveraged her position by 60%, accepting that half a loaf (or 60% of a loaf) is better than none at all.

Determining the right number of options to buy and write takes only a few minutes. Start with the number of shares you are looking to purchase on a cash basis: in our example, this was 1,000. If you are long 1,000 shares, you can write 10 call options. Now start buying the 30 calls. If you purchase 5, you can write 15 of the higher strike calls since you own 1,000 shares and have the right to purchase an additional 500. Buying 5 of the 30 calls costs $1,650, and writing 15 of the 35 calls generates a $2,100 credit. Repeat the exercise for 6 and 16 calls (as above) and then for 7 and 17 (which ends up costing $100). The decision to establish a 6-by-16 rather than a 7-by-17 spread is purely a question of whether or not an investor is willing to pay $100 for the upside potential of an additional 100 shares. This example also shows how situations that may not look viable at first can be turned to an investor's advantage with a little imagination and a sharp pencil.

More Later

Collars, an advanced investment strategy, are discussed in Chapter 8. Even if you have no interest in hedging corporate stock or options, make sure you read about this strategy.

C H A P T E R **6**

ADVANCED
TRADING
STRATEGIES

Bull Call Spreads

Traders who start out by purchasing call options quickly realize that it is best to purchase calls on stocks that will move significantly. High-volatility stocks have a greater probability of moving significantly, but the option premiums on those stocks are correspondingly high. Buying calls on high-volatility stocks is not a slam dunk.

To illustrate this point, take a look at the following 91-day options on Siebel Systems (SEBL), trading at $31.71:

May 27½ call:	$7.00–$7.10
May 30 call:	$5.50–$5.70
May 32½ call:	$4.30–$4.40
May 35 call:	$3.20–$3.40

Table 6.1

	Option Premium	Upside Breakeven	Percentage Increase in SEBL to Break Even
May 27½ call	$7.10	$34.60	9.1%
May 30 call	$5.70	$35.70	12.6%
May 32½ call	$4.40	$36.90	16.4%
May 35 call	$3.40	$38.40	21.1%

Table 6.1 looks at the upside breakeven at expiration in both dollar and percentage terms, assuming the options are bought at the offered price.

Purchasing the slightly in-the-money 30 call requires SEBL to increase by close to 13% just to break even. Few traders are looking just to break even. Of course, if expectations are that this stock will go up by 30% to 40% over the next three months, buying these calls may be an appropriate strategy. But what if a trader is bullish on SEBL but not to the point of purchasing these calls? Should he walk away and start looking elsewhere for trading opportunities? This is where spreads enter the picture.

A *spread* is any option position that combines a long and a short position. A bull call spread involves purchasing one call option and writing a different call with the same expiration date but a higher strike price. For example, a trader could purchase the May 30 call at $5.70 and simultaneously write the May 35 call at $3.20 to create a bull call spread. To understand this spread, it is best to break it down into its component.

Buying the 30 call gives the trader the right to purchase shares of SEBL at $30. By writing the 35 call this trader also assumes the obligation of selling shares of SEBL at $35. The trader does not own any shares of stock, but his short call is considered covered because he has the right to buy shares if necessary (although most brokerage firms require spreads to be done in a margin account).

Bull call spreads fall into the subcategory of debit spreads. This indicates that the position will be initiated for a net debit, $2.50 in our example (the cost of the 30 call, $5.70, less the premium received

Table 6.2

SEBL Price at Option Expiration	Value of Long 30 Call	Value of Short 35 Call	Value of 30–35 Call Spread
$28	$0	$0	$0
$29	$0	$0	$0
$30	$0	$0	$0
$31	$1	$0	$1
$32	$2	$0	$2
$33	$3	$0	$3
$34	$4	$0	$4
$35	$5	$0	$5
$36	$6	($1)	$5
$37	$7	($2)	$5

from writing the 35 call, $3.20). The risk of this spread is limited to the initial debit because the worst-case scenario has SEBL at or below $30 at option expiration, making both options worthless. The best-case scenario has SEBL at or above $35 at expiration, in which case the spread will be worth its maximum theoretical value of $5 (think of it as exercising the 30 call to buy SEBL at $30, being assigned on the short 35 call, and being forced to sell your shares at $35, realizing a $5 profit on the stock purchase and sale). Table 6.2 gives the values of both options and of the spread for various stock prices at expiration.

Note that the far-right-hand column gives the value of the spread at expiration, not the profit or loss realized on the trade. To calculate this last number, the original debit of $2.50 must be subtracted from the final value. This profit and loss at expiration is illustrated in Figure 6.1.

Bull call spreads are limited risk/limited reward positions. (This cannot be said of all spreads.) Some traders believe that the limited profit aspect is a sufficiently negative condition to warrant dismissing this type of strategy altogether. But we view it differently. In the SEBL example a spread with a maximum value of $5 was estab-

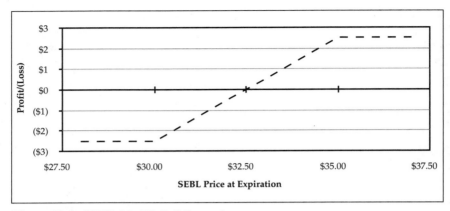

Figure 6.1 SEBL 30–35 Call Spread

lished for a $2.50 debit. The best-case scenario has a trader doubling his initial outlay if the stock rises to $35, or by 10.4%. Table 6.3 looks at the upside moves necessary for the buyers of various calls to double their initial investment at option expiration.

Now we can look at spreads in a totally different light: it's a strategy that will return 100% on the initial investment if the underlying stock is up 10.4% or more at option expiration. To achieve the same magnitude of return with a straight call purchase requires SEBL to rally more than 30%. Does this strategy now sound interesting?

Table 6.3

	Premium	SEBL Price Needed at Expiration to Break Even	SEBL Price Needed at Expiration to Double Premium	Percentage Increase in SEBL Price Needed to Double Premium
27½ call	$7.10	$34.60	$41.70	31.5%
30 call	$5.70	$35.70	$41.40	30.6%
32½ call	$4.40	$36.90	$41.30	30.2%
35 call	$3.40	$38.40	$41.80	31.8%
30–35 call spread	$2.50	$32.50	$35.00	10.4%

There are some downsides to spreads. First, continuing with our example, a double is the best that can be expected. The second disadvantage is the way spreads behave prior to expiration. This is best illustrated by Table 6.4, which estimates the value of the 30–35 call spread for various stock prices and at different times to expiration, assuming no changes in the options' implied volatility.

Table 6.4 is instructive in many ways. First, notice that even if SEBL rallies to $40 in a very short period of time (say 11 days after the trade was initiated) the spread's value only rises to $3.58. Two months later, with only 20 days left until expiration, the spread's value is still only $4.39. Bull call spreads will trade close to their maximum theoretical value only if the options are very close to expiration, or if the stock has risen substantially above the short option's strike price.

Second, notice the impact of time decay. If SEBL remains close to unchanged, the value of the spread will change very little. At a $32.50 stock price, the spread rises very slowly in value. At a $30 stock price, the spread is still worth $1.31 10 days before expiration (remember this position was established for $2.50; so after 80 days, a little over half of the spread's value remains). The passage of time does not have a major impact because the spread consists of one long and one short option. The losses due to the time decay of the long option are largely made up by the gains on the short one.

And third, although Table 6.4 assumes that the volatility assumption remains constant, it is easy to see the impact that changes in this

Table 6.4 Value of 30–35 Call Spread

SEBL Price	Days to Expiration									
	91	80	70	60	50	40	30	20	10	0
$40	3.51	3.58	3.66	3.73	3.81	3.95	4.14	4.39	4.74	5.00
$37.50	3.17	3.21	3.26	3.30	3.42	3.56	3.72	3.94	4.32	5.00
$35	2.85	2.89	2.93	2.98	3.02	3.08	3.14	3.31	3.59	5.00
$32.50	2.41	2.42	2.43	2.43	2.43	2.44	2.46	2.46	2.48	2.50
$30	2.24	1.91	1.88	1.85	1.82	1.78	1.72	1.56	1.31	0.00
$27.50	1.57	1.54	1.47	1.38	1.29	1.18	1.05	0.80	0.48	0.00
$25	1.12	1.07	1.03	0.92	0.80	0.68	0.54	0.33	0.10	0.00

pricing variable would have. A lower-volatility assumption would have the same impact as the passage of time; so under a lower-volatility assumption the value of the spread 40 days before expiration would look more like the values calculated for the 30 Days to Expiration column. An increase in volatility would have the opposite effect, so that at 40 days to expiration the spread would be priced closer to the values given in the 50 Days to Expiration column.

You may have noticed a small quirk in this last table. The spread was established for $2.50 when SEBL was $31.71. A quick rise to $32.50 on the day the spread is purchased results in a theoretical value of $2.41, lower than the starting point. Yes, the value of the spread should be going up, but this anomaly appeared because we did not factor in bid-ask spreads in creating the table.

Maximum Theoretical Value

A bull call spread's maximum theoretical value is equal to the difference between the two calls' strike prices: a 30–35 call spread has a maximum theoretical value of $5, a 105–115 spread, one of $10. Note the use of the word *theoretical*. Because of the options' bid-ask spreads, it is extremely unlikely that a trader will ever be able to sell a spread for its maximum value. A $5 spread is more likely to be sold at $4.90 when it is theoretically worth $5.

This brings up the issue of exit strategy. A trader purchased the SEBL 30–35 call spread and on expiration Friday the stock is trading in the $37–$38 range. Should this trader enter a sell order at $5.00, at $4.95, or at $4.90 or should she take a totally different tack—exercise her long 30 call and wait for assignment on her short 35 call? There is obviously no cost or risk in entering a sell order at $5, even though it is unlikely to be filled. But is this the best strategy? It all depends on transaction costs. Trading out of the spread will incur two option commissions. (Most brokerage firms treat spreads as two different transactions in calculating commissions.) Exercising and waiting for assignment will incur two stock commissions. Based on our experience, commissions for stock trades tend to be lower than those on options. So in many instances exercise and assignment will generate a higher profit than selling the spread, even if one is able to obtain its maximum value. But to determine what's best for you, you will have to compare your broker's equity and option fees and decide accordingly.

An argument often made against spreads concerns trading fees. Purchasing a spread could involve two commissions, plus an additional two to liquidate the position. If the fees are high enough, a trader finds himself in what is known in the industry as an *alligator spread*—where one is eaten alive by the transaction fees. To avoid this fate, one must deal in sufficient quantities (do not attempt 1-by-1 spreads) and one's transaction costs must be toward the lower end of the fee spectrum. More important than fees are the options' bid-ask spreads. A bull call spread involves two initial transactions plus two liquidation trades, each one with a bid-ask spread. It is often possible to shave a nickel or a dime on the total cost of a spread by entering the order as a package, but if the options are trading with wide bid-ask spreads, we would probably back off.

Bid-ask spreads can have a much more significant negative impact on a trade than the direct transaction costs. This is why we would limit most of our spread trades to the more liquid options, where bid-ask spreads tend to be narrower and therefore create less slippage.

Spread Selection

If you thought call selection was confusing, take a look at choosing a call spread. With the four SEBL calls listed above, six different bull spreads can be constructed. This is also a simplified scenario since, in fact, May calls with strike prices from $5 all the way through $50 were available on SEBL when we selected our example. How can this process be simplified?

Observe that the value of the SEBL 30–35 spread in our example, did not change very much over time. To us, this makes spreads better suited for short-term positions and only very rarely adequate for longer-term situations. (We have a hard time justifying spreads using LEAPS, for example.)

In selecting the strike prices for a spread, we first look at selling our target. If you have reason to believe SEBL is poised to rally to $40, you probably do not want to write the 35 call, as this eliminates any possible gains from the stock above $35. Remember that by writing a call with a higher strike price you are in fact selecting a point above which you will no longer participate in the stock's appreciation. You are willing to give up any further upside in exchange for a reduced cost of entry into the position.

Once the upper band of the spread is selected, look for a spread that creates an acceptable risk-reward ratio. Above, we purchased a $5 spread for $2.50, a 1-to-1 risk-reward ratio. We could have also purchased the 32½–35 spread for $1.20 (lower than 1-to-1 risk-reward) or the 27½–35 spread for $3.90 (higher than 1-to-1 risk-reward). We do not like to risk more than the strategy's potential return, but many seasoned traders have no objection to risking more than they can gain on a spread trade. Spreads with extremely favorable risk-reward ratios (say, 1 to 10) will also have a very low probability of reaching their maximum theoretical value.

Entering Orders

Most brokerage firms will let you enter a spread order as a spread. For the SEBL example above, the standard verbal order would be: "Buy 5 SEBL May 30 calls, and sell 5 SEBL May 35 calls for a net debit of $2.50." By entering a spread order as a package you will not end up with half your position—bought the 30s, couldn't sell the 35s or, worse, wrote the 35s, couldn't buy the 30s. And by setting a limit to the debit you are willing to pay, you become indifferent to the individual option prices, as long as you pay no more than $2.50 net. If your order is filled and you paid $5.80 for the 30 calls but wrote the 35s at $3.30, it should be all the same to you.

One fact to keep in mind when you are looking at options quotes. Say the 30 call is offered at $5.70 and the 35 call is bid at $3.20. You enter your order, willing to pay $2.50. Nothing happens. You check with your broker and get a "nothing done" response. Why aren't you getting filled? The two options prices you are seeing on your computer could be coming from two different exchanges: the 30 call is offered in Chicago, the 35 call is bid in Philadelphia. This is a recurring problem with options listed on multiple exchanges but brokerage firms and the exchanges are addressing this issue. We admit that at times we have been tempted to leg into spreads—to execute one leg and hope we can enter the second order before the markets moved. We don't recommend this maneuver, but if you do leg into a spread, always execute the buy order first.

Bear Put Spreads

This strategy, the mirror image of the preceding one, consists in purchasing a put option and writing a different put with the same expiration date but a lower strike price. Bear put spreads are a low-cost alternative to the straight purchase of put options and are usually used with high-volatility options.

As an example, look at the following Emulex (EMLX) 67-day put options:

April 30 put:	$1.50–$1.65
April 32½ put:	$2.20–$2.40
April 35 put:	$2.80–$3.10
April 37½ put:	$3.70–$4.00
April 40 put:	$4.90–$5.10

With EMLX trading at $41.33, a trader who is bearish on this stock over the short term might hesitate to simply buy puts. The at-the-money puts are offered at $5.10, a premium equal to more than 12% of the stock price! But a possible put spread would be to buy the April 40 put at $5.10 and simultaneously write the April 32½ put at $2.20, for a net debit of $2.90. Table 6.5 calculates this put spread's profit and loss at expiration for various ending stock prices.

Table 6.5

EMLX Price at Expiration	Value of Long 40 Put	Value of Short 32½ Put	Value of 32½–40 Put Spread	Profit/(Loss)
$42.50	$0	$0	$0	($2.90)
$40	$0	$0	$0	($2.90)
$37.50	$2.50	$0	$2.50	($0.40)
$35	$5	$0	$5	$2.10
$32.50	$7.50	$0	$7.50	$4.60
$30	$10	($2.50)	$7.50	$4.60

Table 6.6

	Long 35 Put	Long 32½–40 Put Spread
Cost	$2.90	$2.90
Risk	$2.90	$2.90
EMLX Price to Break Even	$32.10	$37.10
EMLX Price to Double	$29.20	$34.20
Maximum Profit	$32.10	$4.60
EMLX Price for $4.60 Profit	$27.50	$32.50

Once again, we created a position with limited risk (the initial debit paid) and limited profit potential (the theoretical maximum value of the spread, $7.50, less the initial debit of $2.90, or $4.60).

An alternative to the 32½–40 put spread would be the straight purchase of the April 35 put, which is offered at $3.10 but which we will assume can be purchased at $2.90. Table 6.6 compares the profitability of this put purchase to that of the 32½–40 put spread.

The advantages of the spread are evident in the preceding table: for the same initial investment, the spread provides a higher breakeven price, a higher price where the initial investment doubles, and a higher point where the value of the position reaches $7.50 and generates a $4.60 profit. (We are dealing with puts here, so higher is better.) The glaring disadvantage of the spread is its limited profit potential.

The other negatives of the spread are the same as those we outlined for the bull call spread strategy: the spread's value will not change dramatically, even if the underlying falls quickly, and the spread's maximum value can only be attained at or near expiration or if the stock falls significantly below the short put's strike price. This is shown in Figure 6.2, which illustrates the value of the 32½–40 put spread at three points in time: the day the position is initiated (67 days before expiration), 10 days prior to expiration, and at expiration.

Note that since Figure 6.2 illustrates the bear put spread's value, the initial cost of $2.90 must be subtracted to calculate the strategy's profit and loss.

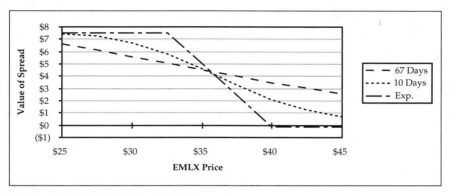

Figure 6.2 EMLX 32½–40 Put Spread

Our comments about limiting spread transactions to options classes that are highly liquid are equally valid for bear put spreads, as are our comments about exiting a position through exercise and assignment. There is also the risk of early assignment on the short put position. This risk was explained in Chapter 4, but we also note that for the short put to be assigned early the underlying stock would have to be trading substantially below this put's exercise price. This means that the stock has behaved as expected and the strategy is profitable. If the short put is assigned, a trader can then exercise the long put to flatten out the position. Because of the overnight delay in being notified of an assignment, there will be a difference of one business day in the settlement of the two stock trades. The trader who is advised on a Tuesday morning that her short put position has been assigned must pay for this stock on Thursday (the holder of the put exercised it on Monday, and so settlement is three business days later). If she turns around and exercises her long put immediately (on Tuesday), the sale of the stock through exercise will settle on Friday, three business days later.

Credit Spreads

Bull call and bear put are both debit spreads. Each has an equivalent credit spread, the topic of this section.

Bull Put Spreads

Our SEBL example was built around a 30–35 call spread. In addition to the calls, the following puts were listed for trading:

SEBL:	$31.71
May 27½ put:	$2.65–$2.80
May 30 put:	$3.70–$3.80
May 32½ put:	$4.90–$5.10
May 35 put:	$6.30–$6.50

A trader bullish on this stock can create a position equivalent to the call spread by writing the May 35 put at $6.30 and purchasing the May 30 put at $3.80, initiating the spread for a $2.50 credit. Let's first analyze this position in terms of rights and obligations.

The spread involves writing the May 35 put: this means the trader assumes the obligation to purchase SEBL at $35. In itself, this short option has all the risk of a long stock position. But the spread's second leg is buying the May 30 put, giving the trader the right to sell shares of SEBL at $30. This is, in fact, a protective put on a stock that the trader does not own but that he could eventually own if his short put position is assigned. So the worst-case scenario in our example is for the trader to be obligated to buy SEBL at $35 (on assignment of the short put) and to turn around and sell these shares at $30 (by exercising the long put). Buying a stock at $35 and selling it at $30 results in a $5 loss, which is reduced by the $2.50 credit received when the position was initiated. So the worst-case scenario turns out to be a loss of $2.50.

The best-case scenario occurs if SEBL rallies past $35 and both put options expire worthless. The trader then keeps the initial credit of $2.50, and this represents his maximum profit potential. The profit and loss on this spread is identical to that on the 30–35 call spread earlier in this chapter: $2.50 profit if the stock is above $35 at option expiration and a maximum loss of $2.50 if SEBL is below $30 at expiration. This is why we refer to the spreads as equivalent.

The spreads may be equivalent, but they are not identical. From a theoretical viewpoint the two strategies have the same profit-and-loss potential, realized under the same conditions. In real life a few practical factors come into play. The first difference is that the bull call spread requires the trader to pay the initial $2.50 debit, whereas the bull put spread generates a $2.50 credit. Isn't it always better to receive money than to pay it out? Yes, the $2.50 will be credited to your account, where it will earn interest or can be used to purchase a Treasury bill. If one takes into account the fact that buying the bull call spread reduces one's account balance by $2.50, the difference between the two strategies is actually the interest earned on $5. So $5 invested for 91 days at 2% (T-bills were yielding around 1.7% when we looked up this example, but we prefer round numbers) will generate nearly $0.03 in interest income. We doubt this will tip the scales one way or the other.

A second, more substantial, difference is that the bull put spread must be margined. The worst-case scenario is a $5 loss on the purchase and sale of the underlying stock, and therefore a $5 margin is required. In other words your brokerage firm does not want to have to phone you up and ask for more money. The margin requirement can be cash, but it can also be the loan value of other securities in your account. If the spread is margined with cash, the $2.50 credit received when the position is initiated can be applied toward the total margin required of $5.

A third minor difference is exiting the position if everything has gone the right way. To realize the maximum profit with a bull call spread, the position must be sold at its maximum theoretical value, which is difficult, or it must be collapsed by exercise and assignment, which incurs two transaction fees. With the bull put spread, if the underlying stock has risen above the upper strike price, nothing needs to be done because both puts expire worthless and the trader pockets the initial credit—a slight advantage in favor of the put spread. On the other hand, if the stock does not perform, the bull call spread buyer need do nothing, unless he can recoup part of the initial investment by selling the spread for a residual amount. The bull put spread will have to be covered at some point, if the stock has not met expectations. It is possible to have to pay more than $5 to cover a $5 spread because of the options' bid-ask spreads. Also, as puts go further in-the-money, they have a tendency to become illiquid, and this is reflected in wider bid-ask spreads.

The last real-world difference is the risk of early assignment. With the bull call spread, the short option is the one furthest out-of-the-money (the one with the higher strike price). If a trader gets assigned on this short call, it is because the underlying has risen sharply, the strategy has worked well, and the position can be closed out by exercising the long call. With the bull put spread, the short put will always go in-the-money before the long one (it has the higher strike price). Early assignment is also more frequent with put options, as discussed in Chapter 4. It is also possible for the short put to be assigned early when the long put is still out-of-the-money. For example, with the underlying at $31, the short 35 put could be assigned and the long 30 put is out-of-the-money, so it does not make economic sense to exit the position by exercising the long 30 put.

Bear Call Spreads

An alternative to the bear put spread on EMLX is to create an equivalent position using calls. The following were listed at the same time as the puts in the example above:

EMLX:	$41.33
April 30 call:	$12.80–$13.20
April 32½ call:	$10.90–$11.30
April 35 call:	$9.20–$9.60
April 37½ call:	$7.60–$8.00
April 40 call:	$6.30–$6.50

To initiate a bear call spread write the April 32½ call at $10.90 and purchase the April 40 call at $6.50, for a net credit of $4.40. The best-case scenario is for EMLX to drop below $32.50 by April expiration, in which case both call options would expire worthless, generating a profit of $4.40.

To understand the worst-case scenario, think in terms of rights and obligations. Writing the 32½ call creates the obligation to deliver shares of EMLX at $32.50, an obligation with theoretically unlimited risk. Purchasing the 40 call limits this risk and creates a situation where if shares have to be sold at $32.50 they can always be purchased at $40, creating a $7.50 loss on the shares' purchase and sale. This loss is reduced by the $4.40 credit generated when entering into the position, for a worst-case loss of $3.10.

You will have noticed that this profit-and-loss profile is slightly different from the one obtained with the bear put spread: $4.40 versus $4.60 profit potential, and $3.10 versus $2.90 worst-case scenario. Half of this difference can be explained by the wider bid-ask spread on the 32½ calls, the other half by slight moment-to-moment fluctuations in the options' premiums. Life on the trading floor is not always textbook perfect.

This bear call spread is equivalent to the bear put spread described earlier, with once again some real-life differences: cash in versus cash out, the cost of exiting if the strategy works according to plan, and the risk of early assignment on the short option (even though this tends to be minimal in the case of call options).

One last note on equivalent strategies: for two strategies to be deemed equivalent, whether two bull or two bear spreads, the expiration date and the two strike prices of the long and short options must be identical. Otherwise we are faced with an apples-to-oranges comparison.

Buying Volatility

We have heard the following reasoning on many occasions: "I am convinced that XYZ stock is about to move one way or another, so if I buy both a call and a put I can't lose: If the stock goes up, I'll make money on the call. If the stock goes down, I'll make money on the put. What could go wrong with this strategy?"

Some people would say nothing could go right with this strategy: If the stock goes up, the investor will lose money on the put. If it goes down, he will lose money on the call.

As in most cases, the truth lies somewhere in the middle. The purchase of a call and a put option, both with the same expiration date and the same strike price, is known as buying a *straddle*. Traders think of this as buying volatility. You don't care what the stock does, as long as it does it a lot. The gains on your one profitable option have to more than make up your losses on the other.

The traditional illustration of straddle goes along these lines: you are looking at the shares of Genentech (DNA) now trading at $50.03 and expect these to move up or down significantly over the next couple of weeks. You purchase a 31-day 50 call at $2.70 and a 31-day 50 put at $2.65, for a total cost of $5.35. Table 6.7 gives the value and the profitability of your straddle trade at option expiration.

Table 6.7

DNA at Expiration	Value of 50 Call	Value of 50 Put	Value of 50 Straddle	Profit/(Loss)
$60	$10	$0	$10	$4.65
$57.50	$7.50	$0	$7.50	$2.15
$55	$5	$0	$5	($0.35)
$52.50	$2.50	$0	$2.50	($2.85)
$50	$0	$0	$0	($5.35)
$47.50	$0	$2.50	$2.50	($2.85)
$45	$0	$5	$5	($0.35)
$42.50	$0	$7.50	$7.50	$2.15
$40	$0	$10	$10	$4.65

The value of the straddle is simply the value of the put added to the value of the call. By expiration, DNA has to either move above $55 or below $45 for this strategy to be profitable. The profit-and-loss graph gives this strategy its name and is illustrated in Figure 6.3.

The foregoing analysis has one severe limitation: it tells us a lot about the straddle's profitability, but only at expiration. What if the trader intends to hold this position only for one week or two—or

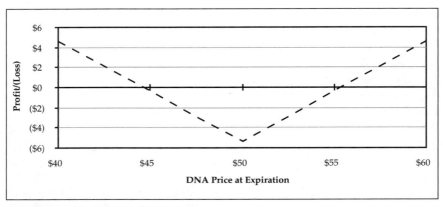

Figure 6.3 Long DNA 50 Straddle

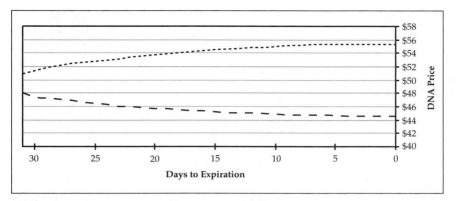

Figure 6.4 DNA 50 Straddle: Breakeven Points

for one day or two? By how much does the underlying stock have to move for the trade to be profitable? Figure 6.4 is a different way to look at a straddle. Assuming a constant volatility estimate, it shows for each day the upside and downside breakeven points for the DNA March 50 straddle.

Perhaps the most surprising aspect of Figure 6.4 is how far apart the breakeven points are 31 days before expiration, on the day the straddle was purchased. Why does the stock have to move to $48 on the downside, or $50.95 on the upside, to break even? Shouldn't the breakeven be the current price of the stock, $50.03?

The breakeven is not the current price of the stock because to break even we must make up the bid-ask spread on both options. (We assumed that we purchased both options at their offered price; to get back to breakeven we need to get back to theoretical prices, which we have taken as midway between the bid and the offer.). Still, $48 on the downside does require some explanation.

If DNA starts moving down, the call value will fall (creating a loss) and the put value will increase (generating a profit). Initially, the call's delta is 0.53, the put's −0.47. So as the stock starts dropping, the losses on the call are greater than the gains on the put. At some point the call and the put have respective deltas of 0.50 and −0.50. But as the stock continues to the downside, the put's delta goes below −0.50 and the gains on the put now become greater than the losses on the call. So if the stock starts moving to the downside, breaking even requires first making up for the straddle's bid-ask spread and then getting to the point where the put is gaining value at a faster rate than the rate at which the call is losing value. If DNA's price drops, the straddle initially falls in value before turning around, and a (small) accrued loss must be recouped before the position starts generating a profit. But all those nickels and dimes start to add up, and on the day the position is initiated, the stock needs to drop by $2 before we can start making money on the downside.

We view Figure 6.4 as the straddle buyer's road map. If you are going to purchase a straddle, how confident are you that the underlying stock will move outside of the two breakeven lines? Does such a move appear realistic? Understanding the map may prevent you from getting lost.

Buying Straddles for Specific Events

Sometimes you just know that a stock is about to move—earnings reports, analyst meetings, contract allocations. One of the better examples is the U.S. government's decision to nominate the lead contractor for its Joint Strike Fighter. This defense contract could eventually become the largest in U.S. history and there were two candidates for the lead position: Boeing (BA) and Lockheed Martin (LMT). Furthermore, the date on which the winner was to be announced was public knowledge: after the market's close on Friday, October 26.

To some, BA was not the ideal vehicle to trade. Too much of its revenue comes from the commercial aircraft side of the business. LMT, on the other hand, was seen as a pure defense play. So at half past noon (you never trade on company time) on the day of reckoning you pull up the LMT option chain and find the following:

LMT:	$50.05
November 50 call:	$3.30–$3.40
November 50 put:	$3.10–$3.20

You know that you will have to hold the straddle three calendar days through the weekend. But what is your risk? The November options have 22 days until expiration, and on Monday they'll have only 19. And this contract is a make-or-break situation for LMT. You punch in your order and buy 10 of the November 50 straddles at $6.60.

The news comes out on schedule, and LMT is the winner. This is good news. But then "bad news" would have been good news to a straddle holder. Monday lunch hour rolls around, and once again you pull up the LMT option chain.

LMT:	$51.41
November 50 call:	$2.90–$3.00
November 50 put:	$1.45–$1.55

The stock is up, but not by much. It now appears that LMT was favored to win, so this was "already in the market." But the stock has still gone up almost $1.50, so this has got to be good for the straddle holders, right? Not quite. The November 50 straddle is now bid at $4.35, a $2.25 drop from your purchase price, or $2,250 on a 10 lot. Ouch!

What happened? For one thing everyone knew when the news was coming out. And everyone—including the options pros—expected a lot of volatility. So the options, on Friday, were priced accordingly. Go back to the Genentech example, where the 31-day 50 straddle was offered at $5.35. DNA is not a low-volatility stock. And the 22-day LMT straddle was offered at $6.60 on the Friday that the news came out. Also refer back to Figure 6.4 and recall that the major assumption underlying this graph was that the volatility estimate would remain constant. With LMT, the volatility estimate obviously did not remain constant. It, as they say on the floor, got crushed.

By Monday morning a lot of uncertainty had been taken out of LMT stock. This translated into lower expected volatility and lower options prices. The lesson is obvious: if everyone knows about something, the options will be priced to reflect the expected news. Another favorite example is Hewlett-Packard (HPQ, previously HWP), which had a habit of reporting earnings after the close on Thursday immediately preceding expiration Friday. The volatility of HWP options was out of this world on the relevant Thursday afternoon, but that's not surprising since options with only hours left in their trading lives would have to absorb the full impact of a technology company's earnings. By 10:10 on Friday morning things were back to normal and HWP options were trading with a more sedate volatility estimate.

Strangles

Strangles, also known as *combinations* (combos), are sometimes referred to as "the poor man's straddle." Instead of purchasing at-the-money calls and puts, some traders buy an out-of-the-money call and an out-of-the-money put on a stock they forecast to be very volatile. Strangles are also preferred over straddles when a stock is trading between strike prices, as in the following Bank of America (BAC) example:

BAC:	$68.02
May 70 call:	$1.45–$1.70
May 65 put:	$1.30–$1.55

A trader who expects BAC to be extremely volatile over the next 45 days could purchase both the 70 call at $1.70 and the 65 put at $1.55, for a total outlay of $3.25. This initial cost represents the trader's total risk on the position, and the profitability of this combo is summarized in Table 6.8.

Table 6.8

BAC at Expiration	Value of 70 Call	Value of 65 Put	Initial Debit	Profit/(Loss)
$85	$15	$0	($3.25)	$11.75
$80	$10	$0	($3.25)	$6.75
$75	$5	$0	($3.25)	$1.75
$70	$0	$0	($3.25)	($3.25)
$65	$0	$0	($3.25)	($3.25)
$60	$0	$5	($3.25)	$1.75
$55	$0	$10	($3.25)	$6.75
$50	$0	$15	($3.25)	$11.75

If BAC remains between $65 and $70 at expiration, both options will still be out-of-the-money and will expire worthless, resulting in a $3.25 loss. A move above $73.25 or below $61.75 at expiration will result in a profit.

Figure 6.5 illustrates the strangle's profitability at expiration, on the day the trade was initiated (with 46 days until expiration), and at the halfway date (with 23 days remaining). The two latter calculations assume an unchanged volatility assumption.

First, notice how the value of the combo changes on the day the position is established. Or rather, notice how its value does not change. If BAC rises to $70 or falls to $65, the total value of the strangle remains close to unchanged as the gain on one option is canceled by the loss on the other. Only when one of the options goes in-the-money does the gain on this option more than make up for the loss on the other. Conclusion: it is difficult to see how this position will be profitable unless the stock moves outside one of the two strikes, even if it rises or falls on the day the position was established.

A second observation is that with half of the time to expiration gone (with 23 days remaining), the profit and loss line is roughly halfway between the initial day profit and loss and that at expiration. Since out-of-the-money options tend to lose value in a linear fashion, this should not be surprising. If a trader expects BAC to move over the next three weeks and buys a six-week strangle, it would be safe to say that her risk is approximately one-half the initial premium paid, assuming she will exit the position in three weeks.

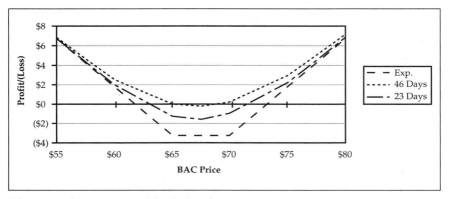

Figure 6.5 BAC: Long 65–70 Combo

Finally, we should point out that strangles, like straddles, have a slightly bullish bias. You will notice that the profit-and-loss graph, except at expiration, is not perfectly symmetrical. Calls have slightly higher deltas than puts (assuming the underlying stock is equidistant from the two strike prices) and also have a tendency to retain more of their time premium as they go in-the-money. (Notice that the 23-day profit-and-loss line converges more rapidly with the expiration date profit-and-loss line as the price of BAC drops.) Creating a combo that is perfectly symmetrical prior to the expiration date would require purchasing slightly more puts than calls, but this is a problem the average trader need not worry about.

Buying Volatility: Call Back Spreads

Buying straddles and strangles creates unbiased long volatility positions. What we mean by unbiased is that the buyer doesn't care whether the underlying stock goes up or down, as long as it moves significantly. But sometimes traders expect a stock to be very volatile but also to have a bias.

For example, a trader has been following the shares of Southwest Airlines (LUV) and is expecting this stock to be very volatile over the next few months. Her forecast is for "high volatility" (an unbiased forecast), but when asked if she believes there is a greater probability of the stock's moving one way or another, her answer is "higher" (a biased forecast). If her expectations were purely bullish, she could simply purchase call options. But we are making a subtle distinction between two forecasts: "I'm bullish" and "I expect a lot of volatility, most probably to the upside." To see the type of position the trader with the second outlook should consider, let's first look at some option quotes:

LUV:	$18.39
June 15 call:	$3.50–$3.80
June 15 put:	$0.20–$0.30
June 17½ call:	$1.75– $1.85
June 17½ put:	$0.75–$0.85
June 20 call:	$0.60–$0.65
June 20 put:	$2.05–$2.25

Table 6.9

LUV at Expiration	Value of Short 15 Call	Value of Long 17½ Calls	Initial Debit	Profit/(Loss)
$27.50	($12.50)	2 × $10.00	($0.20)	$7.30
$25	($10.00)	2 × $7.50	($0.20)	$4.80
$22.50	($7.50)	2 × $5.00	($0.20)	$2.30
$20	($5.00)	2 × $2.50	($0.20)	($0.20)
$17.50	($2.50)	$0	($0.20)	($2.70)
$15	$0	$0	($0.20)	($0.20)
$12.50	$0	$0	($0.20)	($0.20)

Our trader (with the biased forecast) could write one of the June 15 calls and purchase two of the June 17½ calls. Traders usually try to establish this position for even money or for a small credit. Using the quotes above, buying two options at $1.85 and writing one at $3.50 would actually cost $0.20. She could enter the order for even money and hope for a good fill, but let's stick with our $0.20 initial debit.

Writing a call when you are "mostly" bullish may appear counterintuitive. But this call is written to finance the purchase of two calls, so our trader ends up net long one call. It is probably best to start by looking at the position's profitability at option expiration, as is shown in Table 6.9.

The strategy's profit and loss at expiration is illustrated in Figure 6.6.

If our investor's forecast of LUV being volatile to the upside is correct, she will effectively capture all of the stock's rise once it reaches her breakeven point of $20.20. If her volatility forecast is correct but LUV heads south instead of rallying, she will show a very small loss, as long as LUV drops to or below $15. Her risk lies in a relatively flat stock price (i.e., her expectation of high volatility not being realized), with the worst-case scenario having LUV trading at $17.50 at option expiration. At this price, the two long calls are worthless and the short 15 call must be covered at $2.50, for a $2.70 loss on the strategy (the initial $0.20 debit plus the $2.50 required to repurchase the short call).

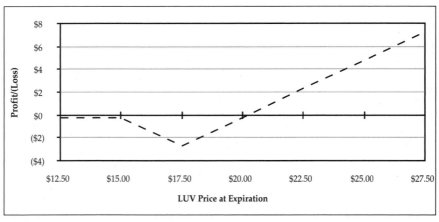

Figure 6.6 LUV: Call Back Spread

Back spreads are sometimes referred to as *pay later options*, but this is a bit of a misnomer. True, the initial debit can be very small (as in our example) or even nonexistent, but the position does include a call credit spread that will have to be properly margined. The cash may not come out of the account until expiration, but brokerage firms want it ready and available.

Comparison to Other Strategies

Our mostly bullish trader could have simply purchased a call option. The 17½ strike was offered at $1.85 and would have provided her with a lower upside breakeven ($19.15 versus $20.20 for the back spread), lower risk ($1.85 versus $2.70) if LUV is at $17.50 at expiration, but a larger loss ($1.85 versus $0.20) if LUV drops below $15.

There is no need to create back spreads by writing one option and buying two. A more bullish position could have been initiated by writing the June 17½ call at $1.75 and purchasing three of the June 20 calls at $0.65, for an initial debit of $0.20. This position is more bullish because the upside breakeven has been raised to $21.35, but above that price the value of the spread increases by $2 for every $1 LUV rallies. You can also see how, by varying the ratio of options bought to options written, positions can be initiated for even money. For example, writing three of the June 17½ calls and buying eight of

Table 6.10

Strike Price	30% Volatility	60% Volatility
$45	$5.60	$7.14
$50	$2.20	$4.27
$55	$0.61	$2.44

the 20s would generate a very small credit (premium received: $175 × 3 = $525; premium paid: $65 × 8 = $520).

The Impact of Volatility

How does higher volatility impact back spreads? Traders will naturally want to establish these types of positions on more volatile stocks, whose options typically trade with higher implied volatility. To find out, we calculated selected theoretical option prices under two volatility assumptions, 30% and 60%, and present these in Table 6.10.

The values in this table assume a $50 stock price, a 4% risk-free interest rate, and no dividends. First, look at writing one 45 strike call and purchasing two of the 50s. Under the 30% volatility assumption this position could be established for a $1.20 credit, but under the 60% volatility assumption there would be a $1.40 debit. So volatility does matter, and a call back spread's breakeven point will rise as the options volatility increases. We can also test the 50–55 back spread with a 30% volatility, where writing one of the 50 calls and buying two of the 55s generates a $0.98 credit. With the higher volatility a trader would have to pay $0.61 for the same 50–55 back spread.

Buying Volatility: Put Back Spreads

If you have read the previous section, it will not come as a surprise that a put back spread involves purchasing more puts than are written and that the strategy is used when high volatility is expected with a greater probability that the underlying stock will move lower. Some option prices on Intel (INTC) with which to start:

INTC:	$30.03
May 27½ put:	$0.75–$0.80
May 30 put:	$1.65–$1.70
May 32½ put:	$3.10–$3.30

The more conservative of the two back spreads we will consider (and we define conservative as having the higher downside breakeven point) can be established by writing one of the May 32½ puts at $3.10 and purchasing two of the 30 puts at $1.70, for a net debit of $0.30. Note that May options have approximately seven weeks until they expire. Table 6.11 looks at the value and profitability of this back spread at option expiration.

The profit-and-loss numbers at expiration are illustrated in Figure 6.7.

The put back spread looks like a mirror image of the call back spread: a move to the upside above $32.50 and all options expire worthless, leaving a small $0.30 loss. An unchanged stock price results in a $2.80 loss, the worst-case scenario. Below $27.20 profits accrue on a dollar-for-dollar basis with the fall of the stock. Compare the 32½–30 put back spread to the purchase of the 30 put at $1.70 and you find that the back spread has a slightly higher risk

Table 6.11

INTC at Expiration	Value of Short 32½ Put	Value of Long 30 Puts	Initial Debit	Profit/(Loss)
$35	$0	$0	($0.30)	($0.30)
$32.50	$0	$0	($0.30)	($0.30)
$30	($2.50)	$0	($0.30)	($2.80)
$27.50	($5.00)	2 × $2.50	($0.30)	($0.30)
$25	($7.50)	2 × $5.00	($0.30)	$2.20
$22.50	($10.00)	2 × $7.50	($0.30)	$4.70
$20	($12.50)	2 × $10.00	($0.30)	$7.20

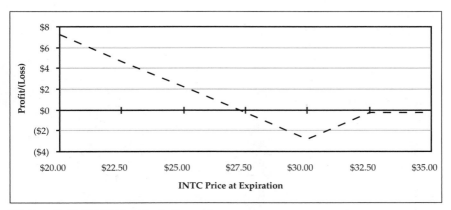

Figure 6.7 INTC: Put Back Spread

($2.80 versus $1.70) and a lower breakeven point on the downside ($27.20 versus $28.30), and it virtually breaks even if INTC rallies above $32.50 (a $0.30 loss versus a $1.70 loss on the long put). The spread's maximum loss is realized only if INTC is trading at $30 at expiration (with the long put, the maximum loss is realized for any INTC price below $30 at expiration). Another way to look at this is that the long put loses $1.70 for any stock price below $30, while the back spread loses $1.70 or more (to a maximum of $2.80) if INTC is trading between $28.90 and $31.10 at expiration.

Alternative Spreads

Two other put back spreads can be created using the options we just quoted: a 30–27½ spread and a 32½–27½ spread. Table 6.12 gives the essential statistics of these two plus those of the 30–27½ spread described above.

The ratios chosen are the ones that allow the position to be established for as close to even money as possible. (Another alternative is to establish the 32½–27½ spread with a 1:3 ratio, for an initial credit of $0.70.) The initial credit or debit also represents the profit or loss of the strategy if INTC rallies above the higher strike price of the two options. The risk is equal to the spread (the difference between the two strikes) plus or minus the initial debit or credit. And the maximum loss is realized at the long option's strike price.

Table 6.12

	30–27½ Spread	32½–30 Spread	32½–27½ Spread
Spread Ratio	1:2	1:2	1:4
Initial Credit (Debit)	$0.05	($0.30)	($0.10)
Downside Breakeven	$25.05	$27.20	$25.80
Risk	$2.45	$2.80	$5.10
Maximum Loss at	$27.50	$30	$27.50

The most aggressive of the three spreads presented is the 32½–27½, which has more than $5 of risk. Of course, if INTC drops below this spread's breakeven point, then the value of the spread increases by $3 for every $1 the stock falls. It is the higher risk–higher reward spread of this trio.

Only three put back spreads were possible in our example because we limited the number of INTC options we quoted. Actually, there were many more strikes available. The number of possibilities can feel overwhelming when you are considering establishing a back spread. To keep your trading as simple as possible, follow these guidelines:

■ Forget about options more than one strike away from the stock's price.

■ Start with the at-the-money option because you will probably want to include it as one of your long or short positions.

■ The wider the spread or the higher the ratio of long to short options, the riskier the position.

In-the-Money Short Put

A last reminder: if a put back spread is established and the underlying stock moves down (the best-case scenario), the short put will become deeper and deeper in-the-money, and, as was pointed out earlier, short puts are prone to being assigned early. Early assignment would not hurt the profitability of the strategy but may require a fair amount of cash relative to the capital being used for the spread. We would therefore advise monitoring closely all in-the-money puts and perhaps taking action when most of their time premium has disappeared.

Selling Volatility: Straddles and Front Spreads

It is a tautology to claim that for every buyer there is a seller. But it is a useful reminder that for every "buyer" of a back spread there is a "seller" of a front spread. We now take a brief look at the latter.

The constant in all back spreads is that the position is long more options than it is short. This means that every short option is to a certain extent covered. The corollary is that in all front spreads there will be a greater number of short options than long ones, leaving at least some of the short options uncovered. This renders these spreads very risky and inappropriate for most traders.

Front spreads, whether constructed with puts or calls, are short volatility plays. This means that these positions will be profitable as long as the underlying stock remains within a narrow trading range. Before we look at front spreads, a quick sidebar on the purest of the short volatility positions, short straddles.

To illustrate, take Hind Quarter Stock (HQS) trading at exactly $25. A trader is convinced this stock is going nowhere over the next 45 days and decides to write the 25 straddle, writing the 25 call for $2.10 and the 25 put for $1.90. The trader's account is credited $4 for writing the straddle. If HQS closes at exactly $25 on expiration Friday, both the call and the put will expire worthless and the trader will have earned the full $4. But HQS is more likely to move away from $25, either up or down, and the trader will have to cover either the call or the put, depending on the direction the stock takes. Table 6.13 summarizes the value of the short 25 straddle at expiration.

The good news is that the straddle writer will see one of the two options expire worthless. The bad news is that he could be forced to buy back the other option for more than the $4 initial credit, resulting in a loss. Potential losses are substantial to the downside (if HQS becomes worthless the 25 put would be worth $25, for a loss on the strategy of $21) and theoretically unlimited to the upside (HQS could get taken over at $40, $45, or $75). The risk of the strat-

Table 6.13

HQS at Expiration	Value of Short 25 Put	Value of Short 25 Call	Initial Credit	Profit/(Loss)
$33	$0	($8.00)	$4.00	($4.00)
$31	$0	($6.00)	$4.00	($2.00)
$29	$0	($4.00)	$4.00	$0
$27	$0	($2.00)	$4.00	$2.00
$25	$0	$0	$4.00	$4.00
$23	($2.00)	$0	$4.00	$2.00
$21	($4.00)	$0	$4.00	$0
$19	($6.00)	$0	$4.00	($2.00)
$17	($8.00)	$0	$4.00	($4.00)

egy makes it of little appeal to the average trader. Potential profit and loss is illustrated in Figure 6.8.

Back to our front spreads. Take a trader who has been following Exxon Mobil (XOM). He feels the stock is going nowhere over the next month and a half but is unwilling to write a straddle because of the potential downside risk in the stock. In other words, our trader does not see XOM moving much, but if it does move, he expects it to head south. With XOM trading at $43.41 he initiates a

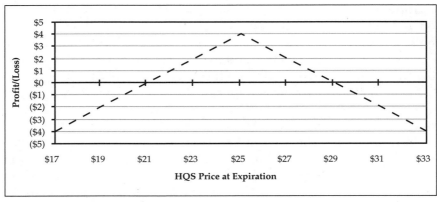

Figure 6.8 Short HQS 25 Straddle

Table 6.14

XOM at Expiration	Value of Long 40 Call	Value of Short 42½ Calls	Initial Debit	Profit/(Loss)
$52.50	$12.50	2 × ($10.00)	($0.10)	($7.60)
$50	$10.00	2 × ($7.50)	($0.10)	($5.10)
$47.50	$7.50	2 × ($5.00)	($0.10)	($2.60)
$45	$5.00	2 × ($2.50)	($0.10)	($0.10)
$42.50	$2.50	$0	($0.10)	$2.40
$40	$0	$0	($0.10)	($0.10)
$37.50	$0	$0	($0.10)	($0.10)

front spread by purchasing one of the September 40 calls at $3.90 and writing two of the 42½ calls at $1.90, for an initial debit of $0.10. Table 6.14 calculates the value and profitability of this front spread at option expiration.

The profit-and-loss numbers are illustrated in Figure 6.9.

Figure 6.9 provides a quick summary of the features of a call front spread. Like the short straddle, it is a strategy with limited profit potential, which is realized only if the underlying stock closes at the short options' strike price. Unlike the short straddle, the call front spread has virtually no risk if the price of the underlying stock

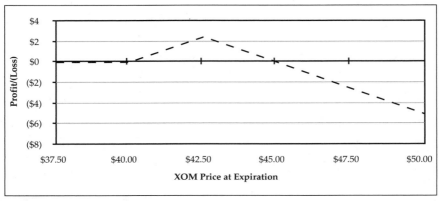

Figure 6.9 XOM: Call Front Spread

moves sharply lower (in our example this risk is limited to $0.10). But like the straddle, the call front spread is net short one call option, which means there is theoretically unlimited risk to the upside.

Another minor point is that unless a stock is trading exactly at a strike price, a call front spread will require a trader to give his position a slight bias. With XOM at $43.41, the 40–42½ front spread in our example had a slightly bearish bias as its maximum profit is realized at $42.50, nearly $1 below the current stock price. A slightly bullish spread could have been created by purchasing the 42½ call and writing the 45s.

Put Front Spread

Finally, take the case of a trader who is very neutral on Illinois Tool Works (ITW), trading at $71.22, expecting it to remain in a narrow trading range over the next few months. If this trader sees any volatility risk in ITW, it is to the upside; in other words, the trader's forecast is for "nothing to happen," but a surprise would more than likely see ITW rallying. She initiates a put front spread by buying one June 75 put at $5.80 and writing two of the June 70 puts at $3 each, for an initial credit of $0.20. Table 6.15 summarizes her option position and its profitability at expiration.

Once again we present the results in Figure 6.10.

Table 6.15

ITW at Expiration	Value of Long 75 Put	Value of Short 70 Puts	Initial Credit	Profit/(Loss)
$85	$0	$0	$0.20	$0.20
$80	$0	$0	$0.20	$0.20
$75	$0	$0	$0.20	$0.20
$70	$5	$0	$0.20	$5.20
$65	$10	2 × ($5.00)	$0.20	$0.20
$60	$15	2 × ($10.00)	$0.20	($4.80)
$55	$20	2 × ($15.00)	$0.20	($9.80)

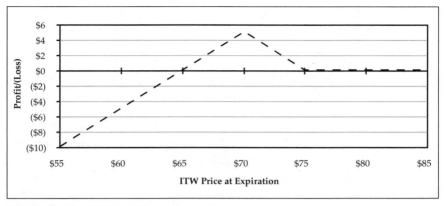

Figure 6.10 ITW: Put Front Spread

We now have the mirror image of the call front spread: limited profit potential, realized only if ITW closes at $70 at expiration, no upside risk, and all of the stock's downside risk.

Both front spreads have half the risk of a short straddle and it should not come as a surprise that their profit potential is somewhat lower. Before entering into any of the strategies in this section we recommend reading the discussion of risk management in Chapter 10.

Synthetics

Sometimes traders have no use for options. They simply want to own a stock for the short term without calculating deltas and coping with time decay. And if they are like a lot of other traders, they'll be buying these shares with borrowed funds since they are already fully invested. Take the situation of a trader who has turned bullish on the shares on Invidia (NVDA) but has no cash left in his trading account. If he has sufficient securities he could purchase shares using borrowed funds, but he should also take a look at the options market, such as the following quotes:

NVDA:	$42.86
June 40 call:	$7.60–$7.80
June 40 put:	$4.60–$4.80

The trader considers the options too pricey and refuses to pay nearly $8 for a call with less than three months until expiration. If he purchased the 40 call and at the same time wrote the 40 put, he would be entering into a strategy that replicates a long stock position, known as long synthetic stock.

Buying the 40 call at $7.80 and writing the 40 put at $4.60 means that the option position is established for a $3.20 debit. At option expiration, NVDA will either be above $40 or below $40. In the first instance, the 40 call would be in-the-money and could be exercised. The adjusted cost of the stock would then be $43.20—the $40 paid upon exercise of the call plus the initial debit of $3.20. If NVDA is below $40, the put will be in-the-money, and if it is not covered it will be assigned, forcing the trader to buy shares at $40. Once again, the adjusted cost on the stock will be $43.20—the $40 paid upon assignment of the put plus the initial debit of $3.20. Yes, there is a third possibility, that of NVDA closing at exactly $40 on expiration Friday. In this case the trader would probably not want to exercise his call because the possibility of being assigned on the puts will still exist. To eliminate the risk of being assigned on his short option the trader would have to buy it back for some nominal amount.

Of course, a trader will not have to exercise or be assigned on his synthetic stock position: he'll be able to trade out of his options any time prior to expiration.

The position and its profitability at option expiration are summarized in Table 6.16 below.

Table 6.16

NVDA at Expiration	NVDA $ Change	Value of 40 Call	Value of 40 Put	Initial Debit	Option Profit/(Loss)
$50	$7.14	$10	$0	($3.20)	$6.80
$47.50	$4.64	$7.50	$0	($3.20)	$4.30
$45	$2.14	$5	$0	($3.20)	$1.80
$42.50	($0.36)	$2.50	$0	($3.20)	($0.70)
$40	($2.86)	$0	$0	($3.20)	($3.20)
$37.50	($5.36)	$0	($2.50)	($3.20)	($5.70)
$35	($7.86)	$0	($5.00)	($3.20)	($8.20)

The profit or loss realized on the option position is equal to the dollar change in NVDA less $0.34. So why not simply buy the stock since the options leave us $0.34 poorer? Because the numbers above do not reflect the cost of capital. If the trader has enough cash to buy the stock, his opportunity cost is $0.21 per share for the next three months. This represents the forgone interest on $42.86 invested at 2% for three months. On the other hand, if the trader plans to borrow the funds to buy the stock, then his interest cost would be $0.64 per share, assuming he borrows $42.86 at 6% for the next three months.

In the end, the difference between the real stock and the synthetic stock will boil down to two minor factors: the fact that establishing the position with options involves two bid-ask spreads versus only one with the stock, and the trader's opportunity or borrowing cost versus the carrying cost imbedded in the price of the options. Remember that options are usually priced using the risk-free interest rate, and the theoretical value of a long synthetic stock will tend to reflect this cost of money.

Choosing Strike Prices

A trader looking to establish a long synthetic position on Home Depot (HD) finds the following quotes:

HD:	$48.43
May 45 call:	$4.10–$4.30
May 45 put:	$0.65–$0.70
May 50 call:	$1.05–$1.10
May 50 put:	$2.55–$2.65

With HD trading between exercise prices the trader must choose between the 45 or 50 strikes. Establishing the long synthetic using the 45 strike would entail buying the 45 call at $4.30 and writing the 45 put at $0.65 for a net debit of $3.65. The effective purchase price of HD would be $48.65 (the 45 strike plus the $3.65 debit). Using the 50 strike options would mean purchasing the 50 call at $1.10 and writing the 50 put at $2.55 for a net credit of $1.45 and an effective purchase price of $48.55 (the 50 strike less the $1.45 credit).

At first glance there are two advantages to using the 50 strike options. First, the effective purchase price is $0.10 lower, probably because of the wider bid-ask spread on the 45 call. And second, the 50 strike synthetic can be established for a credit rather than a debit, and isn't getting paid better than paying?

Yes, but these two advantages must be balanced against the fact that using the 50 strike price involves writing an in-the-money put. Both synthetic positions carry the risk of early assignment on the short puts, but the 50 put is already in-the-money and so carries a higher risk of having to purchase the stock on assignment before option expiration.

Personally, we would probably rather pay up and use the 45 strike to reduce the risk of early assignment. This is not an immediate issue, even with the 50 puts, as they are in-the-money by a little more than $1.50 and are trading with an additional dollar of time premium, but we prefer our short puts to be out-of-the-money.

Another possible solution is to create what is known as a split-strike synthetic: purchase the out-of-the-money 50 call at $1.10 and write the out-of-the-money 45 put for $0.65 for an initial debit of $0.45. This position will behave like stock above 50 and below 45 but not in between the strike prices. If HD is inside the strikes at expiration, both options will expire worthless and the split-strike synthetic will show a loss of $0.45, the initial debit.

Even though long synthetic positions can be initiated for little or no up-front cash, they all incorporate a short put option that must be adequately margined. This is not the illusive free ride.

Short Synthetics

It should come as no surprise that an option position that fully replicates the risk and profit potential of a short stock can be created synthetically. By buying a put a trader obtains all of the downside profit potential of a short stock position, and by writing a call he must assume all of the upside risk. Look at the following quotes on Procter & Gamble (PG):

PG:	$89.12
July 90 call:	$3.30–$3.50
July 90 put:	$4.40–$4.60

Purchasing the 90 put at $4.60 and writing the 90 call at $3.30 would establish a synthetic short position for a $1.30 debit, effectively shorting the stock at $88.70. Is the synthetic short short-changing us by $0.42? This difference is partly explained by the bid-ask on the options (we did not factor in the bid-ask on the stock) and partly by the $0.36 dividend that is expected between the trade date and the options' expiration date. A trader who shorts the stock would have to pay this $0.36 dividend to the brokerage firm from which he borrowed the shares (and it in turn would pay this dividend to the client from whom it borrowed the shares). The synthetic short position does not incur this liability. So the net results are pretty even.

Traders know that certain stocks are difficult to borrow and thus to sell short, so they reason, "If I can't borrow shares of a stock I want to short, why not simply create a synthetic short position?" There is nothing to prevent them from trying to short a stock synthetically, but when traders can't borrow a stock this penury is usually felt streetwide. The market makers or specialists in this option class are probably aware that the stock is difficult (or impossible) to borrow, and since this limits their hedging possibilities, they will be reluctant to take on option positions in which they would have to short the underlying stock to hedge themselves.

In brief, if a trader shorts a stock synthetically, the option's market makers end up buying the stock synthetically and would normally hedge this option position by shorting the underlying stock. If it's impossible to borrow shares, the options market may be rather shallow and the bid-ask spreads wider than normal, imposing an additional cost to option traders.

Buying Calls to Hedge a Short Stock

Some traders have the experience, the capital, and, let's admit it, the stomach to short stocks they believe are about to head south. Buying a call to protect a short stock position appears as a natural option strategy—either to let traders with short stock positions sleep better at night or to let someone who could never assume the risk of a short stock position dip her toes into this bearish strategy.

The logic is straightforward: the risk of a short stock position is seeing the underlying rally on good news, takeover speculation, or a plain vanilla bull market. Buying a call locks in the buying price of the shorted stock, limiting the amount of pain that a runaway stock can inflict. Yes, the buyer of the call option has to pay up, but isn't the option premium a relatively small price to pay for the knowledge that if this one gets away, the risk is limited to so many dollars and not a penny more?

Yes, and no. We are ambivalent about this strategy, but let's start with where we believe it has a role to play. A trader has been short a stock for the last four weeks, waiting for the bad news to hit or, as he sees it, for the market to come to its senses. He realizes that earnings will be released next Tuesday. This could be the catalyst he has been waiting for, or it could sound his death knell. The day before the earnings come out he buys call options to hedge his short stock position. He will hold these options for less than a week, just to see how the market reacts to the company's earnings, or lack thereof. If his bearish outlook remains unchanged after this news hits the tape, he will sell his calls to recoup part of the option premium paid and will maintain his short stock position. This, we believe, is how calls can be effectively purchased to hedge a short stock position.

The Married Call

Let's now turn to another trader who has just turned bearish on McDonald's (MCD). She has never shorted shares and, given her risk tolerance, would probably never do so, but marrying a short stock to a long call would reduce her overall risk to a more comfortable level. MCD is trading at $27.34 and the February 27½ call is offered at $0.85. Her reasoning is straightforward: she can short MCD at the current price, pay $0.85 for the eight-week call, and be able to maintain her short stock position for the next two months, knowing her ultimate risk. Table 6.17 looks at the profitability of her short stock/long call position at option expiration in eight weeks.

Table 6.17 clearly shows how the long call hedges the short stock position: if MCD rallies above $27.50, any losses accruing on the short stock are made up by the increased value of the call option. Of course, our investor will have to absorb the loss of the option premium, but she considers this a small price to pay. The numbers in Table 6.17 are illustrated in Figure 6.11.

Figure 6.11 illustrates the limited upside risk of the position and the substantial profit potential to the downside. This graph bears a striking resemblance to one of the basic strategy graphs presented

Table 6.17

MCD at Option Expiration	Profit/(Loss) on Short MCD	Value of 27½ Call	Cost of 27½ Call	Total Profit/(Loss)
$32.50	($5.16)	$5	($0.85)	($1.01)
$30	($2.66)	$2.50	($0.85)	($1.01)
$27.50	($0.16)	$0	($0.85)	($1.01)
$25	$2.34	$0	($0.85)	$1.49
$22.50	$4.84	$0	($0.85)	$3.99
$20	$7.34	$0	($0.85)	$6.49

in Chapter 1. Look at Figure 1.2, which illustrates a long AVP put position. Both a long call/short stock and a long put position have limited risk if the underlying rallies, and substantial profit potential to the downside. The put buyer's risk is limited to the option premium paid. The risk to the trader who is short stock/long call is equal to the option premium paid plus any out-of-the-money amount, if there is any.

In fact, by shorting MCD and purchasing a call option, our trader has simply purchased a put option. The difference is that her trade is more complicated and carries higher transaction costs. It also adds more layers of risk, such as being forced to cover her short position

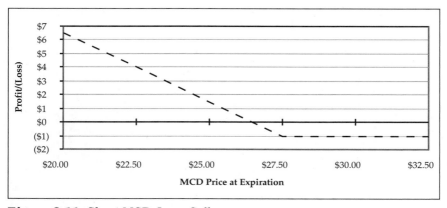

Figure 6.11 Short MCD, Long Call

if her broker can no longer borrow MCD shares, or being liable for any dividends declared by MCD. If she wanted to establish a bearish position with limited risk to the upside and good downside potential, she could have simply purchased the February 27½ put that was offered at $0.90. Her risk would have been $0.90 (versus $1.01 for the short stock/long call position), she would have effectively been short MCD at $27.50 (versus $27.34), and her cost of insurance would have been $0.90 (versus $0.85). Most important, she could have initiated her position with one trade and would have paid one commission instead of two. Getting approval from her broker to purchase puts probably entails much less paperwork than setting up a short stock account.

Although it initially sounds good, the short stock/long call strategy is nothing but a roundabout way of purchasing a put option. Just as we were able to create a synthetic stock position, we can create a synthetic put option (although, in this case, we prefer the 100% natural put). Traders who like the limited risk and substantial downside profit potential of the short stock/long call position will save themselves a lot of trouble (and some transaction costs) by simply purchasing put options. Keep in mind, though, that for the two strategies to be equivalent the expiration dates and strike prices of the options must be identical. When hedging a short stock, traders have a tendency to purchase out-of-the-money calls, which is equivalent to purchasing an in-the-money put. If an out-of-the-money put is purchased to replace a short stock/long out-of-the-money call position, the risk-reward profile will be different—not because the strategies are different, but because of the choice of strike prices.

7

OPTIONS ON EXCHANGE-TRADED FUNDS AND ON INDICES

Options on Exchange-Traded Funds

Options on exchange-traded funds (ETFs) could arguably be lumped with equity options. The main difference between the two is that the underlying of equity options is 100 shares of a specific stock and the underlying of ETF options is 100 shares of a fund.

Think of an index mutual fund. The fund manager purchases the component shares in proportions that are appropriate to the index the fund is designed to track. Investors can buy or sell shares of this fund once a day based on the fund's closing net asset value. Now take a fund, also holding all of the component stocks of an index, and list it on an exchange, giving investors and traders the opportunity to buy it and sell it at any point during the trading day. You now understand the basics of ETFs.

The first ETF to catch investors' attention was the Standard & Poor's Depositary Receipt®, SPDR®, better known as "Spiders" (ticker symbol: SPY), a fund that tracks the Standard & Poor's 500 Index. Today, ETFs are well established, as can be seen by the special section they occupy in the *Wall Street Journal*. The universe of options on ETFs is still small, but these instruments present unique investment opportunities.

Investment Strategies with Options on ETFs

Although options on ETFs can be used for trading purposes, we prefer to use them in an investment context. Traders, especially those who are looking to establish more complex strategies, should probably favor index options, which are discussed later in this chapter.

Writing Puts to Go Long the Market

Say an investor is ambivalent about moving some of his cash into equities. He likes the market, but not enough to stick his neck out, at least at the current levels. He would be more comfortable committing himself to a position in the overall market on a slight pullback. Given the amount he is looking to invest, around $50,000, he is reluctant to purchase individual stocks because it would be difficult for him to attain the level of diversification he feels is necessary for his risk tolerance. He would, however, purchase the Standard and Poor's 100® iShares℠ (OEF), currently trading at $56.72 (note: the OEF are structured to be valued at one-tenth the level of the Standard and Poor's 100 Index, which is at 567.21). Looking at the eight-week options on OEF he finds the following:

OEF: $56.72
April 53 puts: $0.65–$0.85

April 54 puts: $0.85–$1.05
April 56 puts: $1.55–$1.75

Sharpening his pencil, he comes up with the data presented in Table 7.1.

Taking the 54 puts, here is how to interpret these numbers. If the investor writes the 54 put for $0.85 and is assigned, he will effectively be purchasing OEF shares at $53.15 ($54 less the $0.85 premium). This price is 6.3% below the current value of OEF at $56.72. If the investor is not assigned on the puts, he will keep the option premium of $0.85. Remember that he is currently sitting on cash, so the option premium generates an incremental return of 1.57%, which is 10.2% annualized. ($0.85 is earned on every $54 that is set aside to purchase OEF shares if assigned; the return is therefore $0.85 ÷ $54 = 1.57%.)

So which put should this investor write? This is another question that doesn't have just one correct answer. Would a 4% discount to the current market level be an acceptable entry point? If so, writing the 56 puts looks quite attractive and provides an excellent incremental return if not assigned. But this investor should also remember that the higher the put's strike price, the greater the odds of being assigned. So the probability of getting assigned on the 56 puts is significantly higher than the probability of being assigned on the 53 puts. There is therefore less chance of earning the higher incremental return on cash.

For those who like more precision when it comes to probabilities, the probability of being assigned on a put is roughly equal to the absolute value of the put's delta. So a put with a -0.40 delta would have roughly a 40% chance of being in-the-money at expiration and

Table 7.1

	Premium	Effective Purchase Price	Percent Below Current Level	Incremental Return on Cash (Not Assigned)
53 Put	$0.65	$52.35	7.7%	7.9%
54 Put	$0.85	$53.15	6.3%	10.2%
56 Put	$1.55	$54.45	4.0%	18.0%

being assigned. Note that this method of estimating probabilities loses precision the further out the expiration date; so it is fairly accurate for one- or two-month options, but not so accurate for six-month options and LEAPS. The deltas of the options in our example are -0.42 (56 put), -0.28 (54 put), and -0.23 (53 put). Our investor has to balance the probability of being assigned (and going long the market at the discount associated with the put written) and that of not being assigned (and earning the incremental return on his cash).

Writing Covered Calls to Ease Out of a Position

An investor is currently long 1,000 of the Nasdaq-100 Tracking Stock[SM], better known as the "triple Qs" (ticker: QQQ). The QQQ are currently at $34.70, one-fortieth the Nasdaq-100® level of 1388.02. She purchased these shares at a lower price and would not be averse to selling half her position on a rally. Looking at the QQQ options she finds the following three-month calls:

QQQ:	$34.70
May 35 call:	$2.40–$2.50
May 36 call:	$1.90–$2.00
May 37 call:	$1.50–$1.60
May 38 call:	$1.15–$1.25
May 39 call:	$0.90–$0.95

Putting two and two together, she comes up with the data in Table 7.2.

Table 7.2

	Option Premium	Upside	Return from Premium	Total Return (If Called)
35 Call	$2.40	0.9%	6.9%	7.8%
36 Call	$1.90	3.7%	5.5%	9.2%
37 Call	$1.50	6.6%	4.3%	10.9%
38 Call	$1.15	9.5%	3.3%	12.8%
39 Call	$0.90	12.4%	2.6%	15.0%

The upside is the amount by which the call is out-of-the-money and represents the possible appreciation from the ETF's current price to the options' strike price. The return from premium is the percentage of the ETF's price represented by the option premium. If the QQQ price remains unchanged over the life of the option, this would represent her static return (note: these numbers have not been annualized). And finally, the total return is the best-case scenario: her return if the shares rise to or above the options' strike price and she is assigned.

The give and take here is quite simple: a higher total return (which requires the shares to rise to the selected strike price) or a higher return if the shares remain unchanged (which only requires QQQ to remain stable). We can gather that our investor is relatively bullish over the longer term since she only wants to reduce her position by half, not eliminate it. Writing the at-the-moneys (the 35 or 36 calls) probably does not fit in with her overall assessment. She should be looking instead at the 37 or 38 calls, which both provide more than 10% of potential total return over the next three months. You may have a different opinion, and we would not want to change it, as long as you have factored in all the relevant data and weighed the trade-offs.

Other Strategies Using ETF Options

The two preceding strategies are a repeat of the basic investment strategies with equity options. The mindset remains the same, the objectives are similar—only the underlying has changed. It stands to reason that the other investment strategies built around equity options will easily translate to ETFs: the buy/write, the purchase of protective puts, the buying of calls, the repair strategy, covered straddles, and covered combinations. We invite you to review some of the strategies presented in Chapter 5, replacing the equities with ETFs. You should find new investing opportunities.

Index Options: Special Features

Before proceeding with index options strategies we must underscore some of their special features.

Cash Settlement

Think of your car insurance policy. This is a type of option: you paid a fixed premium, the policy has an expiration date, and you have the right to make a claim if this option goes in-the-money. The in-the-money amount is determined by the extent of the damage to your car (the more severe, the deeper in-the-money), and how far out-of-the-money the option (determined by the deductible) is. Note that the right to exercise is completely yours. You may decide not to make a claim if you deem the in-the-money amount to be too small. (You know that making a claim will impact the pricing of future options because the market will view you as a "volatile" driver.)

Now assume that you are involved in a fender bender (yes, it was the other driver's fault) and that you make a claim against your policy. The "insurance option" you hold does not give you the right to buy a new car or to sell the damaged one, but only the right to receive a payment in cash. This payment will be determined by the terms of the policy based on the deductible and the repair estimate from Joe's Garage. Your car insurance policy settles in cash, not in a physical commodity.

Equity options settle in shares of stock: exercise a call and you get 100 shares of the underlying; exercise a put and you have to deliver 100 shares of stock. Index options settle in cash, in the same fashion as your car insurance. Purchasing an index option does not give you the right to buy or sell anything but simply the right to receive a cash amount that will be determined by the terms of the option.

Settlement Amount

The short answer as to how an index option's cash settlement amount is calculated is that it's equal to its in-the-money amount. The longer answer must take into account the fact that there are two different methods of calculating this amount.

Some index options (such as the options on the Standard & Poor's 100 Index, OEX®) are known as P.M. settlement options. The level of the index that is used to calculate the cash settlement is the closing value the day an option is exercised. Assume that on a given day the OEX index closes at 596.40. An investor who earlier had purchased the 580 calls decides to exercise these. His account will be credited $1,640 per contract, calculated by taking the in-the-money amount of $16.40 (596.40 less the strike of 580) and multiplying by 100 (as if the options had 100 shares of underlying). This is the easier of the two methods of calculating the settlement amount, but with the exception of the OEX, very few options are P.M. settlement.

Other index options are classified as A.M. settlement. This does not mean that the settlement value is based on the index's opening value. It's slightly more complicated. As an example, take the options on the Standard & Poor's 500 Index, SPX. There are 500 stocks in this index (don't laugh—there are eleven football teams in the Big Ten Conference), and on the day the options settle each stock opens for trading either on the NYSE or on Nasdaq. Some stocks will open for trading at 9:30 eastern, some will open at 9:31, others at 9:33, and so on, until the last one opens at 9:44, delayed because of an order imbalance. Take the opening prices of all of these 500 stocks, from the first one at 9:30 through the last one at 9:44, and calculate the value of the index. This is the index level that is used to calculate the in-the-money and settlement amounts.

The A.M. settlement calculation has led to some bizarre occurrences. One day, for example, stocks were opening sharply lower than the previous day's close because of some negative news. As the news was reinterpreted in a more neutral light, stocks started bouncing back. Most stocks' opening prices ended up being their lows for the day. And because quite a few stocks had delayed openings, by the time all 500 stocks had started trading, the market was on the mend. The A.M. settlement value ended up falling outside of the index's range for the day. It was lower than the low because it consolidated all of the bad news into one number. Nevertheless, the trend has been toward A.M. settlement and most new index options that are listed for trading fall into this category.

European versus American

No, this is not about figure skating, but about restrictions—or lack thereof—on the right to exercise options. All equity options and some index options are American-style, which means that their holders may exercise them on any business day up to and including their last trading day. Most index options are European-style, meaning that they may only be exercised immediately prior to expiration. Options with no early exercise are becoming the norm with the new index options listings. If this feature sounds like a negative for the option holder, it can also be viewed as a positive for the writer because there is no risk of early assignment.

Last Trading Day

The last trading day for equity options is the third Friday of the expiration month. With index options there are two different last trading days, depending on the option.

- The third Friday of the expiration month, as with equities. OEX, options on the Standard & Poor's 100 Index, is an example.
- The Thursday preceding the third Friday of the expiration month; example: SPX, options on the Standard & Poor's 500 Index. Most index option classes now cease trading at the close of business on the Thursday preceding expiration Friday. With no trading on Friday, these options can have an A.M. settlement based on Friday's opening prices.

Whichever index option class you trade, it is a good idea to verify which is their last trading day. Check the website of the exchange where they trade.

Broad and Narrow

Index options have been listed on most of the obvious candidates: the Dow Jones Industrial Average®, the Standard & Poor's 500 Index, the Russell 2000® Index, and other familiar names. They have also been listed on numerous narrow indices that for the most part cover just one sector of the market. Some, like the Dow Jones Transportation Average℠, you will recognize; others, like the CBOE Gold Index, you may not.

As of this writing 25 broad-based and 39 narrow-based indices have options listed. In terms of liquidity, they run the gamut—from those that can absorb institutional orders for thousands of contracts to those that are traded only by appointment. Check trading volume and open interest before firing in your market orders.

Narrow-based index options and equity options trade until 4:02 P.M. eastern time, for two minutes after the closing bell in New York, whereas broad-based options can be bought and sold until 4:15 P.M. eastern time.

Fractional Underlyings

The most recognized name in indices is the Dow Jones Industrial Average. Are there options listed on this index? Technically no, but in reality yes. There are options listed on the DJX index, which happens to be equal to one one-hundredth of the DJIA. For example, if the DJIA is 10,123.47, then the DJX is set at 101.23 and the options on the DJX trade off this reduced level.

The reason for trading off of a reduced value of the actual index is to keep option premiums at a manageable level. A one-month at-the-money call on an index of 10,000 might be quoted as $200–$210. With a 100 multiplier that would represent $20,000 per contract. This would severely limit the number of participants.

To make life more interesting, some options classes have options on both the full-size index and on a reduced value. For example, the short-term options on the Standard & Poor's 100 Index (OEX) trade off the full value of the index, whereas the LEAPS on the same index trade off one-fifth the index value. It is unclear if the number of options traders gained by keeping the option premiums lower is greater than the number lost due to confusion.

Parallel Universes

Some indices with cash-settled options (as opposed to options on ETFs, discussed earlier) also have exchange-traded funds that track them. For example, SPX, the options on the Standard & Poor's 500 Index, settle in cash; the Spiders (SPY) are an ETF that tracks the S&P 500 Index on a reduced-value basis. SPX and SPY live in parallel universes, both closely tracking the underlying index, but a position in SPX, which settles in cash, will never become or eliminate a position in SPY.

This opens up hedging opportunities, buying SPX puts to hedge an SPY position for example, but the cash settlement feature of the options means that if an investor wants to unwind his total position (long SPY, long SPX puts) she must do so in two transactions (sell

SPY, sell SPX puts) and not through the exercise of the put, as would be the case with options on equities or ETFs.

Strike Price Intervals

Because indices tend to be less volatile than equities, some index option classes have their strike price intervals set at two and sometimes one point, not the $2.50 and $5 intervals associated with equity options.

Index Options: Investment Strategies

There are pluses and minuses to hedging security positions with cash-settled options. The key is understanding what should and what should not be attempted.

Buying Protective Puts

An investor who owns 600 shares of stock and is nervous about the short-term prospects for either this stock in particular or the market in general has one simple hedging strategy to pull out of his bag of tricks: purchase six put options on the stock in question.

What about the investor who owns shares of an ETF on which options are listed, equity mutual funds, or simply a diversified stock portfolio, and who is also looking for some short-term insurance? This is where index options come in, offering the same type of protection, but usually with a twist.

Let's start with a relatively straightforward example. An investor who owns 2,000 shares of SPY (the ETF that tracks the Standard & Poor's 500 Index) is worried about upcoming economic news and would like to hedge his position for the next 60 days by purchasing put options. In this situation the choice of index options is not complicated: SPX options have as underlying the same Standard & Poor's 500 Index, offering perfect insurance.

This investor will have to decide on which expiration date and which strike price to choose, but he will also have to calculate how many put options are required to fully hedge his portfolio. Hedging 2,000 shares usually requires purchasing 20 puts, but if ETFs and index options are involved, one must first verify the "size" of the options relative to the underlying. The following quotes should help us in this process (note: options have eight weeks until expiration):

S&P 500 Index:	1116.84
SPY	$112.14
SPX April 1100 put:	$23.80–$25.80
SPX April 1075 put:	$16.70–$18.20
SPX April 1050 put:	$13.70–$15.20

The SPY shares are valued at one-tenth the level of the index. The slight premium you are seeing reflects the dividends accruing on the Spiders. The index is calculated from the prices of the component stocks ignoring dividends, whereas the Spiders reflect the value of the component stocks plus the dividends that have accrued since the last quarterly ex-dividend date.

Our investor owns 2,000 shares, which have a current value of $224,280. Each SPX option has an underlying value of $111,684, equal to the level of the index times the 100 multiplier. Two puts, not 20, should, therefore, be purchased to hedge this investor's position.

Let's assume our investor decides to purchase the 1050 puts, which are 6% out-of-the-money. He can live with a 6% drop in the value of his portfolio but would like protection below that level. He purchases two of the April 1050 puts at $15.20, for a total cost of

Table 7.3

Index Level at Expiration	Price of 1050 Put	Value of 2 1050 Puts	Cost of 2 1050 Puts	Value of 2000 SPY	Total Portfolio Value
1150	$0	$0	($3,040)	$230,900	$227,860
1100	$0	$0	($3,040)	$220,900	$217,860
1050	$0	$0	($3,040)	$210,900	$207,860
1000	$50	$10,000	($3,040)	$200,900	$207,860
950	$100	$20,000	($3,040)	$190,900	$207,860

$3,040. Table 7.3 calculates the value of his Spiders and put options at option expiration. We assumed that the Spiders will be trading with the same $0.45 premium they currently carry.

The worst-case scenario for this investor is a loss of $16,420, which occurs at an index level of 1050 and comes from the $3,040 put premium and the $13,380 drop in the value of the portfolio. As the index falls below 1050, the losses on the portfolio become larger but are fully compensated by the increase in the value of the put options. If the market goes up in value, profits accrue on the Spiders but are reduced by the $3,040 cost of insuring the portfolio.

If the Standard & Poor's 500 Index is trading below the puts' strike price of 1050 at the April option expiration, our investor will have to decide whether to continue holding his Spiders or to liquidate his shares and move into cash or other investments. If his view is that the market correction has run its course and he wants to maintain his long SPY position, he need do nothing. His puts, being in-the-money, will automatically be exercised and his account credited with the puts' intrinsic value. If the index has dropped to 1000, he will receive $10,000, which he can reinvest elsewhere.

If, on the other hand, this investor decides that the market downturn is just starting and it is now best to move out of equities, he will have to liquidate his long SPY shares in a separate transaction. He still will receive the cash settlement from his long puts, but he will need to place a sell order with his broker in order to move out of his Spiders. For the hedge to be perfect, the price at which he sells his SPY shares would have to be equal to the corresponding index level used in calculating the options settlement value. This will be virtually impossible to achieve.

SPX options are A.M. settlement, and to replicate the option's settlement price, an investor would have to enter market-on-open sell orders for the 500 component stocks. Institutions that actually hold all 500 stocks are able to do this, but our investor owns Spiders, not the 500 component stocks. To minimize slippage, he should probably instruct his broker to sell his Spiders on the opening on expiration Friday. The odds that the price he obtains for his shares and the settlement value of the SPX options will be the same are minimal, but unless there is a sharp drop at the opening followed by a strong rally, the two values should be close enough not be a major source of concern. (A strong opening followed by a sharp decline would probably end up being in his favor.) So the "perfect" hedge we designed falls a little short of that designation.

If the investor above was hedging not Spiders, but shares in an S&P 500 Index mutual fund, every step of the process would remain the same unless the decision was made to liquidate the mutual fund shares. Since most mutual funds are bought and sold based on the trading day's closing value, our investor would have to decide whether to liquidate his fund on the Thursday's close, and assume overnight risk, or the Friday's close, and assume one trading day's worth of risk. Hedging an index fund probably has a bit more slippage risk than hedging the Spiders.

Hedging an ETF, mutual fund, or portfolio of stocks takes on an added level of complexity when there are no options listed on the underlying—whether they be cash-settled or not. The first decision an investor has to make is which option class best tracks a given fund or portfolio.

An investor who is long a small-cap mutual fund will probably want to hedge it using the Russell 2000 Index options. One owning mostly mid-cap stocks will turn to the options on the Standard & Poor's 600™ Index. For investors in large-cap stocks or large-cap stock mutual funds, more choices is not necessarily synonymous with easier choices: Standard & Poor's 100 and 500 indices, the Dow Jones Industrials, and a few other large-cap indices all have listed options.

It also is possible to hedge portfolios or mutual funds that are fully or heavily weighted in one specific sector: investors will find options on the Dow Jones Transportation and Utility averages, the S&P Drug Index™, a couple of competing Nasdaq indices, and, in some instances, indices concocted by the options exchanges when none were available, such as the PHLX Semiconductor Sector and the CBOE Oil Index.

An example will help us work through some of these issues. An investor is holding an equity portfolio heavily weighted in technology stocks. She is looking to purchase some very short-term insurance on her holdings in front of some upcoming economic news. After studying the component stocks of the AMEX Computer Technology Index (XCI), the CBOE Technology Index (TXX), and the PHLX Semiconductor Sector (SOX[SM]) she concludes that the last one best reflects her current holdings. (If you are wondering on which sectors index options are listed, check the *Directory of Exchange-*

Traded Options at www.888options.com). Some of the 17-day options listed are:

SOX:	534.36
January 520 put:	$14.60–$16.60
January 500 put:	$8.70–$10.20
January 480 put:	$4.90–$5.90
January 460 put	$2.50–$3.50
January 440 put:	$1.25–$1.85

This investor's portfolio is composed of various stocks in different quantities. How does she determine the number of puts to purchase? She should start with the value of the portfolio to be insured ($175,000) and the level of the index (534.36). By multiplying the latter by 100 she gets the amount of underlying value covered by each option ($53,436). By dividing the value of her portfolio by the value covered by each option ($175,000 ÷ $53,436) she gets the number of options required to hedge her holdings: 3.27 options. Since she cannot purchase fractional options, she must decide whether to buy only three puts and thus be partially unhedged, or to purchase four and be slightly overhedged. Because of the relatively high cost of the put options (this is a very volatile sector), she decides to risk being slightly underinsured and purchases only three puts, choosing the 480 strike offered at $5.90. The cost of her hedge is therefore $1,770 and will see her through the next two and one-half weeks. Table 7.4 presents some of the possible outcomes, based on the assumption that her portfolio will rise and fall at the same rate as the SOX Index.

Table 7.4

SOX Level at Expiration	Value of 480 Put	Value of 3 480 Puts	Cost of 3 480 Puts	Value of Stock Portfolio	Total Portfolio Value
560	$0	$0	($1,770)	$183,397	$181,627
520	$0	$0	($1,770)	$170,297	$168,527
480	$0	$0	($1,770)	$157,197	$155,427
440	$40	$12,000	($1,770)	$144,097	$154,327
400	$80	$24,000	($1,770)	$130,997	$153,227

Note that the protection offered is not complete because the portfolio is slightly underinsured. But the hedge does an excellent job of stemming the losses once the puts go in-the-money. And, as noted, Table 7.4 is based on the assumption that if the SOX drops by 10%, so will the investor's portfolio. This is a major assumption because even indices that are highly correlated sometimes go their own way. Think of the DJIA and the S&P 500, two blue-chip indices that sometimes head in different directions. A hedge like this could experience severe slippage, which could work for or against our investor. Caveat emptor.

A few words on hedging a mutual fund position: This is not unlike our previous example with an investor choosing an index that best fits the fund's holdings and having to accept the risk of slippage. An additional problem with mutual funds is that their managers have the right to change their holdings. So perhaps a hedge is established based on the funds holdings as of December 31, but by the time the options expire the following March, some major shifts in sector weightings have occurred.

Buying Index Collars

A full discussion of collars (buying a protective put and simultaneously writing a covered call on an equity you own) appears in the next chapter, so you may want to look at what is to come before getting down to what is at hand.

As far as purchasing collars on ETFs, we will consider these to be equity collars, and all of our comments in Chapter 8 stand. This assumes that there are options listed on the ETF in question and that these options are used to create the collar.

The major issue we want to address in this section is purchasing collars to hedge a basket of stocks, a mutual fund, or an ETF with no listed options. It sounds like a great idea. You own shares of an S&P 500 index fund and are looking for some short-term protection. Buying SPX puts is an excellent hedge, but there is a cost involved. Financing the purchase of these puts by writing calls gives you the short-term protection you wanted with little or no cash outlay. Mission accomplished.

Not quite. If you own a mutual fund and purchase puts to hedge this position, your broker will not be concerned. When you buy puts, you have to pay the premium, and this represents your option trading risk, end of story. But if you write an index call to finance the purchase of the put, your broker will more than likely consider the short call position to be uncovered and there the problems start.

When purchasing an equity collar, the short call is covered: you own the underlying stock. When writing an S&P 500 call option (as part of a collar) against an S&P 500 mutual fund, you are not considered to own the underlying. Remember that if the short call is assigned, you cannot deliver your mutual fund shares but must make a cash payment equal to the option's in-the-money amount. In theory, the hedge is perfect: whatever losses you incur on your short call position will be fully offset by gains on the mutual fund. But, from an options trading and a margin perspective, your short call will be treated as uncovered.

There are two downsides to this. First, you must get approval from your broker to write uncovered index options. This is much more difficult than getting approval for covered writing (needed to create a collar with equity options) and requires that you meet various tests in terms of account size and trading experience. (Rumor has it one broker requires a DNA sample.) The second problem is one of margin and possible cash squeeze. If you have the authorization and write uncovered calls, you must margin this short position. In all likelihood your shares of the mutual fund will act as collateral for this short call position. But if you are assigned on your written call, you will have to make a cash payment to settle this assignment. If the only assets you own are the shares of this mutual fund, you could find yourself in a bind. Do you sell some of your shares to meet your obligation, or borrow against your mutual fund? Either way, you are getting caught in a cash squeeze.

If these are the problems created by hedging an S&P 500 mutual fund with short S&P 500 call options, think of the additional headaches created if you are trying to hedge a portfolio of stocks that does not correlate perfectly to an index, or an ETF using options on a "similar" index. You will have to deal not only with uncovered options and a possible cash squeeze, but also with varying degrees of slippage as the underlying and the hedging instrument move in less-than-perfect harmony.

In theory, a collar on a mutual fund or a basket of stocks sounds like a great idea. We could even show you numbers demonstrating the beauty of the strategy. In real life it's a completely different kettle of fish, to be avoided by all but the most sophisticated (or fool-hardy) investors.

Index Options: Trading Strategies

The Continental Divide

The matter of selecting which index option class to trade based on exercise style, American or European, may appear of little importance. Not so if any written options are to be part of the picture.

If you are only going to go long index options, we believe there is little difference in whether you trade American- or European-style options. You'll go long, wait for the profits to pile up, then sell your position. The notion of exercise will probably never enter your mind.

But if you are going to do any type of spreading, long one series, short another, we strongly suggest sticking to European-style options. Think of the following equity option position: short the 60 puts, long the 55 puts. If you are assigned early on the 60 puts, the overall risk of the position will not change: the 60–55 put spread had $5 of risk. If you are forced to purchase the stock at $60 and are still long the 55 put, you still have $5 at risk, no matter what the price of the stock does after you have been assigned.

Now think of the following index option spread, initiated with American-style options: short the 600 puts, long the 550 puts. If you are assigned early on your 600 puts, you will not be obligated to purchase any securities, but will be forced instead to pay the option's in-the-money amount. So assume the underlying index closed yesterday at 540, and this morning your broker calls to inform you that you were assigned on your short 600 puts. Based on yesterday's close, the puts were $60 in-the-money and your account will be debited by that amount. You might think you could collapse your position by exercising your long put, but because the exercise and assignment process is done overnight, if you exercise your put today, the in-the-money amount you will receive upon the exercise of your long 550 puts will be determined by today's closing index value. The market could rally strongly and your 550 puts be out-of-the-money by day's end. In fact, if today is the last trading day for these options, they could be worthless by the closing bell. You have therefore succeeded in losing $60 on a $50 spread! Since early assignments tend to occur relatively late in an option's life, this example is not just a theoretical risk. Too many traders have learned this lesson the expensive way. Stick with European-style options and eliminate the risk of early assignment.

Market Risk

An investor who purchases a stock assumes some risks. These are generally broken down into three levels:

- Market risk: Sometimes everything goes up or down together. Maybe the Federal Reserve Board has changed its interest rate target, or hinted that it is not about to change its target. Maybe consumer confidence is up, or maybe the price of oil is down.

- Industry risk: Also known as sector risk. Sometimes a group of stocks will rise or fall in tandem. Airline stocks might fall on higher oil prices; financial sector stocks might rise on lowered rates; or retail stocks might anticipate above-average Christmas sales. Sectors will also react when a single company announces an unexpected development. All chip stocks, for example, might move down when one chipmaker's inventories are higher than expected.

- Company risk: The market could be going up, with your stock's sector leading the way, yet your stock might be down because its best-selling product is being recalled, or because there is a rumor that the CFO has boarded a plane to Argentina using a one-way ticket, or because the profits of this virtual company turned out to be virtual profits.

Investing or trading in stocks means assuming all three levels of risk. Diversify (buy five bank stocks) and you can reduce company risk. Diversify more (in addition to your bank stocks, buy oil stocks, computer manufacturers' stocks, health care providers' stock, etc.) and you reduce sector risk. Diversify even more (buy all the stocks on all the exchanges) and you still cannot reduce market risk. This is one part of the risk spectrum that cannot be diversified away. And this is the realm of the index options trader.

Buying Calls and Puts

To some, buying index options represents the ultimate trading experience: the individual and the market going one on one. This also is an area where the terms "short-term" and "long-term" take on completely different meanings. Some traders refer to long-term positions as anything they hold more than one hour.

Take a trader who is looking to purchase call options on the Standard & Poor's 100 Index (OEX) and who does not intend to hold these options any longer than a day. The issue of time decay is virtually eliminated, especially if he plans to day trade. He must still decide which strike price to purchase and, looking at the front month options, which have 24 days until expiration, he finds the following listed for trading.

OEX:	549.48	
530 call:	$24.40	+0.75
540 call:	$16.45	+0.65
550 call:	$10.20	+0.50
560 call:	$5.65	+0.35
570 call:	$2.80	+0.21

The prices given are the midpoints between the bid and the ask, and the second number is the options' delta. Our trader calculates, as a first approximation, what his return would be on each option if the OEX rose one point. This is simply the expected gain, i.e., the option's delta, divided by the cost of the option. The results obtained are as follows:

530 call:	+3.1%
540 call:	+4.0%
550 call:	+4.9%
560 call:	+6.2%
570 call:	+7.5%

This first approximation appears to favor the out-of-the-money options. But the above returns ignore one important fact of real-life trading: the options' bid-ask spread. If the expected profit is reduced by $0.10, a relatively tight spread, then the following returns are obtained:

530 call:	+2.7%
540 call:	+3.3%
550 call:	+3.9%
560 call:	+4.4%
570 call:	+3.9%

The out-of-the-money option now looks no better than the at-the-money. The returns that can be expected from the in-the-money options should probably be adjusted for a bid-ask spread wider than $0.10 as in-the-moneys have a tendency to be somewhat less liquid. So where does this leave us? With the at-the-money options.

There are a couple of strong arguments to be made in favor of selecting at-the-money options for short-term trades. The first is liquidity. Traders congregate around at-the-money options, and this has a tendency to narrow the bid-ask spread—not a negligible factor in short-term trading. The second is the fact that the at-the-money options' delta will increase most rapidly if the index starts moving in the anticipated direction. This is discussed in more detail in Chapter 9, in the section on gamma.

If time decay is not really an issue for day traders, the same cannot be said about the options' implied volatility. This can, and does, change from day to day and even during the course of a trading day.

To gauge the importance of daily changes in the volatility level, we looked at the CBOE Volatility Index^{SM} (VIX®) from January 3, 1995, to December 31, 2001. VIX calculates the implied volatility of the at-the-money options (our preferred choice) on the Standard & Poor's 100 Index, and is discussed in more detail in Chapter 9. We calculated the point change in VIX for each trading day and present our results in Table 7.5.

Two observations: The first is that more than 60% of the changes are within plus or minus one point, and more than 80% are within plus or minus two points. Although these small changes will impact the options' values, they are not the ones about which we have to

Table 7.5

Point Change in VIX	Number of Days Change Observed	Percentage of Days Change Observed
Decrease of more than 10	0	0%
Decrease of 9 to 10	1	0.06%
Decrease of 8 to 9	1	0.06%
Decrease of 7 to 8	2	0.1%
Decrease of 6 to 7	1	0.06%
Decrease of 5 to 6	7	0.4%
Decrease of 4 to 5	16	0.9%
Decrease of 3 to 4	21	1.2%
Decrease of 2 to 3	128	7.1%
Decrease of 1 to 2	208	11.5%
Decrease of 0 to 1	557	30.7%
Increase of 0 to 1	540	29.7%
Increase of 1 to 2	198	10.9%
Increase of 2 to 3	70	3.9%
Increase of 3 to 4	37	2.0%
Increase of 4 to 5	14	0.8%
Increase of 5 to 6	5	0.3%
Increase of 6 to 7	3	0.2%
Increase of 7 to 8	1	0.06%
Increase of 8 to 9	3	0.2%
Increase of 9 to 10	0	0%
Increase of more than 10	2	0.1%

be greatly concerned. The second observation is that our study compares VIX from one day's closing level to the next day's closing levels. This could understate some intraday changes.

But it is probably the other 20% of observations that are of most concern to traders: those instances where VIX moves by more than

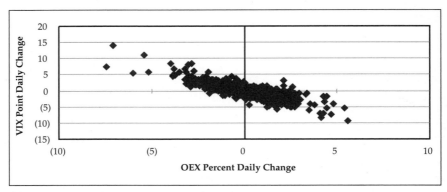

Figure 7.1 OEX/VIX (1995–2001)

two points in either direction. In order to correlate changes in OEX to changes in VIX we graphed all of the 1,815 daily observations, comparing percent changes in OEX to point changes in VIX. Figure 7.1 is what we obtained.

Even though the number of data points turns the central part of the graph into one big blob, a clear picture emerges: VIX has a tendency to rise in falling markets, and vice-versa. Not only is there an inverse relationship, but the larger the market decline, the greater the increase in implied volatility, and the stronger the rally, the more precipitous the fall in implied volatility. (For those statistically inclined, the r^2 of the data is -0.806, a strong negative correlation.) This does have implications for short-term option traders.

Put buyers are the obvious winners, assuming they buy their options before the market declines. If their forecast of a lower market is correct, they'll benefit from both a falling index and higher implied volatility. How should this fact impact strike price selection? Although we have never advocated purchasing far out-of-the-money put options, the observed changes in implied volatility lead one to select at- or slightly out-of-the-money puts. At-the-money puts are pure time premium and will obviously benefit if implied volatility increases, and out-of-the-moneys usually gain the most, on a percentage basis, when volatility goes up. We favor staying relatively close to the at-the-moneys, remembering that 80% of our observations show little change in the volatility level.

The situation is more difficult for call buyers. Knowing that your forecast will be correct and that the market will rise means accepting the fact that implied volatility will decrease, thereby lowering the value of your calls. Does this make it impossible to make money buying calls in rising markets? No, but it does mean that call buyers should favor options that are slightly in-the-money over those that are slightly out-of-the-money so that lower volatility will not be as much of an issue. Remember also that most observations where volatility dropped dramatically corresponded to sharply rising markets. In most instances, call buyers were saved by the market even though volatility collapsed. Call buyers also may want to take a peek at the next section on spreading—a strategy that tries to reduce the impact of changes in volatility, although day traders will find no relief there.

Spreading

Bull and bear spreads, as described in Chapter 6, can be initiated using index options. A few caveats are in order before we look at an example. First and foremost, we would not enter into any index option spreads that involve American-style options. There is no need to deal with the headaches they can create, not to mention the possible adverse financial impact, when European-style options are readily available. Second—and we will return to this later—one should remember that spreads trade at their maximum theoretical value only under limited circumstances: very close to expiration or when both options are deep in-the-money.

Bull and bear spreads were described as strategies that can be used to neutralize the high implied volatility associated with certain stocks. The same can be said relative to the more volatile indices. Take a trader who is short-term bullish on the Nasdaq-100 Index (NDX). He finds the following call options listed for trading.

NDX:	1332.45
April 1300 call:	$45.80–$53.80
April 1325 call:	$31.80–$36.50
April 1350 call:	$20.20–$23.20
April 1375 call:	$11.90–$13.70
April 1400 call:	$6.30–$7.70

Table 7.6

	Buy 1 1350 Call	Buy 2 1375 Calls	Buy 1325–1375 Call Spread
Risk	$23.20	$27.40	$24.60
NDX to Breakeven	1373.20 (+3.1%)	1388.70 (+4.2%)	1349.60 (+1.3%)
NDX to Double	1396.40 (+4.8%)	1402.40 (+5.2%)	1374.20 (+3.1%)

April options have four and a half trading days remaining—half of the Friday preceding expiration week plus the four trading days of expiration week (the last trading day for NDX options is the Thursday preceding expiration Friday). Our trader looks at the following possible bullish strategies: buying the 1350 call at $23.20, buying two of the 1375 calls at $13.70 (total cost of $27.40), or buying the 1325–1375 bull call spread at $24.60 ($36.50 paid for the 1325 call less $11.90 received from writing the 1375 call). All three strategies have approximately the same initial cost. How they will perform at expiration is summarized in Table 7.6.

The spread's attraction is obvious. On a 3.1% move to the upside the trader will double the capital allocated to the trade, while on a similar move the 1350 call will barely be above breakeven and the 1375 calls will still be underwater. The problem with spreads, this trader knows, is that they react relatively slowly to quick moves in the underlying index. This can be seen in Figure 7.2, which estimates the value of the spread on the Friday the trade is initiated, three days before expiration, and at expiration.

Keep in mind that Figure 7.2 represents the spread's value, not the profit or loss on the transaction. Also, any bid-ask spreads there might be on the options were ignored in calculating the values. Note that if NDX rises to 1375 (the spread's upper strike price) on the day the trade is established, the value of the spread barely rises above $30. And a similar move five days after the trade was initiated (with three days left until expiration) sees the spread rise in value to a little under $35. No great guns.

It should be obvious by now that the 1374.20 level given in Table 7.6 as the point at which our trader will double his capital should be qualified by saying that it assumes the spread is held to option

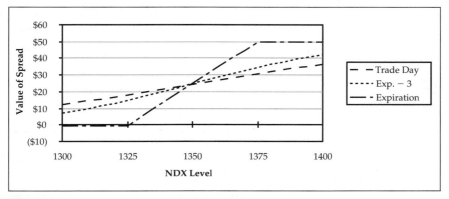

Figure 7.2 NDX 1325–1375 Bull Spread

expiration. And herein lies the trade-off in trading index option spreads: even keeping in mind the limited profit potential of spreads, most traders would opt for the 1325–1375 bull spread based on the data presented in Table 7.6. But the spread comes with a pair of handcuffs that tie the trader to his position until the expiration date. Four and a half days may not seem like a long time to be married to one position, but to some traders it's an eternity. And this should act as a warning that spreading is not for every trader, but for those who have a slightly longer time horizon and are willing to stick with their position. And for those willing to enter into an eight-day spread, there will remain the issue of what to do after option expiration when there are no longer any one-week options listed for trading.

The one area where spreading with index options is simpler than spreading with equity options, is in cases where the spread is held until expiration. With equity options a trader will have to close out the spread or, assuming both options are in-the-money, deal with one exercise and one assignment. With index options being cash-settled, there is no need to do anything. Using the above example, if NDX is below 1325 at expiration, both options will expire worthless; if it settles between 1325 and 1375, say at 1351.47, the short 1375 call will expire worthless and the trader's account will simply be credited $26.47, the in-the-money amount of the long 1325 call. And finally, if NDX is above 1375, say at 1386.55, the trader's account would be credited the full value of the spread, $50, as he would be credited the in-the-money amount of the long 1325 call, $61.55, and debited the in-the-money amount of the short 1375 call, $11.55.

Butterflies and Other Inhabitants of the Menagerie

We have given numerous options seminars over the past two decades, and one of the most often-asked questions before we begin is, "Are you going to talk about butterflies?" One of the most frequent comments after the presentations is, "You didn't talk about butterflies!" Obviously, inquiring minds want to know.

To understand this strategy, start with a trader who expects the Semiconductor Sector (SOX) to be relatively stable over the next five weeks. The purest neutral strategy consists in writing an uncovered straddle. With the SOX at 567.69, the five-week 570 straddle is bid at $68. In dollar terms, this is a huge premium, representing 11.9% of the options' strike price, and Figure 7.3 illustrates this short straddle's profit and loss potential at expiration. But this trader knows that the SOX can be extremely volatile and an uncovered straddle leaves him at risk to both a strong move up and a sharp correction. He probably couldn't sleep at night

To protect himself against a strong rally, he purchases a five-week out-of-the-money call, paying $15.70 for the 620 strike. To insure against a meltdown in this sector he buys an out-of-the-money put, paying $17.90 for the 520 strike. Adding it all up, he pocketed $68

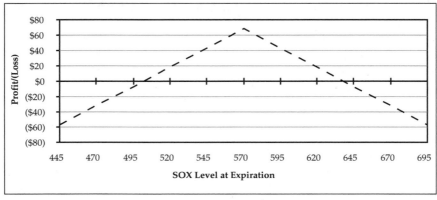

Figure 7.3 Short SOX Straddle

for writing the straddle but paid out a total of $33.60 for his insurance, leaving him with a net credit of $34.40 on the total position. This $34.40 represents his maximum profit potential, which he will realize only if the SOX final settlement level is 570.00 in five weeks. Figure 7.4 plots the butterfly's profit potential at option expiration. This is about half the profit potential of the naked straddle, but it lets him dream sweet dreams.

This trader has just purchased a 50-point butterfly. Yes, the position was established for a credit, but it is still considered a long butterfly (read on for an explanation). The 50-point refers to the difference between the strike prices of the long and short options. It also helps in calculating the spread's risk, which is equal to $50 less the initial credit of $34.40, or $15.60.

So why do we have a problem with this strategy? Count the options involved: two puts plus two calls equals four commissions to initiate the position and another four if it is closed out before expiration. Add four bid-ask spreads getting in, up to four more exiting and the result is one very happy broker. The impact of all this slippage is magnified the narrower the butterfly: look at a $5 butterfly on a $50 stock and there is virtually no way to make it work. The exceptions are the more volatile indices where 40-, 50-, and 60-point butterflies can be easily created. If your options commissions do not change with the premiums—i.e., your transaction costs for a $30 option are the same as for a $3 one—buying one 50-point butterfly at $34.40 generates the same amount of net premium as buying ten

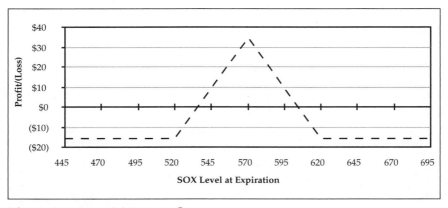

Figure 7.4 Long SOX Butterfly

5-point butterflies at $3.45 but the transaction costs on the 50-point butterfly will be roughly one-tenth those on the 5-point butterfly (roughly because we are ignoring minimum commissions).

Another negative for the retail investor is the margin a lot of brokerage firms demand for butterflies. Some will treat the 50-point butterfly described above as a 50-point bull spread combined with a 50-point bear spread—which it is—but will ask traders to margin both of these spreads even though only one can end being in-the-money at option expiration.

The niche for this strategy is very small. Butterflies use three different strike prices and can be constructed using only three different options (as opposed to the four in the SOX example) if all calls or all puts are used. The 50-point butterfly in the preceding example could also have been initiated by buying one 520 call, writing two 570 calls, and buying one 620 call. Or it could have been done by buying one 520 put, writing two 570 puts, and buying one 620 put. When using either the three calls or the three puts a butterfly will be initiated for a debit; this is why this position is considered a long butterfly. We will leave this for the more adventurous traders to explore.

Another endangered animal is the condor. The aim is the same as with the butterfly, to benefit from a stable market, but the tactic is slightly different. Instead of starting with a short straddle position, a trader will use a short combination. For example, someone who expects the Standard & Poor's 100 Index (OEX) to be relatively stable over the next five weeks could write the 560 call and the 545 put for a total premium of $19.50. The OEX is currently at 552.45, and if it closes anywhere between 545 and 560 on expiration Friday, both out-of-the-money options will expire worthless and our trader will pocket $19.50. This is illustrated in Figure 7.5.

Although a short combination has breakeven points further from the current index level than does a straddle, it still incorporates two uncovered options with all their attendant risks. So our trader decides to buy some protection and purchases the 575 call at $4.20 and the 530 put at $6.00. Her net credit is therefore $9.30, the $19.50 from writing the combo less the $10.20 paid for the long options. Her risk is determined by the difference between the two calls' (or the two puts') strike prices, 15 points, less the initial credit of $9.30, or $5.70. She would incur this loss if the OEX dropped below 530 or moved above 575 at option expiration. This is illustrated in Figure 7.6.

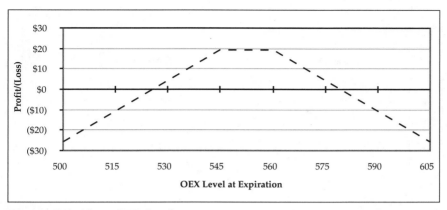

Figure 7.5 Short OEX Combo

Condors are similar to butterflies in that both benefit from low volatility, have limited risk and limited profit potential, and are many-legged strategies. The condor is different in that for the same security or index and the same expiration date it will have a lower profit potential, but this maximum profit can be realized over a range of the underlying's expiration date price, not at just one point. And all of the obstacles relating to butterflies are relevant to condors.

Butterflies and condors can also be sold. Take the case of an investor who expects an index to be very volatile over the short

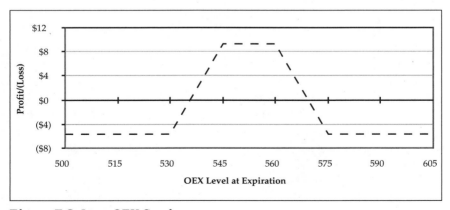

Figure 7.6 Long OEX Condor

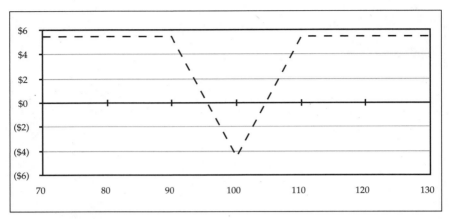

Figure 7.7a Short Butterfly

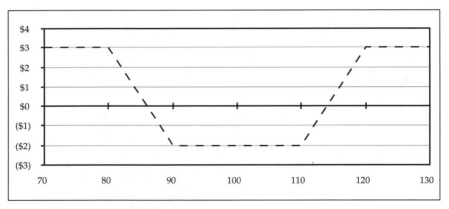

Figure 7.7b Short Condor

term. He could purchase a straddle or a combination, but he could also reduce the cost of these positions by writing one out-of-the-money call and one out-of-the-money put for each straddle or combo purchased. In addition to reducing the cost, the short options will limit the profit potential of these strategies. Generic profit-and-loss diagrams for a short butterfly and a short condor (both assuming a $100 stock and $10 intervals between the options' strike prices) are given in Figures 7.7a and 7.7b.

Variations on these two strategies include directional butterflies and condors (achieved by setting the positions' maximum profit target above or below the current index level), and hybrids where an uneven number of puts and calls are used.

Calendar Spreads

As with butterflies, calendar spreads (which are also known as *time spreads*, or *horizontal spreads*) are designed to take advantage of a stable market. Unlike the former strategy, these do not require trading up to four different option series to establish a position. Start with the following quotes on the Standard & Poor's 500 Index (SPX):

SPX:	1127.93
April 1125 call:	$12.50–$13.90
May 1125 call:	$25.20–$27.20
June 1125 call:	$36.20–$38.20
June (1 year plus) 1125 call:	$103.00–$105.00

Note that the April option has 1½ weeks until expiration, the May 5½ weeks, the June 10½ weeks, and the June of the following year (the option identified as "one year plus" and trading at, yes, $100) just over 62 weeks.

The strategy consists in purchasing a longer-dated option, and writing a shorter-dated one. We will start by buying the May 1125 call at $27.20 and writing the April 1125 call at $12.50, for an initial debit of $14.70.

Calendar spreads are usually initiated with at-the-money options. It is also possible to give the strategy a slight bias by selecting a strike price above or below the current index level. Simply keep in mind that the strategy's profitability reaches its maximum if the underlying index closes at the options' strike price when the shorter dated of the two options expires.

As was seen in Chapter 4, time decay for at-the-money options accelerates as the expiration nears; calendar spreads are designed to benefit from this phenomenon. Assuming the SPX remains at its current level for the next week and a half, both the option we purchased and the option we have written will lose value, but the erosion of the April option's time premium will be more rapid. This means we will lose money on our long option but gain more on our short option. At the April expiration the value of the spread will be a function of both the level of the SPX index and the May option's implied volatility (the April option will be worth its intrinsic value and will not be impacted by any change in implied volatility).

Looking at the time spread at the April expiration, there are two worst-case scenarios. The first is if the market collapses, leaving us with two worthless calls. In this case, the loss would be equal to the initial debit paid to enter into the position, $14.70, although the May call would still have four weeks of life left and it might be possible to recoup part of our initial investment. The second worst case is if the market rallies strongly. Then both our long and our short options would be deep in-the-money—the April trading at intrinsic value, the May not much above its intrinsic. The spread would have to be unwound, the April option covered, and the May sold. And since both options would be trading close to intrinsic, exiting the position would probably be done for a very small credit, or for even money. Assuming the spread is liquidated for even money, the loss would then also be equal to the initial debit of $14.70.

The best-case scenario is for SPX to close at 1125 at April expiration. The short April option would expire worthless and we would be left holding the May option. Assuming no change in the options' volatility, the May 1125 call would be valued at $20.20 and if sold at this price would generate a profit of $5.50 ($20.20 less the initial debit of $14.70). Figure 7.8 illustrates the strategy's profit and loss at the April expiration date, assuming no change in implied volatility.

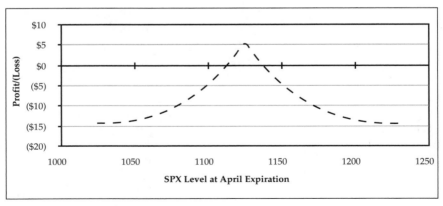

Figure 7.8 SPX Time Spread

Compare the general shape of the graph in Figure 7.8 to that of the long butterfly spread in Figure 7.4. They are similar, with both strategies having limited risk and limited profit potential that is realized when the underlying closes at a specific strike price. Since a butterfly spread can involve up to four different option series and the time spread can be initiated with only two, traders may see an advantage in the latter if only from a transaction's costs point of view.

The major difference between butterflies and time spreads is that the value of the calendar spread at the short option's expiration date will be a function of the market's implied volatility, whereas the butterfly's value at expiration is purely a function of the underlying index's level. This is where time spreads are somewhat counterintuitive. First, they are established for a debit, when for the most part, option strategies that look to take advantage of time decay are initiated for a credit. Second, the value of a time spread will be positively impacted by higher, not lower, implied volatility. Remember that in our example, at the April expiration, the short April call will either be out-of-the-money and worthless, or in-the-money and trading at or close to its intrinsic value. Neither of these outcomes is impacted by volatility. But we will still be long the May option and the higher the implied volatility, the greater the value of the May option and the higher the profit on the transaction. Time spreads actually benefit from higher implied volatility but are hurt by actual volatility.

Why does the risk-reward ratio in our example look so unfavorable? We could lose $14.70 but only stand to make $5.50, and that only if the SPX closes at 1125. The answer is because of the expiration date of the option we wrote, just one and a half weeks away. Consider a calendar spread where we write the May 1125 call at $25.20 and purchase the June 1125 call at $38.20 for an initial debit, and ultimate risk, of $13.00. Given an index level of 1125 at the May expiration, we can estimate the value of the June 1125 call (which will still have five weeks until it expires) to then be $22.45, for a profit potential of $9.45. A longer time frame creates a more favorable risk-reward ratio because the further out the expiration date of the short option, the higher the probability that the market will move away from its current level.

It also should be noted that there is no need to trade options expiring in two consecutive months when initiating a calendar spread. Going back to the quotes given above, a trader could have purchased the June 1125 call at $38.20 and written the April 1125 call at $12.50, probably with the intention, at the April expiration, of either writing the May 1125 call if the April expires worthless or rolling the short April position into May if SPX ends up above 1125 at expiration. And traders who are long-term neutral could purchase the far out June call at $105, write the April, and continue writing short-term options over the next 15 months.

Calendar spreads also can comprise options with different strike prices, in which case they are known as diagonal spreads. The most popular form of this strategy involves buying a longer-dated in-the-money option and writing a shorter-dated option that is either at- or out-of-the-money. Purchasing the in-the-money option will increase the initial cost of the position but will reduce the impact of time decay on this long option. By writing an at-the-money (or slightly out-of-the-money) option, the trader can still take advantage of the accelerating time decay. Finally, puts can be substituted for calls because time decay does not differentiate between calls and puts.

8

HEDGING CORPORATE STOCK AND OPTIONS

The "equity culture" of the late nineties led to many changes in employee compensation as stock purchase plans and option grants worked their way down the food chain. We've all heard the good stories (the hourly worker at Wal-Mart retiring a millionaire through the regular purchase of company shares), the bad (piles of options in dot-bomb companies, accepted as a trade-off for a lower salary, expiring worthless), and the ugly (Enron employees losing their jobs the same week as their 401(k), loaded with company stock, imploded). Increased ownership of company stock and stock options presents new challenges and investment dilemmas in addition to their well-known benefits. This chapter will address some of these issues.

Before taking any action, investors who own shares of or options on their employer's company should verify what is and is not permitted under their company's rules. Some of these rules are explicit (the interdiction to sell designated shares before you are 47 years old), others maybe less so (the prohibition of writing covered calls against company stock). Double-check before taking any action.

Equity Collars

Can one have too much of a good thing? If the good thing is a stock, the answer is yes. Consider these two examples:

- Mrs. Jones has been buying her company's shares for the last 14 years. It's the only stock she owns, and it represents a substantial percentage of her net worth.
- Mr. Smith has just sold the company he founded 12 years ago to a multinational that paid him with its stock, rather than cash.

Sometimes it is difficult or impossible for an investor to reduce an oversized position. The obstacle may be real (the investor is prohibited from selling) or psychological (an employee is afraid of jeopardizing future career prospects if the company interprets the sale of its stock in a negative light). In either case, there may come a point where protection of capital becomes a priority.

It's hard to argue against the advantages of going long some put options to protect an equity position: they limit the downside risk, maintain the stock's upside potential, and help the holder sleep at night. The problem is, buying these puts costs money. Someone who has accumulated a substantial position in the shares of Costco (COST) might hesitate to pay $1.30 to purchase the April 40 puts (with eight weeks until expiration) when the stock is trading at $42.09. The cost of two months' protection is more than 3% of the stock price and could represent a serious cash drain for someone with a substantial number of shares.

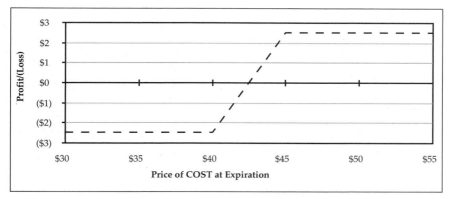

Figure 8.1 COST Collar

But for someone whose main concern is preservation of capital and who may be willing to give up something besides cash, an equity collar may be a viable solution. This strategy consists of purchasing a protective put, for example the April 40 put at $1.30 mentioned above, and financing the purchase by writing a call option, maybe the April 45 call at $0.90. Writing the call does limit the profit potential on the stock, but it also cuts the cost of the hedge to $0.40 per share.

The collar, in fact, accomplishes two things. First, it limits the downside risk on the stock since the put gives the investor the right to sell COST at $40. Second, it limits the upside on the stock from the current price of $42.09 to the call's strike price of $45. Quantifying these numbers we get a risk of $2.49 (the loss from $42.09 to the put's $40 strike plus the $0.40 cost of the position) and a profit potential of $2.51 (the stock's appreciation from $42.09 to the call's exercise price of $45 less the $0.40 cost of the collar). This resulting risk-reward profile is illustrated in Figure 8.1.

What if our investor wants to hedge the position for longer than eight weeks? To determine the cost, let's look at COST option quotes, with the stock at $42.09:

	45 Call	40 Put
April	$0.90–$0.95	$1.15–$1.30
July	$2.00–$2.10	$2.15–$2.25
October	$3.20–$3.30	$3.10–$3.30
January	$4.40–$4.60	$4.00–$4.20

Table 8.1

	Buy 40 Put	Write 45 Call	Cost of Collar
April	$1.30	$0.90	$0.40
July	$2.25	$2.00	$0.25
October	$3.30	$3.20	$0.10
January	$4.20	$4.40	($0.20)

Table 8.1 calculates the cost of the 40–45 collar for various expiration dates.

It may come as a bit of a surprise that the longer-dated collars actually cost less than the shorter-dated ones. In fact, the January 40–45 collar can be established for a small credit. Many investors structure their collars so that the premium received from writing the call fully offsets the cost of the put. This is known as a *zero-cost collar*. This may seem advantageous—more time for less money—but there is another side to the coin, as you will see in the next section.

Anyone who decides to collar his corporate shares should remember that it involves writing a call, and for this call to be covered, the stock cannot be hindered by any selling restrictions. In most cases, the stock needs to be deposited with the broker executing the collar to margin the short call position.

Reality Interferes with Theory

When we pulled up the COST option quotes for our collar example, the risk-free interest rate, as defined by Treasury bills, was hovering somewhere below 2%. Cash was trash. This fact (reality) interfered with a phenomenon (theory) that is usually observed with collars but was not in evidence here. We offer some theoretical option prices in Tables 8.2 and 8.3 to illustrate this point. We created scenarios with 3% and 6% risk-free rates for two stocks, one with 25% volatility (blue-chip range) and one with 50% volatility (high-tech range). Both tables assume a stock price of $42.50. Here is what we found.

Table 8.2

		Volatility = 25%				
		3 Months	6 Months	9 Months	1 Year	2 Years
With 3%	45 Call	$1.26	$2.22	$3.04	$3.75	$6.06
Risk-free	40 Put	$0.96	$1.61	$2.14	$2.57	$3.76
Rate	Difference	$0.30	$0.61	$0.90	$1.18	$2.30
With 6%	45 Call	$1.37	$2.47	$3.44	$4.31	$7.20
Risk-free	40 Put	$0.88	$1.44	$1.87	$2.21	$3.06
Rate	Difference	$0.49	$1.03	$1.57	$2.10	$4.14

Let's start with Table 8.2, looking at the 40–45 collar under the 3% risk-free interest rate assumption. The 3-month collar can be established for a $0.30 credit. This is usually the case for collars when the stock is sitting halfway between the two strike prices, as the call will generally be worth slightly more than the put. As the time to expiration increases, the credit becomes larger, to the point where the two-year collar can be initiated for a $2.30 credit, virtually eliminating all risk from the position. Remember that the worst-case scenario has the stock falling below $40, in which case a $2.50 loss is realized on the stock. If the collar was initiated for a $2.30 credit it virtually absorbs all of this loss.

Moving down to the same collar under the 6% interest rate assumption, we find larger credits, to the point where the two-year collar is not only risk-free, but is generating a profit under all possible outcomes. The $4.14 credit more than makes up for the maximum $2.50 loss realized if the stock goes below $40, leaving a $1.64 profit under the worst-case scenario. A rise of the stock to $45 or higher would generate a $2.50 profit on the stock that, added to the initial $4.14 credit, produces a total gain of $6.64. An ideal "can't lose" situation.

Or is it? An investor who initiates a two-year collar has eliminated not only all of the downside risk, but also most of the profit potential. This investor has, in fact, turned the stock position into something that looks a lot like a fixed-income instrument. There is no out-of-pocket cost to establish the option position, but there are

Table 8.3

		3 Months	6 Months	9 Months	1 Year	2 Years
		Volatility = 50%				
With 3% Risk-free Rate	45 Call	$3.36	$5.26	$6.73	$7.98	$11.82
	40 Put	$2.88	$4.40	$5.53	$6.46	$9.06
	Difference	$0.48	$0.86	$1.20	$1.52	$2.76
With 6% Risk-free Rate	45 Call	$3.49	$5.15	$7.11	$8.48	$12.75
	40 Put	$2.77	$4.17	$5.17	$5.98	$8.16
	Difference	$0.72	$0.98	$1.94	$2.50	$4.59

plenty of opportunity costs. Of course, moving synthetically from an equity position to something that looks like cash may be what someone with an overexposure to one stock is trying to accomplish. (Note that this type of position—where an investor eliminates all risk and virtually all profit potential—has caught the attention of people at the U.S. Treasury. See the section on taxes in Chapter 10 before trying this at home.)

Moving down to Table 8.3, we find results that once again may appear counterintuitive: collars on a 50% volatility stock generate a higher credit than those on a 25% volatility equity. In fact, under the 6% interest rate assumption, the $2.50 credit obtained in establishing the one-year collar is sufficient to completely eliminate the position's risk. Using two-year options generates a $4.59 credit, guaranteeing a $2.09 profit no matter what the stock price at expiration. This, of course, is great news for those looking to reduce or eliminate the risk of a stock position: the hedged position will return 4.9% in the event that the stock drops below $40 and 16.7% if it rises above $45—roughly 2.43% annualized and 8.0% annualized if one assumes annual compounding. One associates returns like these with cash, not with a 50% volatility stock.

Other Potential Collar Buyers

Buying a collar might be of interest to traders and investors who are not necessarily overweighed in one stock. Consider the case of a trader who has held a stock for 11 months, during which time the stock has doubled in value. Selling now would generate a nice profit but would also incur a tax bill based on the short-term capital gains rate. Holding on for one more month would substantially reduce the tax bill, but the reduction could be the result of the stock going down as much as the result of the more favorable tax treatment. The appropriate collar could help reduce the downside risk of the position while the holding period meter keeps running.

An equity collar would also do the job for an investor who finds herself with a substantial long-term capital gain in November or December but wants to postpone the gain until the following tax year, even though she will benefit from the lower tax rate. Before initiating a collar for tax reasons, see Chapter 10 and make sure you have up-to-date information on the tax treatment of collars because the rules change faster than a book can be printed.

The Two Half-Collars: Buying Puts, Writing Calls

If collars can be used to hedge an overweighed stock position, so can half-collars—either writing the calls or purchasing the puts. If an investor owns some shares without any restrictions, she can deposit them with her broker and write covered calls. Another investor might be receiving unrestricted shares in a few months and would still like to write calls against those shares. The only solution for this second investor is to get approval from her broker to write uncovered calls, provide the margin necessary to maintain this position, and monitor the position closely to avoid early assignment. Of course, this assumes she is not prohibited from writing calls on her company's stock. Very few investors will want to put up with all these restrictions. Furthermore, writing covered calls against an overweighed stock position only provides partial downside protection; this is where the strategy falls short of the desired risk reduction.

The last avenue left to explore is the purchase of protective puts. These have the double advantage of offering as much downside protection as an investor desires (through strike price selection) and maintaining the underlying stock's full upside potential. They also can be quite expensive, and we have seen many investors decide to take their chances when we pulled up quotes on put options and told them how much it would cost to insure their holdings.

Buying Partial Insurance

There is no need for an investor with a large stock position to insure every share held. Insurance can be purchased on part of the position to protect the core of the holdings, and the balance of the shares can be held unhedged. It is easy to understand how one would buy puts on only a half, a third, or a quarter of a stock held. In this section, we want to highlight options' flexibility and show that buying partial insurance can mean more than buying 50 puts to hedge half of a 10,000 share position.

Take the situation of a longtime employee who has accumulated 5,000 shares of Plodding Along (PAL), now trading at $100. This employee will be retiring in one year, at which point she will be free to sell any or all of her PAL shares. Having half a million dollars tied up in one security makes her somewhat nervous, especially when this represents the core of her retirement nest egg. Looking at one-year LEAPS she finds the following:

PAL:	$100
100 put:	$12.10
95 put:	$9.80
90 put:	$7.60
85 put:	$5.70
80 put:	$4.10
75 put:	$2.85

Fully insuring her holdings would entail purchasing 50 of the 100 puts, at a cost of $60,500 ($12.10 × 50 × 100). This choice insures all of her shares, with no deductible, but at a cost of 12% of her stock position's value. This is where a lot of would-be hedgers back off: they are all in favor of insurance, but not at this cost.

Our investor needs to determine how much she is willing to spend for insurance. If 12% is too high, what about 6%? There is obviously no correct answer here, but for the purpose of our example, let's see what type of insurance she can buy with a 5% limit.

Hedging fewer than 5,000 shares: in dollar terms, 5% of the value of our investor's holdings represents $25,000. This sum could be used to purchase 20 of the 100 puts, 25 of the 95 puts, 43 of the 85 puts, or 50 of the 80 puts. This last alternative would cost only $20,500 and insure all of her shares; but the amount by which these options are out-of-the-money would force our investor to absorb the first 20% drop in the price of PAL. For argument's sake, let's assume she is most comfortable purchasing 25 of the 95 puts. These insure half of her holdings, and she can easily cope with the options being only 5% out-of-the-money.

Another way for this investor to obtain partial insurance would be to insure all of her shares but to obtain coverage over only a limited range. For example, she could purchase 50 of the 95 puts at $9.80 each and simultaneously write 50 of the 80 puts at $4.10 per contract. Her insurance cost would then be $5.70 per share, slightly higher than her 5% limit. Let's explore this further before begging off because the spending cap has been breached.

Readers will have recognized the long 95/short 80 put position as a bear put spread, described as a trading strategy in Chapter 6. Here we are using what was previously described as a trading strategy to hedge. First let's do a quick analysis in terms of rights and obligations. Our investor purchases 50 of the 95 puts: this gives her the right to sell her 5,000-share position at $95. She can consider herself to be fully insured. She also wrote 50 of the 80 puts, obligating herself to purchase 5,000 shares of PAL at $80. Should she be forced to reestablish her stock position at $80, her newly acquired shares would then be held without any downside protection. In other words, the bear spread insures our investor from $95 down to $80, but no further.

Since this bear spread is purchased on a share-to-share basis with the stock held, the overall position can be easily summarized, as in Table 8.4.

A few comments on Table 8.4. The value of the 80 put appears as a negative number since the investor is short this option and will have to repurchase it at expiration if she does not want to be assigned. The far-right-hand column is the overall profit and loss based on a starting stock price of $100 and the ending value of the bear put spread. We have not asked our investor the average cost of her PAL shares, but we can probably safely assume that since these

Table 8.4

PAL at Option Expiration	Profit/ (Loss) on Stock	Value of 95 Put	Value of 80 Put	Cost of Put Spread	Total Profit/ (Loss)
$110	$10	$0	$0	($5.70)	$4.30
$105	$5	$0	$0	($5.70)	($0.70)
$100	$0	$0	$0	($5.70)	($5.70)
$95	($5)	$0	$0	($5.70)	($10.70)
$90	($10)	$5	$0	($5.70)	($10.70)
$85	($15)	$10	$0	($5.70)	($10.70)
$80	($20)	$15	$0	($5.70)	($10.70)
$75	($25)	$20	($5)	($5.70)	($15.70)
$70	($30)	$25	($10)	($5.70)	($20.70)

have been accumulated over many years it is significantly below the current $100 stock price.

Figure 8.2 compares an unhedged equity position, a partial hedge created by purchasing 95 puts on half the shares held, and a partial hedge created by purchasing the 95–80 bear put spread. Profits and losses are calculated on a per share basis. The result shown for the

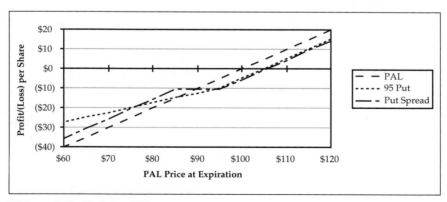

Figure 8.2 Hedging PAL

long 95 put strategy is actually an average of half hedged shares and half unhedged shares.

This figure gives us a visual representation of how two of the possible hedges perform. If PAL's price is up from the current $100 at option expiration, they have very comparable costs: the equivalent of $4.90 per share for the 95 puts (the cost of each put was $9.80, but only half the number of contracts necessary to cover the stock position was purchased), and $5.70 per share for the bear spread. Below $95, the bear spread, at least initially, offers better protection, as the long 95 puts fully hedge the long stock. Below $75, since the bear spread only offered protection down to $80, the half-position in the 95 puts offers a more efficient hedge than the bear spread. Two insurance strategies with similar initial costs but different downside protection. We view this choice as an illustration of the flexibility of options, not as an additional headache.

The bear spread we chose was one of many that are possible. We could also have purchased the 100 puts and written the 80s (for an $8 debit), or bought the 90s and written the 75s for a $4.85 cost. How does one choose which option to buy and which one to write, or at least narrow down the field? We like to start with the approximate amount we are willing to spend on a hedge. In the above example, this was 5% of the stock's value for 12 months of protection. We then look at which spreads such an amount will buy. In addition to the 95–80 spread at $5.70, the 100–90 spread was $4.50. The 100–90 spread was a little less expensive, at-the-money, but the two strike prices were only $10 apart. Spending an additional $1.20 gave us a full extra $5 of protection (when the goal is insuring a long stock position, the wider the spread, the better). Once again, the final decision becomes a function of personal preference, risk aversion, and which spread feels best given what we know of PAL and our perception of potential risk over the next 12 months.

Finally, for those investors who may have skimmed over the spreading strategies in Chapter 6, we would strongly recommend going back and paying special attention to the price behavior of spreads over time and how they tend not to reach their maximum theoretical value until very close to option expiration. Time spent reviewing that section may eliminate some unexpected frustrations down the road.

Hedging Corporate Stock Options

Anyone who is looking to hedge a position in corporate options should begin by verifying what is permissible under corporate policy and that it will not be a "career limiting move."

A Note on Nomenclature

When dealing with exchange-traded options, the standard is to talk in terms of contracts, each covering 100 shares of underlying stock. In the world of corporate options, if someone is granted 5,000 options this refers to options on 5,000 shares, not 500,000. We will try and keep this distinction clear in our discussion.

Also, executive options usually vest after a set time period. Before they are vested, options are, for this discussion, worthless because they cannot be exercised. Needless to say, we assume that the options being hedged have vested.

What and When to Hedge

Hedging corporate stock options seems like a redundancy: options provide a natural hedge with limited risk and full upside potential. And because corporate options are generally granted at no cost to the employee (employees do not have to pay the option's premium, although they will have to pay an amount equal to the option's strike price in order to purchase the stock upon exercise), the limited risk aspect turns out to be no risk, while the full upside potential is obtained. To make the option holders' life even easier, most corporations provide a cashless exercise feature, where the stock under option can be purchased through exercise and sold immediately without the option holder having to put up any capital. So what is there to hedge?

Not the options themselves, but the options when they start acting like the underlying stock; in other words, when they are in-the-money by a substantial amount. In-the-money options represent unrealized gains, and although the gains cannot turn into losses, they can easily disappear. And this is the object of our attention: in-the-money call options that represent accrued but unrealized profits.

If It Looks Like Stock . . .

If an in-the-money call option looks like the underlying stock, behaves like stock, and goes up and down in value like stock, then it is probably wise to treat it like stock. This means that the equity hedging strategies discussed above should apply. The problem is that the option holder is not in possession of the stock, even though he may be free to exercise his options at any point in time. Writing calls, or purchasing a collar (which involves writing calls), would entail margining uncovered options, which is not a very attractive proposition. So are we back to square one?

Studies show that executives place a lower value on their corporate options than the market does. The likely explanation is that to the executives these options represent more of the same: they are employed by the firm, probably own shares of stock, and now are getting options. The end result is too many eggs in the employer's basket, so it is not surprising that an outside investor, whose portfolio is otherwise well diversified, would place a higher value on these same options.

Another possible explanation is that executive options are not all they appear to be. In Chapter 1 we noted that the buyer of a call has to take one of three actions: let the option expire, exercise it, or sell it to close the position. When someone is granted company options, the third choice is not available: the options have to be exercised or, if they are out-of-the-money, kept until they expire worthless. This restriction means corporate options should be discounted when compared to equivalent listed options. This also is illustrated in the frequency of early exercise. With listed options it very seldom makes any economic sense to exercise a call early. But with corporate options, this occurs frequently. To gauge the cost of exercising options early, look at Table 8.5, which calculates the theoretical values of different in-the-money call options with a $50 strike price.

Assume corporate options were granted quite a few years ago, when the stock was at $50 (the price that became the options' strike price). The stock has risen to $75, but the options still have two years until expiration. An employee who wants to lock in some of the stock's gains could exercise and would net $25, assuming a cashless exercise. But if this employee could simply sell her options, she would pocket a little over $30, assuming the options are priced with a 30% volatility. Some would see her as "leaving $5 on the table," or

Table 8.5

		Stock at $75	Stock at $100
30% Volatility	One-Year Option	$27.51	$52.01
	Two-Year Option	$30.42	$54.23
45% Volatility	One-Year Option	$29.26	$52.61
	Two-Year Option	$33.55	$56.04

20% of her realized gain. If the underlying stock is riskier and its options are priced with a 45% volatility, the opportunity loss is more than $8.50, or about 34% of her realized gain. Even with the stock at $100 (and the options 100% in-the-money), early exercise results in an apparent opportunity loss.

Of course, no money is being left on the table because the difference outlined here really represents that between listed and corporate options. But it does open up an interesting strategy. Assume an executive holds some in-the-money options with two years remaining until they expire. If his goal is to generate cash to pay for a new house, a bigger boat, or a divorce settlement, his choice is limited: exercise the option and take the money. But if his primary goal is to lock in the accrued gain, and there is no immediate need for the cash, he could write uncovered call options with an expiration date and strike price as close as possible to those of his corporate options. There will be two obstacles to writing the exchange-traded options: convincing his brokerage firm to approve his account for uncovered call writing and margining the position until expiration.

If our executive holds any financial assets, these can probably be used to margin the uncovered call position. Stocks, bonds, and mutual funds are all marginable, and it should be remembered that margining a short option position does not involve borrowing funds and accruing interest expenses, but simply putting up sufficient assets to show the ability to meet the obligation assumed in writing options. He should be aware of the risks of early assignment on short call options, as discussed in Chapter 4.

Assuming these two obstacles can be overcome, writing uncovered calls against corporate options will have a double benefit: the first is easily measurable in that the premium received from writing

Table 8.6

		Stock at $75	Stock at $100
30% Volatility	One-Year Option	$19.36	$42.65
	Two-Year Option	$23.44	$45.78
45% Volatility	One-Year Option	$22.46	$44.11
	Two-Year Option	$27.73	$48.99

the exchange-traded calls will be greater than the amount that would be obtained by exercising the corporate options. The second advantage may turn out to be tax related. Exercising corporate options immediately creates a tax liability. Writing uncovered calls against corporate options may or may not trigger a taxable event. The tax treatment may hinge on how similar in terms both options are. If they are deemed to be "essentially the same security," the writing of uncovered calls may trigger a taxable event.

Which argues in favor of writing a materially different option. To judge if this makes economic sense, look at Table 8.6, which calculates the theoretical prices of options with a $60 strike price.

To recap, we have an executive with the right to purchase company stock at $50, two years left on his corporate options, and the stock trading at $75. If he exercises his calls, he nets $25. If he writes an uncovered call, with two years until expiration and a $60 strike price he gets a bit more than $23 in option premium (assuming a 30% volatility). So far, he is down $2. But he is now in position to earn an additional $10 since he has a call on company stock at $50 and the obligation to sell these shares at $60. He now has the potential to increase his gain by $8 and defer the tax liability, assuming that the 60 call is materially different from the 50 call in the eyes of the tax people.

If the stock's options trade with a 45% volatility, the premium received is more than $25 and the position has the potential to generate an additional $10 in gains. Obviously, this type of strategy is not for everyone given the capital required to maintain an uncovered short option position for two years, but it does represent one of the few arbitrage possibilities between the corporate and listed options markets.

If the executive in this example also owns company shares, this might turn out to be a good news–bad news situation. The good news is that these shares could be deposited with his broker to cover the call options written. The bad news is that writing calls against his shares (if in-the-money options are selected) may create a taxable event. See the relevant section in Chapter 10 and consult a professional tax advisor.

9

OPTIONS 901: ADVANCED THEORETICAL NOTIONS

Shania Twain is not impressed by rocket scientists, and our goal is not to turn readers into options nerds. Rather, it is to demystify some of the technical terms you may have heard or read about and to underscore their practical applications (or lack thereof) for options traders and investors.

Calculating Historical Volatility

Historical volatilities can be found on various websites, including cboe.com, but for those instances where it is not available, or not available for the required time frame, here is how it is calculated.

First we must choose the period over which we want to calculate the stock's (or index's) volatility. Let's take 20 trading days for Baker Hughes (BHI). Table 9.1 below is an Excel spreadsheet where we have calculated BHI's historical volatility.

In the second column are the stock's daily closing prices. The third column calculates the stock's daily continuously compounded rate of return. One could use straight daily rates of returns, and they would be very close to the continuously compounded rates, at least when the returns are relatively small. There is a slight advantage in using continuously compounded rates in that a move from $100 to $101 and a second move from $101 to $100 will result in the positive and negative rates being of equal magnitude, whereas if simple rates are used, a move from $100 to $101 is equal to a 1.00% return and from $101 to $100 one of -0.99%. To calculate continuously compounded rates use the $=\mathrm{LN}(\ldots)$ formula. For example, to calculate the return from day 1 to day 2 use $=\mathrm{LN}(\mathrm{B2}/\mathrm{B1})$. LN stands for natural logarithm.

At the bottom of the third column we have calculated the standard deviation of the continuously compounded returns. We simply use the built-in formula $=\mathrm{STDEV}(\ldots)$; the result obtained is the stock's daily volatility—in this instance .0237, or 2.37%. This can be converted to an annualized number by multiplying the daily volatility by $\sqrt{256}$. Why 256 and not 365? We are interested in the number of trading, not calendar, days, and there are between 252 and 254 trading days in a year. If one assumes that the Friday to Monday volatility is no greater than that of the Monday to Tuesday volatility and of the volatility between the other weekdays, then one can ignore Saturdays and Sundays. In other words, weekends do not add to a stock's volatility. And why do we not use 253 as an average? Pure laziness: $\sqrt{256}$ is equal to 16, a nice round number and not different enough from $\sqrt{253}$ to make a difference. BHI's historical volatility clocks in at 0.3786, or 38%, a mid-range number for an oil driller.

Table 9.1 BHI: Historical Volatility

Day 1	38.40	
Day 2	38.84	0.0114
Day 3	38.46	(0.0098)
Day 4	36.91	(0.0411)
Day 5	36.43	(0.0131)
Day 6	38.10	0.0448
Day 7	36.89	(0.0323)
Day 8	37.13	0.0065
Day 9	37.48	0.0094
Day 10	37.48	0.0000
Day 11	35.96	(0.0414)
Day 12	36.86	0.0247
Day 13	35.84	(0.0337)
Day 14	35.60	(0.0011)
Day 15	35.13	(0.0133)
Day 16	36.19	0.0297
Day 17	36.84	0.0178
Day 18	36.55	(0.0079)
Day 19	36.41	(0.0038)
Day 20	36.57	0.0044
		0.0237
		0.3786

What Volatility Tells Us About Direction

Table 9.2 gives the closing monthly prices of three fictitious stocks over a 10-month period. Which of these is the most volatile?

If you use the method outlined above, you will be able to calculate these stocks' monthly volatilities (which you can annualize by

Table 9.2

	Bull Run	Bear Cave	Yoyo Corp.
Month 1	100	100	100
Month 2	104	96	104
Month 3	103	97	103
Month 4	107	93	107
Month 5	106	94	106
Month 6	110	90	102
Month 7	109	91	103
Month 8	113	87	99
Month 9	112	88	100
Month 10	116	84	104

multiplying by the square root of 12). The historical volatilities you should obtain: Bull Run 8.5%, Bear Cave 9.9%, and Yoyo Corp. 10.8%. The results are very close because all three stocks fluctuated in similar ways, alternating between $4 changes and $1 changes. It is the magnitude of these changes that is important when calculating volatility, not the direction. The volatilities are not identical because the monthly returns were slightly different. For example, from the end of month 2 to the end of month 3, Bull Run was down $1 but this was $1 on a base of $104. Bear Cave was up $1, but from a starting point of $96, which represents a higher percentage than for Bull Run.

The unfortunate conclusion is that calculating a stock's historical volatility tells us absolutely nothing about its direction, either past or future.

Do the Markets Have the Monday Morning Blues?

In the previous section we assumed that interday volatility between Fridays and Mondays was the same as the volatility between the other days of the week. We decided to test this hypothesis and crunched some numbers.

We looked at the closing level of the Standard & Poor's 500 Index (SPX) from December 30, 1994, to December 31, 2001, giving us seven years of data. We first calculated SPX's volatility looking only at the changes between Fridays' closes and Mondays' closes. Where long weekends occurred, we used the Thursday to Monday change or the Friday to Tuesday variation. We then calculated SPX's volatility for all the other days: Monday to Tuesday, Tuesday to Wednesday, Wednesday to Thursday, and Thursday to Friday.

Finally, we had to decide how to account for the change in the market between September 10, 2001, and September 17, 2001. As we all unfortunately remember, the markets were closed on September 11 and on the three following business days. Should we include the change from September 10 to September 17 in our Friday to Monday data or not? To let everyone see the impact, we decided to perform calculations that both included and excluded this one outlier. The results are presented in Table 9.3.

Ignoring the market change between September 10 and September 17, we note that the markets are slightly more volatile over the weekends than during the week, with volatility at 18.8% versus 17.6%. As a point of reference, for the complete period, the volatility of the SPX (taking all days into account) was 17.97%, 17.87% if the September 10/September 17 change is excluded.

So it appears that the weekends do add a bit of volatility to the markets on Mondays, but the impact is less than three days of volatility compressed into one. We will leave it to the academic researchers to tell us exactly how long the weekends are from a volatility perspective.

Table 9.3

	Friday to Monday Volatility	Weekdays Volatility
Including Sep. 10/Sep. 17	19.25%	17.62%
Excluding Sep. 10/Sep. 17	18.79%	17.62%

Calculating Implied Volatility

Remember the equation for distance traveled? It looked like this:

$$s = v \times t$$

In this equation s stands for distance, v for speed, and t for time. If you traveled 47 miles in 1.2 hours, what was your average speed? You would solve this problem by rearranging the terms of the equation as follows:

$$v = s \div t$$

You would easily find your average speed to have been 39.2 miles per hour. This general type of problem was known as solving for x. At first glance, calculating an option's implied volatility would appear to be a simple case of solving for x. We are given the answer (the option's value) and all but one of the variables (volatility). We just rearrange the option pricing equation to isolate volatility on the left side of the equal sign, and voilà!

There is only a slight problem. If you try to isolate volatility on the left side of the equal sign in the Black-Scholes option pricing equation, you will find it impossible. (If you decide to try this, you will either waste a lot of time or end up winning a Nobel Prize.) So calculating implied volatility is not as straightforward as it may appear.

Implied volatility must be calculated through an iterative process (read: trial and error). Assume you want to calculate the implied volatility of an option trading at $3.40. Start with a mid-range volatility assumption, say 35%, and calculate the value of this option based on 35% volatility. You get $2.95. Your volatility assumption was too low; try again with a higher number, say, 40%. You get $3.55. Too high; try again with a number somewhere between 35 and 40%. And so on.

Solving for implied volatility by hand would be cumbersome and time consuming to say the least. Fortunately, you probably have as much computing power in your personal computer as some corporations had in 1973 when Professors Black and Scholes published their findings. The process now takes approximately 12 seconds and can be done on various websites.

Implied Volatility of Different Option Series

Assume you are looking to purchase calls on a particular stock. Obviously you want to pay as little as possible. In terms of volatility, this means buying the call with the lowest implied volatility. Is it worth your time to calculate the implied volatility of the September 45 call and that of the October 50 call to see which is trading at a lower volatility and therefore represents the better buy? We do not think so.

If you start calculating implied volatility for various series in one class, you will find very few discrepancies. This should not be surprising as professional traders earn their living looking for the smallest anomalies in option prices and stepping in when they find one. They also have a major advantage over the trader sitting at home at his computer: they are physically present on the trading floor, giving them a few seconds' advantage over the living room trader. (If you would like to know how much this few seconds' head start is worth, check out the prices of seats on the options exchanges.) Floor traders also have much lower transaction costs, meaning they can execute trades at a profit, while at-home traders would see all of their gains eaten up by commissions.

If you find major differences in options' implied volatility this should raise a red flag and not be taken as a signal that you have found a great buying or writing opportunity. For instance, maybe the April options are trading near a 35% volatility and the May options at roughly 40% volatility. The reason: earnings are scheduled to be announced in early May. This means that the April options will not be impacted by the earnings news, but the May options will bear the full brunt of unexpected news, good or bad. This is a relatively common occurrence. Other events that may be reflected in diverging implied volatilities: special dividend, spin-off of a subsidiary, announced stock buyback. If you find something that looks too good to be true, it probably is.

The Market's Implied Volatility

With the options software now available, calculating implied volatility is relatively easy. For the options on the Standard & Poor's 100 Index (OEX) it is even easier because this task is performed by the CBOE and the result disseminated to quote vendors under the ticker symbol VIX.

When you ask your broker for a quote on VIX, or when you pull one up from the Internet, what you are getting is the implied volatility of eight options on the OEX, four calls and four puts, four options from the next monthly expiration, and four from the second month out, four options from the first strike above the current level of the index, and four from the strike immediately below the index. These eight options (the near-term, at-the-money options) tend to be the most liquid, so there are numerous trades and a lot of up-to-the-minute information is available.

VIX Levels

Just knowing at what level VIX is currently trading does not impart much information. But when the current level is compared to historical levels, one can see if it is relatively high or relatively low. It is also interesting to compare the level of VIX to the ups and downs of the underlying index. Figure 9.1 charts the progress of VIX and OEX for the calendar year 2000.

What is striking in this graph is how closely VIX mirrors the ups and downs of the OEX: a higher market leads to a lower VIX, and vice-versa. The mirror image is not a perfect one, but it is fairly consistent (the correlation factor for the year, comes in at −0.71).

Relatively long declines in the OEX, such as the one from the beginning of September through mid-October, are reflected by a steadily higher implied volatility. Short-term drops, such as the severe sell-off in late April, also cause sharp spikes in VIX.

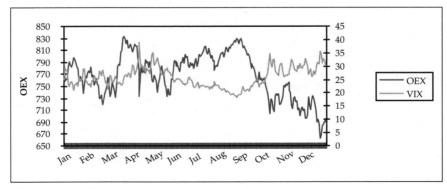

Figure 9.1 2000

This is not too difficult to understand if one thinks of options as insurance. In a falling market, the value of insurance is obvious to everyone. Investors increase their coverage by purchasing puts, and traders jump on the bandwagon hoping to benefit from the down-draft. Since the laws of supply and demand are still in force in the options market, the price of insurance (i.e., the options' implied volatility), increases.

As markets drift up, investors become more comfortable and do not see any need to insure their holdings. Demand dries up, option writers settle for lower premiums as they see little risk in the mar-ket, and, as can be seen in the graph, VIX moves to a lower level. Not to belabor the point, but take a look at Figure 9.2, which tracks OEX and VIX during calendar 2001.

The same general pattern emerges. Note here that VIX had already risen to a closing level of 33.87 on September 10 before jumping to 44.94 on September 17 and peaking at 49.04 on Septem-ber 20. For the year, the correlation coefficient clocks in at −0.60. For readers interested in looking at prior years or up-to-date data, both VIX and OEX levels can be downloaded from the CBOE's website.

VIX is often referred to as the "fear index": the more nervous investors and traders are, the more they are willing to pay for options. A lesser-known index, the VXN, calculates the implied volatility of options on the Nasdaq-100 Index, providing a second measure of fear.

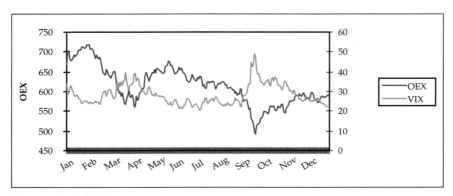

Figure 9.2 2001

How should investors use this index? VIX is a thermometer—it tells the current temperature in terms of implied volatility. When volatility is relatively high, options buyers are paying top dollar and strategies that could be negatively impacted by a return to "normal" volatility (such as the straight purchase of puts and calls) should probably be passed over in favor of those strategies that are less affected by changes in implied volatility (such as spreads).

For those whose primary interest is equity rather than index options, let us add our personal observations, which lead us to conclude that the same phenomenon happens with stock options' implied volatility. If a stock's price is hit hard due to bad earnings or other news, implied volatility will rise more often than not. As the stock settles down and later begins to rally, one can expect a return to more normal levels.

VIX: Thermometer or Barometer

Implied volatility is the market's estimate of future volatility. Options are priced based on expectations, and the price at which an option trades represents an agreement between buyer and seller about future price fluctuations.

How accurate is the forecast of future volatility embedded in implied volatility? Are the professionals pricing options by gazing into their crystal balls, or do they have one eye on the rearview mirror? We looked at VIX over a seven-year period, from December 30, 1994, through December 31, 2001, and compared it to the index's actual volatility over the following 10 and 20 trading days. This gave us a way to measure how well VIX could forecast future volatility. To obtain a second point of reference we also measured how VIX correlated to the past 10 and 20 trading days. Our results are presented in Table 9.4.

A perfect correlation would have an r^2 of 1.00; if there is no correlation between VIX and past or future volatility, the r^2 would be 0.00. Our results show a higher correlation to past volatility than to future volatility, meaning VIX's major appeal is as a thermometer (it tells us how "hot" volatility is at the present), not as a barometer (which would tell us if we should expect a "high"- or a "low-pressure" system).

Table 9.4

	r²
Correlation to Next 10 Trading Days	0.663
Correlation to Next 20 Trading Days	0.669
Correlation to Past 10 Trading Days	0.768
Correlation to Past 20 Trading Days	0.826

If this is a bit of a disappointment, remember that looking at the outdoor thermometer can help you decide how to dress before stepping out. Taking a peak at VIX can help you tailor your option strategies for the prevailing volatility climate.

The Greeks: Gamma

As was mentioned in Chapter 4, deltas change. And as was illustrated in Figure 4.4, deltas change at various rates. Gamma measures how rapidly deltas change. One could say that gamma is delta's delta.

Most options software will give you gamma in addition to theoretical price and delta. If we go back to the market maker with the complex position in ABCDE options (whom we met in Chapter 4), we can calculate her overall gamma just as we calculated her overall delta (see Table 9.5). But note that gamma's sign is determined by whether a position is long or short, not by whether it involves puts or calls. Buying options, puts or calls, creates positive gamma. Writing options results in negative gamma.

Once again we have multiplied the results by 100 to adjust for the number of shares per option. Call gamma is 71.9, put gamma is −181.0, for a total gamma of −109.1. But what does negative gamma mean?

Negative gamma tells us that if the price of the stock moves up, the position's total deltas will decrease—in this case by about 110 deltas for a $1 rise in the underlying. Remember that the options' position total delta (before hedging with short stock) was 1,010, the equivalent of being long 1,010 shares of stock; if ABCDE goes from

Table 9.5

Strike Price	Calls			Puts		
	Quantity	Gamma	Q × Gamma	Quantity	Gamma	Q × Gamma
45	+17	.039	66.3	−22	.039	−85.8
50	−32	.063	−201.6	−32	.063	−201.6
55	+37	.056	207.2	+19	.056	106.4
		Total Call Gamma	71.9		**Total Put Gamma**	−181.0

$50 to $51, the position's total delta would decrease from 1,010 to 900. This is not good. Our trader is losing deltas as the underlying stock is going up. Yes, she is still making money as the stock goes up (remember she has positive deltas), but the higher the stock rises, the less money she is making, and her positive delta position could eventually become negative.

What if the stock goes down? She has 1,010 deltas to start; if the stock goes down, her deltas would increase by 110, to 1,120 on a $1 fall of ABCDE. She is now picking up deltas (also referred to as *getting longer*) as the price of the stock goes down. Not a good idea. Being long 1,010 deltas means she loses $1,010 as the stock goes from $50 to $49. At $49 she is now long 1,120 deltas, which means she would lose $1,120 on a further drop from $49 to $48. Being short gamma reduces her gains as the stock rises, increases her losses as it drops.

No need to be a rocket scientist to figure out what happens when a trader is long gamma. As the underlying stock goes up, the position picks up deltas and becomes more and more profitable. As the underlying stock drops, the position loses deltas, reducing losses in a falling market.

The starting point for the analysis above was a position with net long deltas. Had the initial position been net short deltas, the general results would have been similar. If one starts with negative deltas and negative gamma, the position's net deltas become more negative as the stock rises and less negative as the stock drops. Starting with negative deltas and positive gamma means that the deltas become less negative as the stock increases in price and more negative as it declines.

Another way to look at this is that a position that is long gamma benefits from volatility in the underlying, which is why a long gamma position often is referred to as being *long volatility*. Conversely, a position with short gamma will get hurt if the underlying moves and is therefore known as being *short volatility*.

Long Straddle/Short Straddle

If this theoretical discussion about long/short gamma has your head spinning, take as a starting point a long at-the-money straddle. A long at-the-money straddle has one long call with a delta of approximately 0.50, and one long put with a delta of approximately −0.50. The straddle's total delta is therefore close to zero, which tells us that for a small move in the price of the underlying stock the value of the straddle is not expected to change because the gain on one option will be offset by the loss on the other.

Now think what happens if the underlying stock starts going up. The delta of the call slowly increases as this option goes in-the-money; the delta of the put increases as it goes out-of-the-money (which, since it started at −0.50, means that it is converging toward zero). The straddle's total delta becomes positive as the price of the stock rises. And the more the stock advances, the more positive the straddle's delta becomes. Gains on the call are greater and greater as losses on the put are smaller and smaller. This is good.

Now think what happens if the price of the stock starts to fall. The put's delta starts dropping below −0.50, and the call's delta also is decreasing; the straddle's delta is becoming negative as the price of the stock drops. Once again, this is a good thing. A long straddle is the purest form of a long gamma (or long volatility) position.

Conversely, a short straddle is a position with short gamma (short volatility). The straddle writer is hoping that the price of the underlying will go nowhere. The short straddle's initial delta is close to zero, with −0.50 delta from the short call and 0.50 delta from the short put. But if the price of the stock starts to rise, the delta of the short call will get more negative, going from −0.50 to, say, −0.60, and the delta of the short put will become less positive, going from 0.50 to, say, 0.40. The straddle's delta is becoming negative as the price of the stock is rising. Not a good idea. The same holds true if the stock starts to fall: the put's delta starts increasing, and so does the call's. The result is that the straddle's net delta becomes more positive as the price of the stock heads south. The short straddle is the simplest illustration of short gamma (or short volatility).

The Greeks: Theta

In Chapter 4 we saw how options lose value over time, all else being equal. Some options (in- and out-of-the-money options) decay in a rather linear fashion while others (at-the-money options) start out losing time premium at a constant rate but see this erosion accelerate as expiration nears. Theta quantifies this time decay.

Theta is calculated for a given time period: one-day theta, five-day theta, seven-day theta, and so on. The number of days represents calendar, not trading, days. For instance, your option pricing software may give the seven-day theta for a specific option as −0.08. This tells you, everything else being equal, that over the next seven days this option will decay by $0.08. Note that this theta does not tell you what would happen to your option position in the subsequent seven days. Calculating what this option's seven-day theta will be one week from now, we get −0.12, an indication that time decay is accelerating.

Purchasing options creates a position with negative theta, as both puts and calls will decay over time. Writing options generates positive theta, as a short option position will benefit from the passage of time. A note of caution: not everyone agrees with assigning negative theta to long and positive theta to short options positions. Some authors and computer programmers inverse the signs. Make sure you are on the same wavelength as the author you are reading.

As with other Greeks, the theta from various options can be added together. You created a convoluted spread where you are long 6 options (each with a seven-day theta of −0.14) and short 10 (with a seven-day theta of −0.07). Will the passage of time help or hurt you? Simply calculate your total theta: $(6 \times -0.14) + (-10 \times -0.07) = -0.14$. You are short theta, so time will hurt your overall position, but only to the tune of $14 over the next seven days for the complete position.

The Greeks: Vega

Vega is not a Greek letter; it just sounds like one. Vega measures the impact a change of 1% in an option's volatility estimate will have on that option's value. Table 9.6 illustrates the vega of three puts and three calls, all calculated assuming a stock price of $40, an initial volatility of 35%, three months until expiration, a risk-free interest rate of 3%, and no dividends.

From Table 9.6 we can see that the 40 call is valued at $2.90 under a 35% volatility assumption. Since vega measures the impact of a 1% increase in volatility, a 36% volatility assumption would raise the call's value by approximately $0.08. The value of the 40 put would also increase by $0.08. Puts and calls with the same strike will have similar if not equal vegas, and vega is highest for at-the-money options. Both puts and calls have positive vegas, signifying that option buyers benefit when volatility increases. Writing options will create a position with negative vegas—one that will be hurt by higher-volatility estimates but that would benefit from a lower assumption.

One fact not obvious from Table 9.6 is that vega is linear. This is illustrated in Figure 9.3, which looks at the value of the 40 strike call and put under a range of volatility assumptions.

Figure 9.3 shows that options premiums increase at a constant rate as the volatility estimate goes up: a 10% increase in volatility will result in a premium increase equal to 10 times the increase caused by a 1% rise in volatility.

Table 9.6

	Call		Put	
	Premium	Vega	Premium	Vega
35 Strike	$6.02	0.048	$0.77	0.048
40 Strike	$2.90	0.078	$2.63	0.078
45 Strike	$1.18	0.075	$5.91	0.072

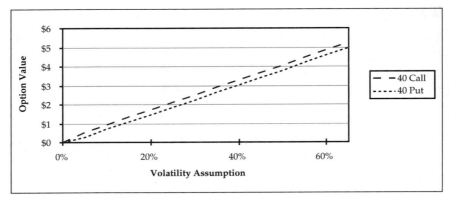

Figure 9.3 Option Prices vs. Volatility

The Greeks: Rho

The last of the Greeks is rho, which measures the impact a 1% change in the risk-free rate will have on option prices. Take the following option prices as a starting point:

Stock:	$50
3-month 50 call:	$3.69
3-month 50 put:	$3.24

The prices above assume a 35% volatility, a 4% risk-free rate, and no dividends. If we recalculate the options' prices assuming a 5% risk-free rate, we obtain the following:

3-month 50 call:	$3.75
3-month 50 put:	$3.19

Our first observation is that higher rates lead to more expensive calls and lower values for puts. But we know from experience that when short-term rates increase by 1% we have more important issues to worry about than the value of our options going up or down by $0.05 or $0.06. Calculating rho may be of interest to market makers and specialists, but for the average investor and trader, this is one Greek lesson they can skip.

The Relationship Among the Greeks

If you think gamma, delta, and theta spell confusion, hang in there because this is where we try to tie it all together. Start with Table 9.7, where we recap which Greek is associated with which option position (we have left out rho because it is of little practical value).

Stock positions are relatively easy: long stocks, by definition, create a long delta position; short stocks result in negative delta. Since a stock's delta will always be 1.00, it has 0 gamma (the delta doesn't change), and a stock's price does not incorporate any time premium so it has neither theta (no time decay) nor vega (no volatility premium).

It gets interesting when we start comparing the Greeks associated with various options positions. Notice that all options positions have the same sign for gamma and vega; all options positions have opposite signs for gamma (and vega) and theta. Is this coincidental or meaningful?

A long call position will benefit if the stock is volatile (long gamma) and if the option's implied volatility increases (long vega), but it will suffer from the passage of time (short theta). The same can be said for a long put position, even though the call buyer is anticipating volatility to the upside, while the put buyer is forecasting volatility to the downside. The straddle buyer is looking for pure volatility (up or down). He will benefit if implied volatility increases and will have to endure the negative impact of time decay.

It all ties in. Options buyers are looking for movement in the price of the underlying and higher option prices due to increased implied

Table 9.7

	Delta	Gamma	Theta	Vega
Long Stock	+	0	0	0
Short Stock	−	0	0	0
Long Call	+	+	−	+
Short Call	−	−	+	−
Long Put	−	+	−	+
Short Put	+	−	+	−

volatility, but they must be prepared to see the value of their options erode as expiration nears. Translated into Greek this last sentence becomes: long option positions result in long gamma, long vega, and short theta.

For option writers, a mirror image is created. Writers are hurt by high stock volatility (short gamma), but they benefit from decreased implied volatility (short vega) and the passage of time (long theta).

The Greeks are tied to one another: if the gamma of a position is known, then so are its vega and theta. A position's complete picture can therefore be drawn from its delta (which tells us if it's bullish, bearish, or neutral) and from its gamma (long volatility or short volatility).

When traders talk about buying volatility or shorting volatility, they are usually referring to positions that have little or no directional bias (i.e., neither bullish nor bearish), but will either benefit from movement in the underlying (buying volatility) or its lack thereof (shorting volatility). A long volatility position is created by being net long options, a short volatility position by being net short options. But heed this warning: a position that is net long options—by being long in-the-money calls and short a greater number of deep out-of-the-money calls, for instance—can turn into a position that is net short options if the underlying moves by a sufficient amount in the wrong direction.

Understanding the Black-Scholes Option Pricing Equation

The first time you saw the Black-Scholes option pricing model you probably dismissed it as rocket science and moved on with your life. We can help you make sense of the model in the next few paragraphs.

First, it is important to understand that the assumption underlying the Black-Scholes model is that a call option can be replicated by trading the underlying security. Take a look at the equation, where C is the value of a call option:

$$C = SN(d_1) - Xe^{-rt} N(d_2)$$

There are two parts to the main body of the equation. The first one is $SN(d_1)$. Buying a call is a bullish position. If one is going to replicate a call option by trading the underlying stock one must purchase shares of this stock. That is the S in the first part of the equation. How many shares of stock should be purchased? We have seen that a stock and its options move up and down at different rates, and we have defined the rate at which options move as delta. $N(d_1)$ calculates delta. If investor A buys a call option on a stock and investor B buys delta shares of the same stock, their profit or loss will be the same for small moves in the price of the stock. So $SN(d_1)$ tells us that to replicate a call, we need to purchase delta shares of stock.

But buying delta shares of stock is bound to cost more than purchasing an option. This is where the second part of the equation comes in. The second part is $-Xe^{-rt}N(d_2)$. Let's start with e^{-rt}. This is the formula used to calculate present value; it takes a given dollar amount in the future and calculates the value of those dollars today based on an interest rate (r) and the time period involved (t). X is the option's exercise price. So Xe^{-rt} is the present value of the option's exercise price. Think about it this way: if you know with 100% certainty that you are going to exercise a call option when it expires, how many dollars do you need to set aside today to have sufficient funds to pay for the stock upon exercise? The answer is the number of dollars that will, while earning interest, end up being equal to the option's strike price. This is Xe^{-rt}.

Notice next that there is a negative sign in front of the Xe^{-rt}. This tells us to borrow funds (the positive sign in front of the $SN(d_1)$ told us to invest funds). But the amount to be borrowed is not the full Xe^{-rt} rather it is adjusted by $N(d_2)$. This last expression calculates the probability that the call option will be in-the-money at expiration. So the amount of funds to be borrowed is equal to the present value of the option's strike price multiplied by the probability that the call will end up in the money.

To summarize: the Black-Scholes equation tells us that we can replicate an option by purchasing delta shares of the underlying stock and by financing part of this purchase with borrowed funds. The shares create upside potential, and the borrowed funds give us the leverage so many options buyers are seeking.

As underscored in Chapter 4 and again in this chapter, delta does not remain constant. So an investor replicating a call by purchasing delta shares of stock would have to increase the number of shares held by purchasing additional shares as the stock went up (remember, delta is increasing) and decrease the number of shares held by selling part of the original position if the price of the stock fell (delta is decreasing). If this sounds difficult, it is. Some investors were at one point (mostly before the market break of October 19, 1987) replicating long put positions to insure their stock portfolios using stock index futures and adjusting their positions by selling more/buying back some of their short contracts as the market dropped or rallied. The technique was then known as dynamic hedging (or portfolio insurance), but it proved to be ineffective on the one day they needed it most.

A Note on Beta

Throughout our deciphering of the Greek alphabet no mention has yet been made of beta. Yet this is probably the first Greek letter investors learn, in such expressions as "high-beta stock" and "low-beta portfolio." How does this letter relate to options?

In fact, it doesn't. Beta is a measure of relative risk, which could be taken as a proxy for relative volatility. Beta tells us how risky a stock is relative to a given benchmark. Benchmarks can vary. The Standard & Poor's 500 Index is sometimes used, but so is the NYSE Composite Index® and the Wilshire Total Market Index. A stock with a beta of 1.00 can be expected to rise 1% when the benchmark goes up 1%, and falls 1% with a market drop of 1%. Stocks with betas greater than 1.00 are expected to rise and fall more than the benchmark; those with betas lower than 1.00 will fluctuate less.

The problem with beta is that it does not tell you how volatile a stock truly is. If High Flying Inc. has a beta of 1.40 we expect it to be more volatile than the overall market, but what is the overall market doing? Is it staying in a narrow trading range, or is it rising and falling by a few percent on a daily basis? When we calculated historical volatility in one of the earlier sections, we only needed the stock's price. We made no reference to any benchmark and were looking at volatility independently of other stocks or indices.

Option Pricing and Interest Rates

We noted earlier in this chapter the impact changes in interest rates had on the value of puts and calls (see "The Greeks: Rho"). You will recall that higher rates mean higher call prices and lower put prices, assuming everything else is held constant. You also will recall that changes in interest rates have a relatively minor impact on premiums: a change from 4% to 5% in the risk-free rate increased the value of the at-the-money 50 call by $0.06, from $3.69 to $3.75. Most investors will consider this to be small change.

There are, however, some option market participants for whom interest rates are central: specialists and market makers. Take the YAWN 45-day calls and puts, which in Chapter 4 (see the section on interest rate and dividends) we valued at $1.81 and $1.55 respectively, based on a 4% interest rate assumption. Let's round the call price to $1.80 to make things more true to life. And finally, let's assume that a market maker purchases 100 shares of YAWN at $60, buys one 45-day 60 put at $1.55, and writes one 45-day 60 call at $1.80. What is this market maker's risk and profit potential?

There is no risk to the downside because the market maker is long the 60 put. If the price of the stock drops, the put can be exercised and the stock sold for $60. There is also no upside potential. If YAWN rises in price, the 60 call will be assigned and the market maker will be forced to sell 100 shares at $60. If the stock closes at exactly $60 at option expiration, then the call and put will both expire worthless and the market maker will keep the 100 shares, which will be worth $60.

So, with YAWN moving lower, the final value of the position is $60. If YAWN rises, the final value of the position will be $60; ditto if YAWN remains unchanged. No matter what the price action in the stock, this position will be worth $60 at option expiration. Is this good or bad? The net cost to establish the position was the $60 paid for the stock, plus the $1.55 to purchase the put, less the $1.80 received from writing the call, or a net cost of $59.75. The market maker realizes a profit of $0.25, which represents a 0.42% return, which in turn annualizes to 3.39%. Not great, but in line with the risk-free rate of 4%.

Yet market makers usually post two-sided markets that include a bid-ask spread. So the market on the 60 call could be $1.75 to $1.85 and the market on the 60 put could be $1.50 to $1.60. What happens if the market maker is able to purchase the put at his bid price of $1.50 and write the call at his offering price of $1.85? The total position can then be initiated for $59.65, will generate a profit of $0.35 and return 0.59%, or 4.76% annualized. The market maker is now earning more than the risk-free rate on his "risk-free" option position. Not bad, even if our numbers do not take into account the market maker's (very low) transaction costs on options and stock.

There are two lessons to be learned here. The first is that it is possible to build no-risk, or low-risk positions using options. This is useful for specialists and market makers whose primary goal is to remain in business. (The secondary goal is to make money, but it is very difficult to make money if you have gone out of business.) The second lesson is that there is more than one way to skin a cat. Let us illustrate.

The position built by the market maker was:

$$+\text{Stock}+\text{Put}-\text{Call}$$

This turned out to have a final value of $60 no matter what the price of the stock at option expiration. This position is known as a conversion. It was, in fact, a $60 "Treasury bill." So the position really was:

$$+\text{Stock}+\text{Put}-\text{Call}=\text{T-Bill}$$

Buying a stock and a put and writing a call (assuming the options' strike prices and expiration dates are the same) looks like a T-bill. This equation is known as the *put-call parity equation*. It shows how to build a risk-free position, but it also shows how to build equivalent positions. Take the case of an investor who is long a stock and purchases a put option to protect it. She is long stock, long put, and by rearranging the terms of the above equation we get the following:

$$+\text{Stock}+\text{Put}=\text{T-Bill}+\text{Call}$$

This investor could replicate her long stock/long put position by purchasing a Treasury bill and a call option. Note that the positions are only equivalent if the T-bill's maturity value is equal to the option's strike price and if the expiration dates and exercise prices of the put and the call are identical. Think back to some of the payoff diagrams in earlier chapters. How does the buy call diagram compare to the protective put diagram? They both have limited risk to the downside and unlimited profit potential to the upside. This is not surprising since they are equivalent strategies. (Compare also bullish credit and debit spreads in Chapter 6.)

Note that equivalent strategies are not identical. The main difference is usually in the risks of early assignment. A strategy short in-the-money options will have a greater probability of early assign-ment than the equivalent strategy with long in-the-money options. Still, it is useful to know that a short stock/long call position (where a trader buys a call to protect a short stock position) is equivalent to a long put position (an issue we discussed in Chapter 6). The latter position is easier to initiate (only one trade), has lower transaction costs (one option commission versus one stock and one option com-mission), does not require borrowing stock, and will be more read-ily approved by most brokers.

Extra! Options Offered Below Intrinsic Value!

The above headline was inspired by the following quotes:

SPX: 999.44
Mar 1250 put: $245.80–$247.80

Back to basics: an option's intrinsic value is equal to its in-the-money amount, that is, the difference between the value of the underlying and the option's strike price. By doing the math on the March 1250 put we see that this six-month option has an intrinsic value of $250.56, yet it is offered at $247.80. Is this, as the numerous offerings in our mailbox keep telling us, a "free gift"?

Not quite. Options on the Standard & Poor's 500 Index (SPX) are European style, only exercisable immediately prior to expiration. If this option were American style, could it not be purchased and exer-cised immediately to capture its full intrinsic value? Yes, and no, and there are two lessons to be learned from the above.

The first point is that deep-in-the-money European-style put options frequently trade at a discount to their intrinsic value. The reason is as follows: if a trader purchases this put at $247.80 because it is trading at a discount to its intrinsic, he must wait a full six months before exercising it. Obviously holding this option for six months creates a major market risk. The SPX could rally and the option would be in-the-money by only 200 or even 100 points by expiration date. (Yes, as the bulls keep reminding us, it could also be out-of-the-money). To capture the option's discount the trader would have to hedge his long put position by buying the compo-nent stocks of the S & P 500 Index. Any loss realized on the put as the market rallied would then be made up by gains on the stocks. This would tie up a lot of money, although this trader would end up collecting all of the dividends paid by the component stocks over the coming six months.

If we take the midpoint of the option's bid-ask spread, $246.80, the discount to intrinsic value is $3.76. This represents 0.38% of the index's value, or a 0.76% annualized discount (since this is a six-month put). This 0.76% represents the difference between the cost of borrowing funds and the yield on the Standard & Poor's 500 Index. Unfortunately, there is no free lunch: the discount on the put simply reflects the net cost of carrying the index's component stocks until option expiration. Whatever is gained by buying the option at a discount is taken away through the cost of the hedge.

The second lesson is that even if this put were an American-style option, buying it at $247.80 would not necessarily lock in a risk-free profit. Remember that an American-style index option will settle, if exercised, based on the closing value of the index on the day it is exercised. If this option is purchased with a few hours left in the trading day and is later exercised, the amount obtained upon exercise may end up being worth less than its purchase price. Occasionally, you will see American-style index options trading at a discount to intrinsic. This usually happens when the market is moving strongly in one direction and option traders start pricing options based on where they expect the market to be in a few minutes, rather than where it is at the present.

So the next time you see an option quote that looks too good to be true, it probably will be.

C H A P T E R

10

TACTICAL
CONSIDERATIONS

T he preceding chapters in this book focused on strategies that can be easily implemented. In this last chapter we review some of the tactical considerations that complement those strategies.

Risk Management

Some investors have sworn off options and other derivatives. They argue that if Long-Term Capital Management (with its star-studded staff that included a Nobel Prize winner), Enron (M.B.A.s from the best schools, political connections, and top-flight accountants), and their cousin Jeff (who devised this "can't lose" trading system) all went up in smoke trading options and other derivative securities, why should they stick their necks out only to have their heads handed to them on a platter?

In presenting the strategies in this book, we made every effort to explain the associated risks. To these we would like to add three general risk management guidelines that can minimize your risks of implosion.

The "It'll Never Go There" Attitude

Upon learning of an option strategy that has a 99% chance of being profitable you: (a) hit the speed-dial to call your broker because the markets are closing in 12 minutes; (b) dismiss it out of hand because it sounds too good to be true; (c) investigate further because you want to know what happens the 1% of the time when it is not profitable.

Obviously, you chose (c) and learned that if things go the wrong way, your trading account would get wiped out. But there is just a 1% chance that this will happen, so what do you do? Do you go ahead and risk it? Before making a decision, look at the probability of getting wiped out (POGWO) as a function of the number of times this strategy is initiated.

Strategy used once	POGWO: 1%
Strategy used 4 times (quarterly over one year):	POGWO: 3.9%
Strategy used 12 times (monthly over one year):	POGWO: 11.4%
Strategy used 50 times (weekly over one year):	POGWO: 39.5%
Strategy used 250 times (daily over one year):	POGWO: 91.9%

If you played Russian roulette with a 100-chamber gun and only one of the chambers contained a bullet, the probabilities of blowing your brains out would be identical to the ones above.

Certain aggressive options strategies are nothing more than a game of Russian roulette. We do not know why traders enter into these strategies—if it's the thrill of pulling the trigger and hearing the hammer fall on an empty chamber, or if it's the profound conviction that "it will never happen to me" because "the stock will never go there"—but we do know that the odds have a tendency to catch up with these players.

Writing deep out-of-the-money options appears to be the weapon of choice for those who like Russian roulette. Although short call positions have theoretically unlimited risk, most of the damage has been caused by short puts, both equity and index options. The largest binge of aggressive put writing in a bull market ended in October of 1987 with bodies littered all over the street. As a result, brokerage firms tightened up their options trading requirements, but we still come across traders holding guns to their heads. The only way to reduce one's POGWO to zero is to throw away the gun.

Leverage

Options are often blamed for various financial disasters when the true culprit is leverage. It is possible, for instance, to wipe out an account's total value by purchasing U.S. Treasury bonds (fully guaranteed by the U.S. government) if the position is leveraged sufficiently.

Chapter 3 showed how leverage works both ways. Does this mean it should simply be avoided? We do not think so. Take the example of an investor with $100,000 who has decided to allocate this sum to an option writing program. He plans to write puts on stocks he is willing to own and, if assigned on the puts, to write covered calls on these stock positions. All positions will be of equal dollar value, fixed at $10,000. If this investor writes puts on 10 stocks, no leverage will ever be involved: if all 10 put series are assigned, he will be forced to purchase $100,000 worth of stocks for which he has the cash.

This investor also could decide to write puts on 11 stocks. His reasoning is as follows: if the stocks are properly diversified the odds are relatively low that all 11 puts would be assigned at the same time. If some stocks are purchased on assignment at the first option expiration, calls will be written immediately. By the second option expiration more puts may be assigned, but there is also a chance that some of the calls will be assigned and some of the stock holdings sold. For all 11 puts to be assigned would probably require the overall market to correct substantially, in which case he would be forced to buy $110,000 worth of stock. Under this scenario he would have to borrow $10,000 from his broker. That's a conservative use of margin and a comfortable degree of leverage.

Now think of this same investor writing puts on 12 stocks, or 15, or 20, 25, 30, or even 50 stocks. At some point he would become uncomfortable. If not, he would end up short puts on 50 different stocks and have to assume the obligation to purchase $500,000 worth of shares with only $100,000 to back him up. This, by the way, is about as far as he could leverage his put writing, assuming his broker's margin requirements are the exchange minimum.

Holding 50 short put positions will not be a problem as long as the market (or at least the relevant stocks) cooperates, i.e., remains stable or rises. But any downturn will generate a margin call, even if none of the puts has been assigned. There is no room to maneuver. This investor will have to meet the margin call by covering some of his short puts or selling stocks he may have bought on option assignments. He is being forced out of his position at what is probably the worst time to liquidate. He is selling low instead of selling high.

Leverage can be a useful tool, but many traders and investors have been forced to liquidate because they had leveraged positions to the last nickel. As options strategists at a brokerage firm we would get phone calls from brokers that went like this: "I have a client with $22,544 of excess margin. How many of the XYX December 40 puts can he write?" These clients—and their brokers—were using our firm's margin requirements as a trading guideline: "If my broker lets me write 12, it must be okay to write 12." Remember that your brokerage firm's margin requirement is for their protection, not yours.

Overleverage proved to be the downfall of Long-Term Capital Management. The company was correct in predicting that the spread between different debt instruments would narrow. The problem was that it was leveraged to such an extent that when the spreads started to widen the company did not have the necessary staying power and had to call it quits. Part of their problem may have been of the "it'll never go there" type (i.e., these spreads are at historically high levels—they cannot get any wider). Don't wait until you are awarded a Nobel Prize to learn from this experience.

Diversification

In the late 1990s, none of us held enough tech stocks as they repeatedly hit new highs. Then, during the tech bust and the demise of the dot-coms, we all held too many tech stocks. It takes discipline not to pile into the sector of the month—to hold energy stocks when biotech is all the rage, or banking stocks when health care is the only outperforming sector.

Even conservative investors who limit their options trading to buy/writes should diversify across sectors. There is nothing new here, but how often is this pillar of sound investing ignored?

Earning Your Stripes

Most brokerage firms have different levels of approval for options trading. A representative example would be:

- level 1: covered writing
- level 2: buying calls and puts
- level 3: spreading (usually within certain limits)
- level 4: writing equity puts
- level 5: writing uncovered calls (sometimes two levels—one for equity options, one for index options)

If you are new to options trading you will have to earn your stripes. Don't expect more than a level 2 approval until you have gained some experience. And when you are refused approval at a specific level, don't take it personally. When we returned to the U.S. after a few years offshore, we moved our option account to a nationally recognized firm. Our application was rejected for writing puts for lack of trading experience (although they did permit us to write covered calls). We had at that point been trading options for close to two decades and had, in fact, trained the said firm's brokers in the uses of options. A follow-up letter straightened things out, but don't forget that most firms will err on the side of caution when looking at your option account application.

Options in Tax-Deferred Plans

At some point you may want to know what you can and cannot do with options in your tax-deferred account (IRA, 401(k), SEP, etc.). This line of inquiry will make getting approved for options in your regular account look like a piece of cake. The only constant we have found among brokerage firms is that they all will let you write covered calls. Besides this strategy, anything goes: some firms let you buy protective puts, others don't; some firms let you buy call options, others don't; some firms permit the writing of equity puts, others don't. There is even one firm that completely disallows LEAPS.

You should also be aware that some firms have two sets of rules for their tax-deferred accounts: there are the general rules, which permit covered writing and maybe the purchase of puts and calls, and the preferred client rules, which allow more strategies. A preferred client can be someone who has an established trading record with the brokerage or a sufficiently large portfolio. It may be worth asking your broker what it takes to get upgraded if you are looking to venture beyond covered call writing in your tax-deferred account.

Options and Taxes

Of the two inevitable facts of life, death and taxes, we would much have preferred to write about the former. Unfortunately, we could not find enough relevance to the topic at hand. This section must be read with the following caveat in mind: the IRS can change the rules at any time, and given the lag inherent in published material, any or all that follows could be completely out of date. Do not take any tax-related action without consulting your tax advisor.

In a nutshell, options are securities (like stocks and bonds), and option transactions create capital gains and losses. For simple trades, buying an option and selling it later, the tax treatment is straightforward: short- or long-term capital gains (or losses) will be generated. Writing options also generates capital gains, although writing LEAPS of more than 12 months results in a short-term, not a long-term, gain or loss, even if the option position is closed out or expires more than 12 months after the option was written. Writing options does not create a tax liability: the option's premium is held in suspense, and a gain or loss is realized when the option is closed out or when it expires.

Covered Writing

It is late November and a stock you purchased a little under a year ago has finally proven you right and has just doubled to $100. You are now sitting on a nice unrealized gain, but you are not as willing to liquidate as you probably should be. You reason that if you can hold on just a little longer, your short-term position will become a long-term one and benefit from the lower tax rate. And if you carry this stock into the new year, you can delay paying the capital gains tax another 12 months. You think of buying protective puts, but the stock's recent volatility makes them prohibitively expensive.

Then you think of writing a covered call. Since the run-up in the stock is recent, there are some nice in-the-money calls, such as the January 70, that you could write for a little over $30. You would immediately pocket $30, hedge your position down to $70, and ride into the new year with little to worry about. Does it sound too good to be true? It is.

The covered write in the preceding example does not fit the definition of a qualified covered call (QCC). If you wrote this call, the stock's holding period would be reset to qualify for long-term capital gain status and you would have to hold the stock another 12 months. For stocks trading between $60.01 and $150, the option written to create a qualified covered call cannot be more than two strike prices below the stock's closing price on the previous trading day and, in certain circumstances, cannot be more than $10 in the money. So with your stock trading at $100, you could write the 90 calls, which would qualify as a QCC, but this would suspend your holding period; the time meter is turned off but not reset to zero.

As noted at the beginning of this section, we are dealing with the tax laws as of this book's writing, and things may have changed. So how do you write covered calls without having first to consult your attorney and your tax advisor? The short answer is to stick to at- or out-of-the money calls. If you do, you will not have to worry about the QCC rules. If you would like to write an in-the-money option, then a call will either qualify as a QCC (in which case the holding period of stocks held short term is suspended) or it will not (and the holding period of stocks held short term will be terminated). The intent of the law is to prevent investors from writing deep in-the-money calls and retaining a stock position with very little risk. As you have guessed, the difference between a QCC and one that isn't is the amount by which the call is in-the-money, and this varies as a function of the stock's price.

A further wrinkle to the QCC rules was added in 2002. Effective July 29, 2002, a further adjustment must be made if the calls written have a term of more than one year. To determine the amount by which a call is in-the-money, the price of the stock has to be adjusted upward by 2% per quarter (uncompounded) and the old QCC rules applied. For a 13-month option, the price of the stock would be adjusted upward by 8%. So a $100 stock would be deemed to be at $108, making the 100 calls the lowest strike to qualify for a QCC (the 100 calls are deemed to be two strikes in-the-money, the most allowable). For a 22-month option, the price of the stock would be adjusted upward by 14%, so for the same $100 stock, the lowest strike to qualify under QCC rules would be the 105. Finally, under the new rules, no call with a term of more than 33 months can qualify as a QCC, regardless of its strike price.

The Wash Sale Rule

The wash sale rule is designed to prevent the following: it is mid-December and you are sitting on 1,000 shares of Big Loser Corp. bought earlier in the year at $44 and now trading at $33. A short-term capital loss of $11,000 would ease the pain this coming April. You sell your shares to realize a short-term capital loss, and a week later you repurchase another 1,000 shares because you are convinced that things will turn around and you don't want to be left behind when the train leaves the station.

Wash sale rules will not let you recognize your capital loss on the above trades. A sale is deemed to be a washed sale if a "substantially identical" security to the one sold is purchased within 30 days of the sale. Within 30 days means 30 days before as well as after the sale date.

You have two choices in this situation: double your risk for 30 days by buying 1,000 shares in mid-November and selling your original shares in mid-December, or go 30 days without owning the stock after you realize your loss and hope the stock doesn't get away from you. A variation on the first choice would be to purchase call options more than 30 days before you sell your shares and exercise these more than 30 days after you have sold your stock position. Yes you have to double your exposure to the stock, but the capital required is bound to be significantly less than a straight double up.

The Collar Saga

Collars, as discussed in Chapter 8, are a great way to reduce the risk of a stock position. Sometime in the mid-1990s, some U.S. Treasury employees started wondering if investors who "collared" a stock were reducing both their risk and their upside potential to such an extent that they were effectively out of their position. The idea surfaced that collaring a stock too tightly would be treated as an effective sale; that is, any accrued profit on the stock would have to be realized. Then came a debate as to the meaning of "too tightly" and how this related to the options' time to expiration. Another idea was floated that any collar involving LEAPS would trigger a tax liability. The decade, century, and millennium have come and gone without this issue being resolved.

As of this writing, collars are on the back burner. But they have moved from there to the front burner and back numerous times. Before initiating a collar make sure new rules have not come into play.

Tax Advice from the Experts

Ernst & Young LLP has written a publication titled *Taxes & Investing: A Guide for the Individual Investor* that can be found on the Chicago Board Options Exchange's website. We recommend downloading this document because it was prepared by tax specialists, not by an options strategist.

Finding Your Style

We noted in the Introduction that we would limit ourselves to strategies that can be implemented in the real world by investors and traders. Readers should not take this as a challenge to go out and initiate every strategy that was described in this book. As you read through the various chapters you probably thought, "This strategy is something I can see myself doing," and at other times you thought, "Who in their right mind would want to try this?"

A lot of investors and traders limit themselves to a few main strategies, with the occasional use of something more exotic. Some option writers, for example, limit themselves to writing puts on stocks they wish to acquire and calls on stocks they would be happy to sell. They might occasionally use the repair strategy or buy a protective put, but, for the most part, they stick to writing. Some spreaders love to purchase longer-dated options (mostly LEAPS) and write shorter-term options against them. They rarely ever own stocks. We also know some options buyers who would never get caught with a short option position.

Your goal should be to identify the strategies that fit your investing and trading style and are appropriate for your level of risk tolerance. You can then proceed to master these strategies and to develop your own options trading style.

INDEX